P9-CKR-569

The Presidential Election Game

The Presidential Election Game

Steven J. Brams

LCCC LIBRARY

New Haven and London, Yale University Press

Published with assistance from the foundation
established in memory of James Wesley Cooper of the
Class of 1865, Yale College.

Copyright © 1978 by Yale University. Second printing, 1979.
All rights reserved. This book may not be reproduced, in
whole or in part, in any form (beyond that copying permitted
by Sections 107 and 108 of the U.S. Copyright Law and
except by reviewers for the public press), without written
permission from the publishers.

Designed by John O. C. McCrillis and set in Baskerville
VIP type. Printed in the United States of America by
The Murray Printing Company, Westford, Mass.

Published in Great Britain, Europe, Africa, and Asia
(except Japan) by Yale University Press, Ltd., London.
Distributed in Australia and New Zealand by Book &
Film Services, Artarmon, N.S.W., Australia; and in
Japan by Harper & Row, Publishers, Tokyo Office.

Library of Congress Cataloging in Publication Data

Brams, Steven J.
    The Presidential election game.
    Includes index.
    1. Presidents—United States—Election.
I. Title.
JK528.B73   329'.00973   78-5815
ISBN 0-300-02254-9 clothbound
        0-300-02296-4 paperbound

To Julie and Michael

Strategy, I told myself; we needed a strategy.

John Dean, *Blind Ambition*

Contents

Figures

Tables

Preface

There is nothing to match the hoopla, pageantry, and excitement of a presidential campaign in American politics. No less dramatic, though quieter, are the strategic, gamelike features of a presidential campaign, which often are a good deal more consequential.

The use of the term "game" in the title of this book is intended to convey both the competitive character of presidential elections and the strategic interdependence of decisions made by the players at each stage in a presidential campaign. A game, by definition, is the sum total of the rules that describe it. (Parenthetically, players in a game are referred to throughout the book by masculine pronouns, but this is simply a convenience: women play games, too.)

In this book, the tools of modern decision theory and game theory are used to analyze presidential campaigns and elections. Much of the analysis is quite involved and probably will not be easy going for the reader unaccustomed to arguments of a more formal, mathematical nature. I would stress, however, that this book is written for, and I believe can be understood by, any conscientious reader with a reasonably good background in high school mathematics.

Since there are other books on presidential elections that require less perseverance to read, it is fair to ask what added benefits mathematical analysis brings to the study of presidential elections. I will respond in two ways.

First, it offers more than good hindsight in trying to determine better and worse strategies in presidential campaigns. For example, consider what good hindsight would say after replaying the "mistakes" of the 1972 campaign: Jimmy Carter should not run for his party's nomination in all states in 1976 because Edmund Muskie had done so in 1972 and lost. Of course, this good hindsight is now bad hindsight, since Carter followed this very strategy and won, which illustrates the dubious scientific status of hindsight.

In contrast to the hindsight approach, I have attempted to develop scientific models that can impart a deeper and more general understanding of underlying factors at work in the presidential election process. By "models" I mean simplified representations that abstract the essential elements of some phenomenon or process one wants to study. By deducing consequences from models, one can see more clearly what is happening than one can by trying to deal with reality in all its unmanageable detail.

The second reason for using mathematical arguments (and models) is relevant particularly to those with normative concerns who are interested in reforming the system. I can see no way to estimate the probable effects of alternatives to the system without modeling them and then testing the models—insofar as possible—by applying them to empirical data. My arguments, for example, for abolishing the Electoral College and switching to the popular-vote election of a president in chapter 3, and for adopting approval voting in chapter 6, would not be persuasive if they were simply asserted without the backup theoretical and empirical analyses. Good reform, I believe, depends on good analysis.

An overview of the book may be helpful to prospective readers. In the first three chapters, I develop models to analyze the three major phases of the presidential election game—state primaries, national party conventions, and the general election. While the evidence presented in chapter 1 is mostly suggestive—examples from presidential primary campaigns that seem roughly in accord with the implications of the spatial models are discussed—the evidence in the second and third chapters is more systematic and quantitative. Specifically, data on bandwagon and underdog effects in all national party conventions since 1832 in which there have been multiballot nominations of presidential and vice-presidential candidates are analyzed in chapter 2, and data on resource allocations by presidential and vice-presidential candidates in the 1960 through 1972 general-election campaigns are analyzed in chapter 3.

Three different models are developed in chapter 4 around the theme of coalition politics, which is central to the building and maintenance of a presidential candidate's support both within and outside his party. Several examples from early and recent presidential campaigns illustrate how coalitions form and break up.

President Nixon's resignation in 1974 was unprecedented, and his confrontation with the Supreme Court that precipitated his resignation is analyzed in chapter 5 as a case study in how an election mandate can be upset. Finally, in chapter 6, the most technical of all the chapters, a new form of voting is proposed, its theoretical properties are analyzed, and its likely empirical effects are assessed.

This, in capsule form, is the sum and substance of *The Presidential Election Game*. The game is not a frivolous one: its stakes are high, and the material and emotional investments made by the candidates and their supporters are substantial. I believe that the search for scientific models that illuminate the complexities of this game is a challenging and fascinating intellectual task. When a better understanding of the game also suggests how some of its problematic features might be solved, and the rules of the game are changed to correct these features, then there may be practical payoffs as well.

Acknowledgments

I am grateful to William H. Riker and Philip D. Straffin Jr. for their detailed and very helpful comments on a first draft of this book. Neither should be held responsible for deficiencies that remain.

I would also like to thank Marian Neal Ash at Yale University Press for the strong support she gave to the book, and Dianne W. Zolotow for her excellent editing of the manuscript. Several journals, acknowledged in the footnotes, kindly gave permission to use previously published material.

As always, my wife, Eva, gave me unstinting encouragement and support. Our children, to whom this book is dedicated, campaigned hard for their fair time. I venture to say they could have offered some political candidates good lessons on effective, attention-getting strategies.

1 The Primaries:
Who Survives the Hurdles?

1.1. Introduction

In this and the next two chapters, I shall examine the three major phases of the greatest spectacle in American politics— the quest for the presidency. Campaigns for the presidency may commence a year—or even several years—before the first state caucuses and primaries in a presidential election year as the early entrants lay the groundwork for their campaigns by putting together staffs and sounding out local political leaders and potential contributors. The campaigns of most presidential candidates do not attract wide news coverage, however, until the first caucuses and primaries, which now begin in January (Iowa caucus) and February (New Hampshire primary) of an election year. Then ensues a whirlwind of activity for the next nine months or so that culminates on Election Day in November.

More than half the fifty states today—twenty-nine in 1976, plus the District of Columbia—hold primaries from the middle of winter through the late spring of a presidential election year.[1] The remaining states choose delegates to the Demo-

This chapter is based largely on Steven J. Brams, *Spatial Models of Election Competition*, Monograph in Undergraduate Mathematics and Its Applications Project (Newton, Mass.: Education Development Center, 1979), which also includes exercises and their solutions.

1. Although now quite dated, the most comprehensive study of presidential primaries is James W. Davis, *Presidential Primaries: Road to the White House* (New York: Thomas Y. Crowell, 1967); see also William H. Lucy, "Polls, Primaries, and Presidential Nominations," *Journal of Politics* 35, no. 4 (November 1973): 830–48; Daniel C. Williams et al., "Voter Decisionmaking in a Primary Election: An Evaluation of Three Models of Choice," *American Journal of Political Science* 20, no. 1 (February 1976): 37–49; and James R. Beniger, "Winning the Presidential Nomination: National Polls and State Primary Elections, 1936–1972," *Public Opinion Quarterly* 40, no. 1 (Spring

cratic and Republican national party conventions in caucuses in which voters at the local or district level elect delegates to statewide conventions, who in turn elect delegates to the national party convention. These successive elections of delegates may be carried through two or more stages until national party convention delegates are chosen.

The bewildering variety of rules governing delegate selection in different caucus states makes it impossible to model a "typical" caucus state. Rules that govern the selection of national party convention delegates in primary states also differ considerably, but all primary states share one feature: the voters vote directly for a slate of delegates or the candidates in one election, whereas in caucus states the election occurs in stages and is, therefore, indirect.

To be sure, some primary states, like California, also use caucuses in the preliminary selection of slates of delegates. Moreover, primaries may be open or closed, depending on whether voters can "cross over" and vote for delegates or candidates in the other party contest (open) or must stick to their own party contest (closed). In addition, while the outcomes of most primaries are binding on the delegates, some are only advisory—"beauty contests" is the term that has been coined.[2]

The fact that the primary states include virtually all the large states with the most delegates makes performance in them a critical factor in securing the nomination of one's party. Of course, if no candidate succeeds in gaining a decisive lead over his opponents in the primaries, the locus of decision shifts to the national party convention, which is the

1976): 22–38. On the politics of party nominations generally, see William R. Keech and Donald R. Matthews, *The Party's Choice* (Washington, D.C.: Brookings Institution, 1976).

2. For further information on different kinds of primaries, and an analysis of their effects on voter turnout in 1976, see Austin Ranney, *Participation in American Presidential Nominations, 1976* (Washington, D.C.: American Enterprise Institute for Public Policy Research, 1977); also, Richard L. Rubin, "Presidential Primaries: Continuities, Dimensions of Change, and Political Implications" (paper delivered at the 1977 Annual Meeting of the American Political Science Association, Washington, D.C., September 1–4).

second phase in the presidential election game that I shall take up in chapter 2. But no candidate defeated in the primaries is ever likely to reach this phase, even if he is the incumbent president.[3]

State primaries, then, are the crucial first phase in a candidate's quest for the presidency. If a candidate, by winning a large proportion of pledged delegates in the primaries, effectively wraps up his party's nomination in this phase, then the party convention provides merely a rubber stamp for the nomination game he has already won. But to win the nomination game is not to win the election game, whose third and final phase—the general election—I shall consider in chapter 3.

1.2. The Primacy of Issues and Their Spatial Representation

The *presidential election game* comprises the two phases of the *nomination game*—primaries and the national party conventions—and the *general election game*. There are obvious interactions among these phases, some of which I shall discuss in chapters 2, 3, and 4, but in this chapter the subject will be restricted to state primaries.

I start from the assumption that voters respond to the positions that candidates take on issues. This is not to say that nonissue-related factors like personality, ethnicity, religion, and race have no effect on election outcomes but rather that issues take precedence in a voter's decision. Indeed, sometimes these "nonissues" become issues, but in the subsequent analysis I shall assume *issues* to be questions of public policy—what the government should and should not do on matters that affect, directly or indirectly, its citizens.

The primacy of issues in presidential elections has been

3. Although Lyndon Johnson chose not to run in the Democratic primaries in 1968, Eugene McCarthy's "strong showing" in the New Hampshire primary (while losing with 42 percent of the vote to Johnson's 50 percent write-in vote) and his expected win in the second primary (Wisconsin) seem to have been important factors in inducing the incumbent president to withdraw from the 1968 race just prior to the Wisconsin primary.

reasonably well documented over the last ten years.[4] Although most of the research that has been conducted applies to the general election, it would seem even more applicable to primaries, in which party affiliation is not usually a factor. Particularly in states where primaries are closed, with only registered Democrats and registered Republicans eligible to participate in choosing delegates to their respective conventions, it is the issue positions of the candidates running for their party's nomination, not their party identification, that assume paramount importance in primaries.[5]

4. See V. O. Key, Jr., with the assistance of Milton C. Cummings, Jr., *The Responsible Electorate: Rationality in Presidential Voting, 1936–1960* (Cambridge, Mass.: Belknap Press, 1966). For a general discussion of the role of issues in presidential elections, see the articles, comments, and rejoinders by Gerald M. Pomper, Richard W. Boyd, Richard A. Brody, and John H. Kessel, *American Political Science Review* 66, no. 2 (June 1972): 415–70. A more recent assessment can be found in Herbert B. Asher, *Presidential Elections and American Politics: Voters, Candidates, and Campaigns since 1952* (Homewood, Ill.: Dorsey Press, 1976), pp. 86–121, 196–99, and references cited therein; see also Gerald Pomper, *Voters' Choice: Varieties of American Electoral Behavior* (New York: Dodd, Mead, 1975), chap. 8; Norman H. Nie, Sidney Verba, and John R. Petrocik, *The Changing American Voter* (Cambridge, Mass.: Harvard University Press, 1976), chaps. 10, 16–18; *Controversies in American Voting Behavior*, ed. Richard G. Niemi and Herbert F. Weisberg (San Francisco: W. H. Freeman, 1976), pp. 160–235; and Donald S. Strong, *Issue Voting and Party Realignment* (University: University of Alabama Press, 1977). Still more recently, the significance of issues in a voter's decision has been challenged in Michael Margolis, "From Confusion to Confusion—Issues and the American Voter (1956–1972)," *American Political Science Review* 71, no. 1 (March 1977): 31–43, where it is argued that candidate evaluations and party images— among other factors—still hold important sway; for empirical support, see Stanley Kelley, Jr. and Thad Mirer, "The Simple Act of Voting," *American Political Science Review* 67, no. 2 (June 1974): 572–91. This criticism, however, ignores the *origins* of candidate evaluations and candidate images, which, it seems plausible to assume, ultimately spring from the issue positions of candidates and parties—though perhaps as seen in earlier elections. Moreover, as Gerald M. Pomper pointed out in an exchange with Margolis in "Communications," *American Political Science Review* 71, no. 4 (December 1977): 1596–97, issue voting trends through 1972 remained strong. In 1976, however, issue voting declined in importance. See Warren E. Miller and Teresa E. Levitin, *Leadership and Change: Presidential Elections from 1952 to 1976* (Cambridge, Mass.: Winthrop, 1976), chap. 7.

5. William H. Flanigan and Nancy H. Zingale, *Political Behavior of the*

Thus, the rule that excludes nonparty candidates from participating in a party's presidential primary would appear to have a rather important political consequence.[6] It forces voters in a primary election to make choices other than on the basis of party affiliation, which is, of course, the same for all candidates running for their party's nomination.

To be sure, a candidate in a primary may claim that he is the only "true" representative of his party's historical record and ideology. But by making this claim, he is not so much invoking his party label to attract votes as saying that his positions on issues more closely resemble those of his party forebears than the positions of his opponents.

How can the positions of candidates on issues be represented? Start by assuming that there is a single overriding issue in a campaign on which all candidates must take a definite position. (Later candidates will be allowed to fuzz their positions—and thereby adopt strategies of ambiguity—as well as take positions on more than one issue.) Assume also that the attitudes of party voters on this issue can be represented along a left-right continuum, which may be interpreted to measure attitudes that range from very liberal (on the left) to very conservative (on the right).[7] I shall not be concerned here with spelling out exactly what "liberal" and "conservative" mean but use this interpretation only to indi-

---

American Electorate, 3d ed. (Boston: Allyn and Bacon, 1975), pp. 130–40. Even in open primary states that permit crossovers (fourteen of thirty in 1976), those voters who cross over from one party to another are probably inclined to do so precisely because of the issue positions of candidates not running in their own party's primary.

6. Formerly, the winner-take-all feature of voting in primaries was also significant, but now a proportional rule governs the allocation of convention delegates in most primary states. (The main exception in 1976 was the Republican primary in California.) In the general election, however, in which the plurality winner in a state wins all its electoral votes, the winner-take-all feature has significant consequences that will be discussed in chapter 3.

7. An issue on which attitudes can be indexed by some quantitative variable, like "degree of government intervention in the economy," obviously better satisfies this assumption than an issue that poses an either-or question—for example, whether or not to develop a major new weapons system.

cate that the attitudes of voters can be scaled along some policy dimension to which the words "liberal" and "conservative" can in some way be meaningfully attached.

The positions candidates take on this dimension or issue are assumed to be perceived by voters in the same way—that is, there is no misinformation about where on the continuum each candidate stands. Like all theoretical assumptions used to model empirical phenomena, this assumption simplifies the reality of the positions candidates take and their perceptions by voters, but it serves as a useful starting point for this analysis.

To derive the behavior of voters from their attitudes and the positions candidates take in a campaign, some assumption is necessary about how voters decide for whom to vote. I am not concerned with the attitudes of *individual* voters, however, but only with the *numbers* who have particular attitudes along some liberal-conservative scale.

For this purpose I postulate a *distribution* of voters, as shown in figure 1.1. The vertical height of this distribution, which is defined by the curve in figure 1.1, represents the number (or percentage) of voters who have attitudes at each point along the horizontal continuum.[8]

8. This spatial representation of voter attitudes and candidate positions was first used in Anthony Downs, *An Economic Theory of Democracy* (New York: Harper & Row, 1957). For a critical assessment of this work, see Donald Stokes, "Spatial Models of Party Competition," *American Political Science Review* 57, no. 2 (June 1963): 368–77; David Robertson, *A Theory of Party Competition* (London: Wiley, 1976), which tests predictions of the theory for the British electorate; and Norman Frohlich, Joe A. Oppenheimer, Jeffrey Smith, and Oran R. Young, "A Test of Downsian Voter Rationality: 1964 Presidential Voting," *American Political Science Review* 72, no. 1 (March 1978): 178–97. For a review of the more recent literature on party-competition models, see William H. Riker and Peter C. Ordeshook, *An Introduction to Positive Political Theory* (Englewood Cliffs, N.J.: Prentice-Hall, 1973), chaps. 11 and 12; Kenneth A. Shepsle, "Theories of Collective Choice," in *Political Science Annual, V: An International Review*, ed. Cornelius P. Cotter (Indianapolis: Bobbs-Merrill, 1974), pp. 4–77; Michael Taylor, "The Theory of Collective Choice," in *Handbook of Political Science: Micropolitical Theory*, vol. 3, ed. Fred I. Greenstein and Nelson W. Polsby (Reading, Mass.: Addison-Wesley, 1975), pp. 413–81; Peter C. Ordeshook, "The Spatial Theory of

Figure 1.1
Two Candidates: Symmetric, Unimodal Distribution

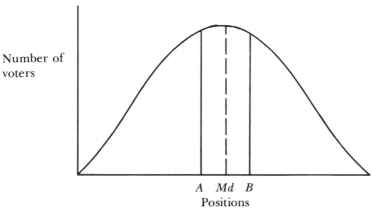

Number of
voters

A Md B
Positions

Because the postulated distribution has one peak, or mode, it is characterized as *unimodal*. Since the curve has the same shape to the left and the right of its median, which is the point where the vertical dashed line intersects the horizontal axis, the distribution is *symmetric*.[9]

I have also postulated in figure 1.1 the positions of two candidates, A and B, at points along the left-right continuum. Assume that candidate A takes a position somewhere to the left of the median and candidate B a position somewhere to the right. How attractive are these positions to the voters? This is the question I turn to in section 1.3, where the analysis is restricted to competition between just two candidates; in

Elections: A Review and a Critique," in *Party Identification and Beyond*, ed. Ian Bridge, Ivor Crewe, and Dennis Farlie (New York: Wiley, 1976), pp. 285–313; and Benjamin I. Page, "Elections and Social Choice: The State of the Evidence," *American Journal of Political Science* 21, no. 3 (August 1977): 639–68.

9. A *median* divides the area under a distribution curve exactly in half, which means in this example that half the voters have attitudes to the left of the point where the median line intersects the horizontal axis and half the voters have attitudes to the right of this point. Moreover, because the distribution is symmetric—the curve to the left of the median is a mirror image of the curve to the right—the same numbers of voters have attitudes equal distances to the left and right of the median.

section 1.4, I shall consider what happens when more than two candidates enter the race.

1.3. Rational Positions in a Two-Candidate Race

I assume that both voters and candidates have goals in an election, and they act rationally to satisfy these goals. To act *rationally* means simply to choose the course of action that best satisfies one's goals.

The rationality assumption is rather empty unless *particular* goals are postulated for voters and candidates. For voters, assume that they will vote for the candidate whose position is closest to their own along the continuum. For candidates, assume they will try to choose positions that maximize the total number of votes they receive, in light of the voters' rationality.[10]

While the *attitudes* of voters are a fixed quantity in the calculations of candidates, the *decisions* of voters will depend on the positions the candidates take. Assuming the candidates know the distribution of voter attitudes, what positions for them are rational?

Assume that there are only two candidates in the race, and the distribution of voters is symmetric and unimodal, as illustrated in figure 1.1. If candidates A and B take the positions shown in figure 1.1, A will certainly attract all the voters to the left of his position, and B all the voters to the right of his position. If both candidates are an equal distance from the median, they will split the vote in the middle—the left half

10. Alternative models in which candidates have policy preferences and view winning as a means to implement them—rather than more cynically adopt policy positions as a means to winning—are developed in Donald Wittman, "Parties as Utility Maximizers," *American Political Science Review* 66, no. 2 (June 1973): 490–98; Donald Wittman, "Candidates with Policy Preferences: A Dynamic Model," *Journal of Economic Theory* 14, no. 1 (February 1977): 180–89; and Donald Wittman, "Equilibrium Strategies by Policy Maximizing Candidates" (mimeographed, University of Chicago, 1976); see also Richard D. McKelvey, "Policy Related Voting and Electoral Equilibria," *Econometrica* 43, nos. 5–6 (September-November 1975): 815–43. Policy considerations, based on the assumption that utilities are associated with different candidate positions, will be introduced in a model in chapter 4.

going to A and the right half going to B. The race will therefore end in a tie, with half the votes (to the left of the median) going to A and half the votes (to the right of the median) going to B.

Could either candidate do better by changing his position? If B's position remains fixed, A could move alongside B, just to his left, and capture all the votes to B's left. Since A would have moved to the right of the median, he would, by changing his position in this manner, receive a majority of the votes and thereby win the election.[11]

But, using an analogous argument for B, there is no rational reason for him to stick to his original position to the right of the median. He should approach A's original position to capture more votes to his right. In other words, both candidates, acting rationally, should approach each other and the median. Should one candidate (say, A) move past the median, but the other (B) stop at the median, B would receive not only the 50 percent of the votes to his left but also some votes to his right that fall between his (median) position and A's position (now to B's right). Hence, there is not only an incentive for both candidates to move toward the median but not to overstep it as well.

The consequence of these calculations is that the median position is "optimal" for both candidates. Presumably, if they both adopted the median position, voters would be indifferent to the choice between the two candidates on the basis of their positions alone and would make their choice on some other grounds.

More formally, the median position is *optimal* for a candidate if there is no other position that can guarantee him a better outcome (i.e., more votes), regardless of what position the other candidate adopts. Naturally, if B adopted the posi-

11. I assume for now that A does not suffer any electoral penalty at the polls from changing his position, though fluctuations along the continuum may evoke a charge of being "wishy-washy," which is a feature of candidate positions that I shall analyze in section 1.7. Alternatively, the "movements" discussed here may be thought to occur mostly in the minds of the candidates before they announce their actual positions.

tion shown for him in figure 1.1, it would be rational for A to move alongside him to maximize his vote total, as I have already demonstrated. But this nonmedian position of A would not *ensure* him of 50 percent of the votes if B did not remain fixed but instead switched his position (say, to the median). Thus, the median is optimal in this example in the sense that it guarantees a candidate at least 50 percent of the total vote no matter what the other candidate does.

The median is also "stable" in this example because, if one candidate adopts this position, the other candidate has no incentive to choose any other position. More formally, a position is *in equilibrium* if, given it is chosen by both candidates, neither candidate is motivated unilaterally to depart from it. Thus, the median in the example is both optimal (offers a guarantee of a minimum number of votes) and in equilibrium (once chosen by both candidates, there is no incentive for either unilaterally to depart from it).

A surprising consequence of all two-candidate elections is that *whatever* the distribution of attitudes among the electorate, the median loses none of its appeal in a single-issue election. Consider the distribution of the electorate in figure 1.2, which is bimodal (i.e., has two peaks) and is not symmetric. Applying the logic of the previous analysis, it is not difficult to show that the median is once again the optimal, equilibrium position for two candidates.

In this case, however, the *mean (Mn)*, which is the point at which the voters, weighted by their positions along the continuum, are balanced on the left and right of *Mn*, does not coincide with the median. This is because the distribution is skewed to the right, which necessarily pushes the median to the right of the mean. A sufficient condition for the median and mean to coincide is that the distribution be symmetric, but this condition is not necessary: the median and mean may still coincide if a distribution is nonsymmetric, as illustrated in figure 1.3.

The lesson derived from figure 1.2 is that it may not be rational for a candidate to take a "weighted average" position on an issue (i.e., at the mean) if the distribution of attitudes of the electorate is skewed to the left or right. Figure 1.3 indicates, however, that the noncoincidence of the median and mean is not necessarily related to the lack of symmetry in a distribution: half the voters may still lie to the left and half to the right of the mean (as well as the median) if the distribution is nonsymmetric.

Given the desirability of the median position in a two-candidate, single-issue election, is it any wonder why candidates who prize winning try so hard to avoid extreme positions? As in figures 1.2 and 1.3, even when the greatest concentration of voters does not lie at the median but instead at a mode (the mode to the right of the median in both these figures), a candidate would be foolish to adopt this modal position. For although he may very much please right-leaning voters, his opponent, by sidling up to this position but still staying to the left of the mode, would win the votes of a majority of voters.

Voters on the far left may not be particularly pleased to see

Figure 1.2
Nonsymmetric, Bimodal Distribution in Which Median
and Mean Do Not Coincide

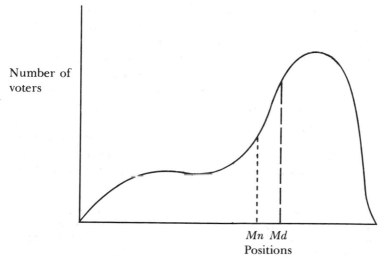

Number of
voters

Mn Md
Positions

Figure 1.3
Nonsymmetric, Bimodal Distribution in Which Median
and Mean Coincide

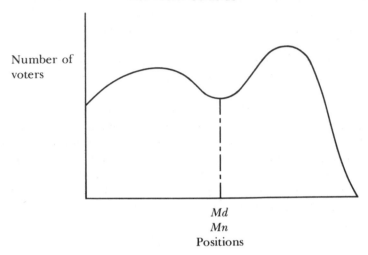

both candidates situate themselves at the median near the
right-hand mode in figure 1.2, but in a two-person race they
have nobody else to whom to turn. Of course, if left-leaning
voters should feel sufficiently alienated by both candidates,
they may decide not to vote at all, which has implications for
the analysis that will be explored in section 1.7.

I conclude this section by mentioning a rather different
application of the analysis as it has been developed so far.
This application is to business, which in fact was the first
substantive area to which spatial analysis was applied.[12] Consider two competitive retail businesses that consider locating
their stores somewhere along the main street that runs
through a city. Assume that, because transportation is costly,
people will buy at the department store nearest to them. Then

12. Harold Hotelling, "Stability in Competition," *Economic Journal* 39, no.
153 (March 1929): 41–57; A. P. Lerner and H. P. Singer, "Some Notes on
Duopoly and Spatial Competition," *Journal of Political Economy* 45, no. 2 (April
1937): 145–86; and A. Smithies, "Optimum Location in Spatial Competition," *Journal of Political Economy* 49, no. 3 (June 1941): 423–29.

the analysis says that, however the population is distributed along (or near) the main street, the best location is the median. If the city's population is uniformly distributed (i.e., not concentrated at one end or the other of the main street), then this location will, of course, be at the center of the main street.

Indeed, clusters of similar stores are frequently bunched together near the center of the main street, though these stores may not be particularly convenient to people who live far from the city's center (i.e., median/mean, if the city's population is uniformly distributed)—and, consequently, not in the public interest since their location discriminates against these people.[13] To accommodate shoppers in the suburbs as their density has increased over the years, however, shopping centers have sprung up, which—in terms of the previous analysis—says that new candidates have been motivated to enter the race.

The rationality of entry into a political race is an interesting but almost totally neglected question in the study of elections. Because presidential primaries, especially at the start of the sequence, tend to attract many candidates, it seems useful to ask what conditions make entry in a multicandidate race attractive.

1.4. Rational Positions in a Multicandidate Race

If there are no positions that a potential candidate can take in a primary that offer some possibility of success, then it will not be rational for him to enter the race in the first place. For a potential candidate, then, the rationality of entering a race and the rationality of the positions he might take once he enters really pose the same question.

Assume that two candidates have already entered a pri-

13. Hotelling, "Stability in Competition," p. 53. The social optimum, Hotelling argues, would be for the stores to locate at the one-quarter and three-quarters points along the main street so that no customer would have to travel more than one-quarter the length of the street to buy at one store. On the other hand, one might argue that if both stores were located at the center, the public interest would be served because greater competition would be fostered.

mary, and, consistent with the analysis in section 1.3, they both take the median position (or positions very close to it so that they are effectively indistinguishable). Is there any "room" for a third candidate?[14]

Consider figure 1.1, but now imagine that A and B have both moved to the median and therefore split the vote since they take the same position. Now if a third candidate C enters and takes a position on either side of the median (say, to the right), it is easy to demonstrate that the area under the distribution to C's right may encompass *less than* one-third of the total area under the distribution curve and still enable C to win a plurality of votes.

To see why this is so, in figure 1.4 I have designated, for a position of C to the right of A/B (at the median), the portion of the electorate's votes that A/B on the one hand, and C on the other, would receive. If C's area (shaded) is greater than half of A/B's area (unshaded), he will win more votes than A or B. (Recall that A and B split their portion of the vote since they take the same median position.)

Now C's area includes not only the voters to the right of his position but also some voters to his left. More precisely, he will attract voters up to the point midway between his position on the horizontal axis and that of A/B: A and B will split the votes to the left of this point; C will win all the votes to the right of this point. Since C picks up some votes to the left of his position, this is why less than one-third of the electorate can lie to his right and he can still win a plurality of more than one-third of the total vote.

By similar reasoning, it is possible to show that a fourth candidate D could take a position to the left of A/B and further chip away at the total of the two centrists. Indeed, D could beat candidate C as well as A and B if he moved closer to A/B (from the left) than C moved (from the right).

14. This question is considered briefly in Robertson, *Theory of Party Competition*, appendix 1, in the context of an electorate that changes with the enfranchisement of new voters. In light of the subsequent analysis, Robertson's statement that "all that we say [about a two-party system] can be generalised to multiparty systems without too much difficulty" (p. 7) is hard to accept.

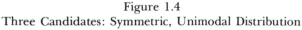

Figure 1.4
Three Candidates: Symmetric, Unimodal Distribution

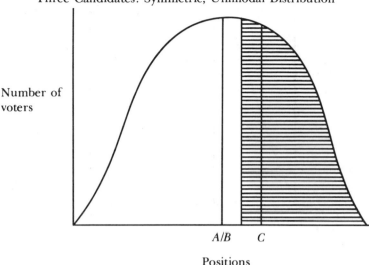

Clearly, the median position has little appeal, and is in fact quite vulnerable, to a third or fourth candidate contemplating a run against two centrists. This is one lesson that centrist candidates Hubert Humphrey and Edmund Muskie learned to their dismay in the early Democratic primaries in 1972 when George McGovern and George Wallace mounted challenges from the left and right, respectively. Only after Muskie was eliminated and Wallace was disabled by an assassin and forced to withdraw did Humphrey begin to make gains on McGovern in the later primaries, but not by enough to win.

In fact, there are *no* positions in a two-candidate race, for practically any distribution of the electorate,[15] in which *at least one* of the two candidates cannot be beaten by a third (or fourth) candidate.[16] I have already shown that *both* candidates

15. For details, see Steven J. Brams, "The Entry Problem in a Political Race" (mimeographed, New York University, 1978).

16. Given certain assumptions, there are equilibrium positions as the number of candidates increases and the original candidates are free to change their positions, too, but this fact does not inhibit the entry of new

Figure 1.5
Two Candidates: Symmetric, Bimodal Distribution

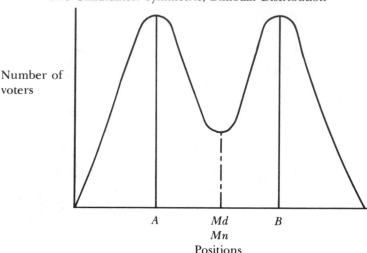

in a two-candidate race can be beaten by a third (or fourth) candidate if they both adopt the median position. Indeed, it is easy to show that *whatever* positions two candidates adopt (not necessarily the same), one will always be vulnerable to a third candidate; if the other is not, he will be vulnerable to a fourth candidate.

To see why this is so, assume two candidates, perhaps anticipating other entrants and realizing the vulnerability of the median, take different positions, as illustrated in figure 1.5. In this example, because the distribution is bimodal (as well as symmetric), positions at the modes would seem strong positions for each of two candidates to hold.

But enter now a right-leaning third candidate *C*, who would like to push candidate *B* out of the race. Excluding the possibility of ties, either there are (1) more voters to the right of *B* than between *B* and the median/mean or (2) the opposite is

candidates (see note 18). Lerner and Singer, "Notes on Duopoly and Spatial Competition," pp. 176–82, provide details on equilibria in multicandidate races, though their analysis is developed for buyers and sellers in a competitive market.

true. If (1) is true, then C can beat B by moving alongside B to his right; if (2) is true, then C can beat B by moving alongside B to his left. In either event, B is vulnerable to a third candidate C (and A would be vulnerable to a fourth candidate D for similar reasons). Hence, a third (or fourth) candidate can, by himself, knock out at least one of the two original candidates (A and B) in the example.

The vulnerability of *any* positions that two candidates might take in single-issue races to third (or fourth) candidates can be demonstrated generally, given very nonrestrictive assumptions about the distribution of voter attitudes. There is, in fact, *always* a place along a left-right continuum at which a new candidate can locate himself that will displace one or more nearby candidates.

This conclusion is in direct conflict with Anthony Downs's assertion that "there is a limit to the number of parties [candidates in the present analysis] which can be supported by any one distribution. When that limit is reached, no more parties can be successfully introduced."[17] On the contrary, no such limit exists, for reasons already given.[18]

This analysis thus provides an explanation, in terms of the rational choices of both voters and candidates, why many candidates may initially be drawn into the primary fray. As cases in point, in the first Democratic primary in New Hampshire in 1976, four candidates each received more than 10 percent of the vote, while in the second primary in Massachusetts seven candidates each received at least 5 percent of the

17. Downs, *Economic Theory of Democracy*, p. 123.

18. Downs seems falsely to have thought that (1) his assumption that a party is not perfectly mobile—"cannot leap over the heads of its neighbors" once it has come into being—would prevent disequilibrium; (2) once equilibrium is reached, "new parties . . . cannot upset" it (Downs, *Economic Theory of Democracy*, p. 123). With respect to (1), a form of cooperation—not just competition with restricted mobility—that allows the parties to make simultaneous adjustments seems also necessary for parties to reach equilibrium positions (assuming they exist); with respect to (2), the concept of equilibrium implies only that no old party can benefit from unilaterally shifting its position but says nothing about the benefits—discussed in the text—that may accrue to new parties that take up other positions along the continuum.

vote. In neither primary did the front-runner (Jimmy Carter in New Hampshire, Henry Jackson in Massachusetts) receive as much as 30 percent of the total Democratic vote.

1.5. The Winnowing-Out Process in Primaries

So far I have restricted the spatial analysis of presidential primaries to a single election in which the positions that candidates take on a single issue totally determine the vote they receive. Unlike the general election, however, in which the party affiliation of a presidential candidate may account for a substantial portion of his vote independent of the position he takes on any issue, the assumption that a candidate's position on an issue is determinative does not seem an unreasonable one from which to launch an analysis of primaries. Indeed, most candidates in presidential primaries tend to be identified as "liberal," "moderate," or "conservative," based on their positions on a range of domestic and foreign policy questions. (In section 1.8, however, I shall show that if there are multiple issues on which candidates are simultaneously evaluated, the simple one-dimensional spatial analysis heretofore described may not yield optimal positions that are in equilibrium.)

The spatial analysis in section 1.4 suggested why many candidates are drawn into the presidential primaries. To be sure, if an incumbent president or vice president is running, or even contemplates running, members of his party may be deterred from entering the primaries because of the built-in advantages that his incumbency brings.[19] But, it should be pointed out, incumbency did not stop Eugene McCarthy from challenging Lyndon Johnson in the 1968 Democratic primaries, Paul McCloskey from challenging Richard Nixon in the 1972 Republican primaries, or Ronald Reagan from challenging Gerald Ford in the 1976 Republican primaries (for an analysis of the Ford-Reagan race, see section 4.9).

Generally speaking, most primary challenges that have been mounted against an incumbent in recent presidential

19. For a rational-choice analysis of this question, see Steven J. Brams, *Paradoxes in Politics: An Introduction to the Nonobvious in Political Science* (New York: Free Press, 1976), pp. 126–35, and references cited therein.

elections have been single-man crusades and can be viewed, therefore, as essentially two-candidate contests. On the other hand, when an incumbent does not run, the field opens up and many candidates are motivated to stake out claims at various points along the left-right continuum, as I showed earlier.

To explain the entry of multiple candidates into primaries, I considered the contest for the nomination *as if* it were one election in which each candidate sought to maximize his vote total. But this limited perspective clearly does not explain the exit of candidates from primaries. Indeed, probably the most important feature of presidential primaries distinguishing them from other elections is their sequential nature; it is performance *in the sequence*—not in one primary election—that is crucial to a candidate's success.

This fact is conveyed quite dramatically by statistics from the 1972 Democratic primaries. In these primaries, roughly 16 million votes were cast, with George McGovern polling 25.3 percent of the total primary vote and Hubert Humphrey 25.4 percent, despite entering late.[20] Nonetheless, though McGovern received fewer primary votes than Humphrey, and little more than a quarter of the total, he went on to win his party's nomination on the first ballot at the national convention.

Bone and Ranney attribute McGovern's success "to certain breaks,"[21] but it seems that a winning strategy in a series of primaries is more than a matter of luck. I shall not try to analyze McGovern's success specifically, however, but rather attempt to identify optimal strategies over a sequence of elections generally.

As an institution, one is immediately struck by the fact that primaries play less of a role in selecting candidates than in eliminating them. Candidates who have won or done well in the primaries, such as Estes Kefauver in the 1952 Democratic primaries or Eugene McCarthy in the 1968 Democratic

20. Hugh A. Bone and Austin Ranney, *Politics and Voters* (New York: McGraw-Hill, 1976), p. 81.
21. Bone and Ranney, *Politics and Voters,* p. 81.

primaries, have, despite their impressive showings, lost their party's nomination to candidates who did not enter the primaries (Adlai Stevenson in 1952, Hubert Humphrey in 1968). No candidate who has been defeated in the primaries, however, has ever gone on to capture his party's nomination in the convention.

Once a candidate enters the primaries, his first-priority goal is not to be eliminated. In a multicandidate race, this goal most often translates into not being defeated by an opponent or opponents who appeal to the same segment of the party electorate.

To facilitate the subsequent analysis, assume that there are three identifiable segments of the party electorate: liberal, moderate, and conservative. This trichotomization of the electorate may not always be an accurate way of categorizing different positions in multicandidate races, but these labels are commonly used by the media and the public.

A candidate who takes a position on the left-right continuum will, I assume, fall into one of these three segments. Depending on the segment he is identified with, he will be viewed to be in a contest—at least in the first primaries—with only those other candidates who take positions in this segment.

What is likely to happen if there are at least three candidates contesting the vote in each segment? More specifically, who is likely to beat whom in the first-round battles and survive the cuts of candidates in each segment?

If the distribution of the electorate is symmetric and unimodal, as pictured in figure 1.1, then the liberal segment will appear as in figure 1.6, with the median of this segment to the right of the mean. For reasons given in section 1.3, the median will be attractive in a two-candidate liberal contest, but should a third candidate battle two candidates who take the median position in this segment, then his rational strategy would be to move to the right of the median—and toward the center of the overall distribution—where voters are more concentrated in the liberal, and adjoining moderate, segments.

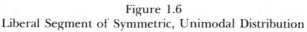

Figure 1.6
Liberal Segment of Symmetric, Unimodal Distribution

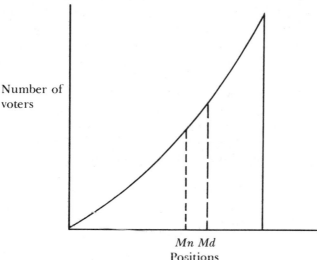

This movement toward the center may be reinforced by two considerations, one related to the concentration of votes near the center and the other by an anticipation of future possibilities in the race. As discussed in section 1.7, if voters become alienated by a candidate whose position is too far from their own and respond by not voting, a candidate would minimize this problem by being to the right rather than the left of the median in figure 1.6, where a loss a given distance from his position would be numerically less damaging. In addition, a position to the right of the median is more attractive as moderate candidates are eliminated and the liberal survivor can begin to encroach on voters who fall into the moderate segment.

Thus, liberal candidates will be motivated to move toward the moderate segment and, for analogous reasons, conservative candidates will also be motivated to move toward the moderate segment (though from the opposite direction).

What should the moderates do in their own segment (see figure 1.7)?

If two candidates take the median position, which is also the mean because of the symmetry of this segment, then a third moderate candidate would be indifferent to taking a position to the left or right of the median/mean since voters are symmetrically distributed on either side. To illustrate the consequences of a nonmedian position, assume that the third candidate takes a position somewhat to the right in the moderate segment. He thereby captures a plurality of the moderate votes against his two opponents at the median (for reasons given in section 1.4 for the entire distribution) and eliminates them from the contest.

If, as I argued earlier, a moderate-leaning liberal and a moderate-leaning conservative are advantaged in their segments in multicandidate contests, they can eliminate their median opponents from the respective contests on the left and right. As a consequence of these outcomes, the election

Figure 1.7
Moderate Segment of Symmetric, Unimodal Distribution

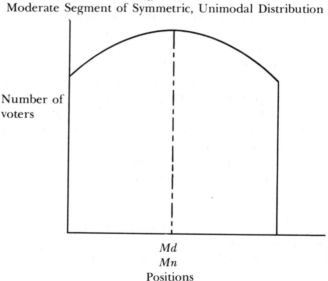

Number of voters

Md
Mn
Positions

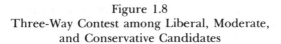

Figure 1.8
Three-Way Contest among Liberal, Moderate,
and Conservative Candidates

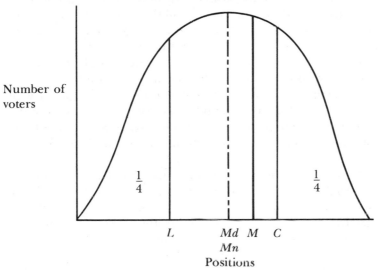

would reduce to a three-way contest among a liberal (L), a
moderate (M), and a conservative (C), with positions approximately as shown in figure 1.8. (As indicated earlier, I assume
that the moderate takes a position to the right of the
median/mean.)

In this manner, the initial primaries serve the purpose of
reducing the serious candidates in each segment to just
one. But the elimination process does not stop here. In fact, if
as few as one-fourth of the voters lie to the left and one-
fourth to the right of the liberal and conservative candidates,
respectively (see figure 1.8), it is unlikely that the moderate
candidate will get the most votes. For, by the previous assumption, he is not at the median but to its right, so he will in
all likelihood receive hardly more than one-half of those votes
in the middle (or one-fourth of the total, since one-half of the
total falls between L and C).[22]

22. If the moderate candidate's position were at the median, he would

Hence, the moderate candidate will probably receive fewer votes than the liberal candidate and perhaps fewer than the conservative candidate as well. For both the liberal and conservative candidates will pick up all the votes to their left and right, respectively (one-fourth of the total), plus all votes in the moderate segment up to the point midway between their positions and those of the moderate candidate. In fact, if the liberal and conservative candidates can each supplement their one-fourth liberal and one-fourth conservative support with as few as an additional one-twelfth of the total votes from the moderate segment, they would each receive a third of the total and thereby also limit the moderate candidate to one-third.

This is why a liberal candidate like McGovern could win with slightly more than 25 percent of the primary votes. More generally, a moderate candidate can be squeezed out of the race by challengers on both sides of the spectrum even when the bulk of voters falls in the middle. If most voters are not concentrated in the middle, but tend instead to be either liberal or conservative, then of course the problems of a moderate are aggravated.

Even if most voters are concentrated in the middle, the moderate may face another kind of problem. Contrary to the model postulated earlier, more than one moderate may attract a sufficient number of votes to survive the early primaries. But opposed by just one surviving liberal and one surviving conservative in the later primaries, the two or more moderates who divide the centrist vote will lose votes as the primaries proceed, relative to the liberal and conservative candidates who pick up votes from those in their segment

---

receive more than half the votes between the points L and C since voters are more concentrated around the median than at L or C. But being to the right of the median, the votes that would be divided between him and the liberal candidate at the point midway between L and M would, if he were sufficiently far away from Md/Mn, give the advantage to the liberal candidate. The conservative candidate would get fewer votes the closer the moderate candidate approached him, but, depending on the distribution, it is certainly possible that the liberal and conservative could both beat the moderate in the three-way contest depicted in figure 1.8.

whom they eliminate. The 1964 Republican primaries are an example of this situation, in which Henry Cabot Lodge, Jr., a moderate, lost out to Nelson Rockefeller and Barry Goldwater, the liberal and conservative candidates who fought a final climactic battle in the California primary that Goldwater won.

Moderates are not inevitably displaced in a sequence of primaries—as the case of Jimmy Carter in the 1976 Democratic primaries demonstrates—but this has been one trend in recent years in heavily contested primaries in both parties. As I have tried to show, spatial analysis enables one to understand quite well the weakness of moderates when squeezed from the left and right in a series of elimination contests.

1.6. The Factor of Timing

Primaries, I have suggested, are first and foremost elimination contests that pare down the field of contenders over time. Implicit in the previous analysis has been the assumption that the key to victory in the primaries is the position that a candidate takes on a left-right continuum *in relation to the positions taken by other candidates*. Thus, a candidate's goal of avoiding elimination, and eventually winning, cannot be pursued independently of the strategies other candidates follow in pursuit of the same goal. This quality of primaries, and elections generally, is what gives such contests the characteristics of a game, in which winning depends on the choices that *all* players make.

Since the rules of primaries do not prescribe that these choices be simultaneous,[23] there would appear to be advantages in choosing *after* the other players have committed

---

23. In some states, these choices are not made by the candidates at all but by a state official who places the names of all recognized candidates on the ballot, whether they have formally announced their candidacies or not. In other states, there are filing dates that must be met if one's name is to appear on the ballot. But even these can be ignored in most states if one runs as a write-in candidate. However, successful write-in campaigns, especially by nonincumbents, are rare, notwithstanding the write-in victory of Henry Cabot Lodge, Jr., in the 1964 Republican primary in New Hampshire.

themselves and the strengths and weaknesses of their positions can be better assessed. Indeed, some candidates avoid the early primaries and join the fray at a later stage on the basis of just such strategic calculations. Robert Kennedy, for example, stayed out of the 1968 Democratic primaries until the weakness of Lyndon Johnson's position as the incumbent became apparent, and Johnson had withdrawn from the race, before engaging Eugene McCarthy in Indiana and the later primaries.

A more extreme case of a late-starter was Hubert Humphrey, who stayed out of the 1968 Democratic primaries altogether, apparently believing that as the incumbent vice president he stood his best chance in the national party convention. He was not to be disappointed, winning on the first ballot in the convention, though his only serious opposition came from McCarthy because of the earlier assassination of Kennedy after the California primary.

The advantages of starting late, when the positions of one's opponents are known and their weaknesses can be identified and exploited, must be balanced against the organizational difficulties one faces in launching a campaign hurriedly. Last-minute efforts by even well-known candidates have often fizzled out.

The campaigns of some late-starters do take off, however, as illustrated by Robert Kennedy's run for the 1968 Democratic nomination before he was assassinated. True, it is usually only already well-known contenders who enjoy the privilege of holding out on announcing their candidacies. Candidates who come from nowhere, like Eugene McCarthy in 1968, George McGovern in 1972, and Jimmy Carter in 1976, have no choice but to start their campaigns very early to acquire sufficient recognition to make a serious run.

How can spatial analysis be used to model the factor of timing? Consider the situation in which several candidates to the left and right of the median struggle for their party's nomination in the early primaries. Assume that their various positions fall within the shaded bands pictured in figure 1.9, in which the distribution of voter attitudes is assumed to be symmetric and unimodal.

Figure 1.9
Bands Encompassing Positions of Candidates on Left and Right

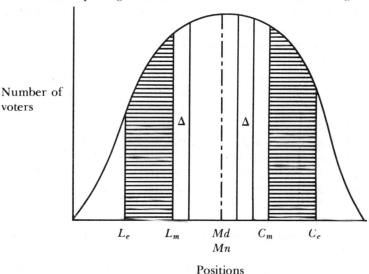

Number of
voters

L_e L_m Md C_m C_e
Mn

Positions

Assume that a prominent moderate politician considers making a bid for his party's nomination by positioning himself somewhere near the median/mean. He calculates that his chances of winning his party's nomination are good if extreme (e) candidates are the ones to survive in the early primaries on the left and right (at positions L_e and C_e), since he will be able to capture the bulk of the votes in the middle of the distribution. On the other hand, if moderate (m) candidates are the ones to survive in the early primaries (at positions L_m and C_m), he will probably be squeezed out by one or the other if he runs, for reasons given in section 1.5.

Thus, to gain a better picture of his chances, the prominent moderate may decide to await the results of the early primaries before making his decision, even if it means postponing the building of a campaign organization that would enable him to make a stronger bid. Aside from the problem of organizing an effective campaign late in the game, however, there may be a more compelling reason to avoid an announcement, based on spatial considerations.

Assume that the survivors of the early primaries are an extreme liberal candidate (at L_e) and a moderate conservative candidate (at C_m). Thus, if the moderate runs, he would be squeezed more from the right than from the left. Clearly, his chances are not so favorable as they would be if he faced two extreme candidates on the left and right. Nonetheless, spatial analysis clarifies how he can capitalize on the information he gains from awaiting the results of the early primaries to position himself optimally against his two surviving opponents at L_e and C_m.

Although one might think initially that a holdout moderate could maximize his vote total by taking a position midway between L_e and C_m, a glance at figure 1.9 will show this to be a poor strategy. Instead, he should take a position to the right of the median/mean near C_m.

The latter strategy follows from the fact that the votes he gives up to his L_e opponent as he moves to the right of the median/mean are more than compensated for by the votes he gains from his C_m opponent as he moves toward his position. Visually, it can be seen from figure 1.9 that there are more votes in the Δ-region just past the midway point between the median/mean and C_m than in the Δ-region just past the midway point between L_e and the median/mean. Therefore, a moderate gains more votes (in the right Δ-region) than he loses (in the left Δ-region) as he moves rightward toward C_m.

It is evident, then, if the distribution of voter attitudes is symmetric and unimodal, a late-starting moderate's best weapon against opponents on his left and right is *to move toward his more moderate opponent*. The qualitative analysis does not say exactly how far he should move, but this problem can easily be solved if the distribution of voter attitudes is known.[24]

The analysis in this section can be extended to different-shaped distributions and can incorporate different assump-

24. Solutions to examples involving both discrete and continuous distributions are given in Brams, *Spatial Models of Election Competition*; and Brams, "The Entry Problem in a Political Race," wherein general optimality results are given.

tions about the positions of committed candidates and the timing of the announcement of an uncommitted candidate. My main purpose, however, has been to introduce with a simple example the factor of timing into the spatial analysis of primaries, not to try to treat this subject exhaustively. It is a subject that deserves much more systematic attention than it has received in the literature.

1.7. Fuzzy Positions and Alienation

In section 1.6 I considered the possibility that there may be several candidates to the left of the median and several candidates to the right whose collective positions can be represented by bands, rather than lines, on the distribution. This same representation can also be used to model the positions of candidates that are *fuzzy*—that is, that cover a *range* on the left-right continuum instead of occurring at a single point.

Fuzzy positions in campaigns are well-known and reflected in such statements as, "I will give careful consideration to . . ." (all positions are open and presumably equally likely), "I am leaning toward . . ." (one position is favored over the others but not a certain choice), and "I will do this if such and such . . ." (choices depend on such-and-such factors). Such ambiguous statements may be interpreted as probability distributions, or lotteries, over specific positions and have been shown, under certain circumstances, to be rational choices not only for candidates but for voters as well.[25]

To model fuzzy positions, I shall not introduce probabilities into the spatial analysis but instead shall analyze some implications of band versus point positions. First, however, to motivate the subsequent analysis, consider why a candidate may not want to adopt a clear-cut position on an issue.

Perhaps the principal disadvantage of clarity in a campaign is that, while attracting some voters, it may alienate others, independently of the positions that other candidates take.

25. See Brams, *Paradoxes in Politics*, pp. 53–65, and references cited therein.

That is, voters sufficiently far from the position that a candidate takes at a particular point on the continuum may feel disaffected enough not to vote at all, even given the fact that his position is closer to theirs than that of any other candidate.

Much has been made of the "alienated voter" in the voting behavior literature, with many different reasons offered for his alienation.[26] If there is not universal agreement on why voters are alienated, the fact of alienation—as measured, for example, by the number of citizens who fail to vote—is indisputable. To be sure, some voters fail to vote because of such legal restrictions as residency requirements, but the vast majority of nonvoters in a presidential election—an average of about 40 percent in recent presidential elections,[27] which climbed to a historic high of 46 percent in 1976[28]—are eligible but choose not to exercise their franchise. In competitive primaries, by comparison, an even greater proportion of eligible voters—an average of about 60 percent in recent elections—do not vote,[29] though typically there are more candidates from whom to choose than in the general election.

Spatially, I shall assume that the alienation of a voter is a direct function of his distance from the position of the candidate closest to his position. If this distance is sufficiently great, then the voter's alienation overcomes his desire to vote for the candidate closest to him and he becomes a nonvoter. In the economist's language, if the demand for a product (candidate) is elastic (i.e., depends on its price), that product (candi-

26. The classic study is Murray Levin, *The Alienated Voter: Politics in Boston* (New York: Holt, Rinehart and Winston, 1960). For recent analyses, see James D. Wright, *The Dissent of the Governed: Alienation and Democracy in America* (New York: Academic Press, 1976); and the several articles on "Political Alienation in America," in *Society* 13, no. 5 (July/August 1976): 18–57.

27. Bone and Ranney, *Politics and Voters*, p. 35, figure 3.

28. Gerald Pomper et al., *The Election of 1976: Reports and Interpretations* (New York: David McKay, 1977), p. 72.

29. Austin Ranney, "Turnout and Representation in Presidential Primaries," *American Political Science Review* 66, no. 1 (March 1972): 24, table 1. On factors that affect turnout in primaries, see William D. Morris and Otto A. Davis, "The Sport of Kings: Turnout in Presidential Preference Primaries," *American Political Science Review* (forthcoming, 1978); and Ranney, *Participation in American Presidential Nominations, 1976.*

date) will not be purchased if the price for a customer (voter) becomes too high (voter is too far from a candidate's position).

The alienation of voters "too far" from any candidate's position may contravene findings from the earlier analysis. For example, alienation will tend to undermine the desirability of the median/mean in figure 1.3, and enhance the desirability of the two modes in this figure, as the optimal positions in a two-candidate race.

The reason is that the number of voters alienated a given distance from the median/mean may be more than the numbers alienated the same distance from either mode. The decrease in the number of alienated voters at the modes implies an increase in voter support, making the modal positions more attractive to the candidates.

Thus, a bimodal distribution in which alienation is a factor may induce rational candidates to adopt polarized positions on the left and right of an issue rather than locate themselves near the median. While advocates of "responsible" parties (and candidates) that present clear and distinct choices to the voters will view this polarization as salutary, advocates of compromise will not be enamored of the black and white choices that such polarization entails.

One way that a candidate can reduce his distance from voters, and possibly avoid the vote-draining effects of alienation, is to fuzz his position. Given that voters perceive a candidate's ambiguity as favorable to them, a strategy of ambiguity will increase the broadness of his appeal.

To illustrate the possible advantages of ambiguity, assume that a candidate's *true position* is at the center of the band in figure 1.10. If the candidate does *not* fuzz his position, assume that the "reach" of this position along the continuum is that shown as "true" in figure 1.10.

If the candidate fuzzes his position, however, he might be able to extend its reach from the left extreme to the median, assuming that voters on the left extreme interpret his position to be the left boundary of the band and voters at the median interpret his position to be the right boundary of the band. On the other hand, if voters, assuming the worst, make the

Figure 1.10
Fuzzy Position of a Candidate

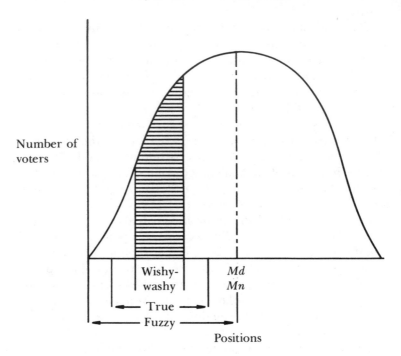

opposite interpretation—the boundaries of the band *farthest* from them are the actual positions of the candidate—an ambiguous candidate may perversely succeed in contracting (rather than expanding) his support when he fuzzes his true position. Call this interpretation of a candidate's position by voters "wishy-washy" and assume its reach to be only the bandwidth itself, versus the "fuzzy" range, in figure 1.10.

Thus, a danger may attend a strategy of ambiguity, depending on what voters perceive to be the actual position of a candidate. Or, given that they recognize the ambiguous strategy of a candidate to be a band rather than a point on the continuum, their choice may then depend on whether they view this ambiguity to represent a desirable flexibility or an undesirable pusillanimity.

Apparently, voters respond to ambiguity differently in different elections. Nobody ever accused Richard Nixon of forthrightness in his 1968 presidential campaign when he said "I have a plan" to end the war in Vietnam. But, judging from the results of the Republican primaries and general election in 1968, more voters believed in his competence to deal with the Vietnam situation than believed in the more specific proposals of his opponents.

In contrast, as George McGovern became increasingly vague about specific proposals he had made in the early Democratic primaries in 1972, and then withdrew his initial "1,000 percent" support of his vice-presidential choice, Thomas Eagleton, after the convention, voters began to see him as irresolute. At the polls, they overwhelmingly chose the by then better-known quantity, incumbent Nixon, in the 1972 election. Of course, only a few months after this election, the unraveling yarn of Watergate turned Nixon's presidential image into a shambles (see chapter 5).

Jimmy Carter's positions before and after the 1976 election present an interesting blend in contrasts. During the campaign he was quite unspecific on a number of issues, but after his election he developed a number of detailed programs (e.g., on energy and welfare) that he presented to Congress. Should he run for reelection in 1980, his campaign strategy as an incumbent president will undoubtedly emphasize less moral and spiritual themes and stress more his specific accomplishments as president.

These examples would seem to indicate that a strategy of ambiguity may be productive or unproductive, depending on how the candidate is viewed by the voters. From a spatial perspective, an ambiguous strategy would seem least risky for a candidate who tries to push his support toward the extremes, given that he can also hold onto more moderate voters with another position near the center. On the other hand, a candidate squarely but ambiguously in the center is more likely to have to counter attacks from both his left and his right, which may dissolve his centrist support on both sides, especially if his opponents can represent his position to be at the boundary of the band farthest from them.

Admittedly, these conclusions are rather speculative, principally because very little is known about what kinds of factors engender support for or opposition to fuzzy positions. In the absence of such knowledge, I can make only tentative assumptions about the relationship between ambiguous strategies and voting behavior and indicate the consequences each entails.

I suggested earlier that voter alienation is pervasive, but its implications are not entirely clear, especially in primaries. To begin with, citizens may fail to vote in the early primaries not so much because they find the candidates unattractive as they know very little about them. This might be called *indifference due to ignorance*: voters may not even know how to bracket the candidates, much less their specific positions.[30] However, as the field narrows in later primaries, and more information is generated about the races in both parties, the positions of candidates—specific or ambiguous—become clarified. Then *alienation due to incompatibility*, which I stressed earlier, may begin more and more to manifest itself.[31]

As early contenders are eliminated and the appeal of the surviving candidates broadens, each will feel less need to draw a fine line between himself and the other survivors, who will generally be spaced farther apart along the continuum. Hence, there will be an incentive for a candidate to extend his position from a point to a band to take in voters who otherwise would be alienated because they fall between or—if situated at the extremes—too far away from positions that have been eliminated.

30. Three out of five supporters of Eugene McCarthy, the antiwar candidate in the Democratic primary in New Hampshire in 1968, believed that the Johnson administration was wrong on Vietnam because it was too dovish rather than too hawkish—a complete inversion of McCarthy's views. Richard M. Scammon and Ben J. Wattenberg, *The Real Majority: An Extraordinary Examination of the American Electorate* (New York: Coward, McCann and Geoghegan, 1970), p. 91.

31. Riker and Ordeshook draw a similar distinction between "indifference" and "alienation," though they use the former concept to refer to a "cross-pressured" voter, not one who simply lacks information. See Riker and Ordeshook, *Introduction to Positive Political Theory*, pp. 323–30.

But then the danger of being seen as wishy-washy or eva-
sive, especially when sharpened by attacks from the opposition, may inspire contraction as well. The frequently observed
consequence of buffeting by these contradictory forces is to-
and-fro movements as candidates hew to basic positions but
at the same time scamper for pockets of support somewhat
removed from these positions. It is fascinating to watch this
dance performed along the continuum, even if it does not
always seem well rehearsed.

1.8. Multiple Issues in Campaigns

The dance along the continuum may be complicated if
there is more than one issue or policy dimension on which
candidates take positions and voters base choices. For then a
voter's distance from a candidate's position must be measured
in two- or higher-dimensional space, and optimal positions of
candidates with respect to different distributions of voter
attitudes become considerably harder to determine.[32]

The problem is rendered more difficult if voters weight the
various issues differently. Some voters, for example, may
attribute more importance to a candidate's position on economic issues than foreign policy issues, while others may
reverse this attribution. In general, the *salience* of issues for
voters, or the relative importance they attach to candidate
positions on them, obviates any simple extension of the one-
dimensional spatial analysis to higher dimensions, especially
when salience is correlated with the attitudes of voters on
issues.[33] In addition, the interrelatedness of some issues may
invalidate their representation as independent dimensions on
which candidates are separately evaluated.

Despite these difficulties, it is important to try to analyze
some elementary consequences of multi-issue campaigns. For

32. A geometric treatment of optimal positions in two dimensions is given
in Gordon Tullock, *Toward a Mathematics of Politics* (Ann Arbor: University of
Michigan Press, 1967), chap. 4.

33. John E. Jackson, "Intensities, Preferences, and Electoral Politics," *Social Science Research* 2, no. 3 (September 1973): 231–46.

Table 1.1
Preferences of Three Voters for Platforms

Voter	Preference
1	$(xy,\ xy',\ x'y,\ x'y')$
2	$(xy',\ x'y',\ xy,\ x'y)$
3	$(x'y,\ x'y',\ xy,\ xy')$

this purpose, consider a simple example of a campaign in which there are just two issues, X and Y.

Assume that each candidate can take only one of two positions on each issue (e.g., for or against), which I designate as x and x', y and y'. Altogether, there are four possible *platforms*, or sets of positions on both issues, that a candidate can adopt: xy, $x'y$, $y'x$, or $x'y'$.

Assume that the electorate consists of three voters, and their preferences for each of the platforms are as shown in table 1.1.[34] For each voter, the first platform in parentheses is his most preferred, the second his next most preferred, and so on.

Assume that there are just two candidates, and one is elected if a majority of voters (two out of three) prefers his platform to that of the other candidate. What platform should a candidate adopt if his goal is to get elected?

To answer this question, one might start by determining which position on each issue would be preferred by a majority if votes were taken on the issues separately. Since x is preferred to x' by voters 1 and 2, and y is preferred to y' by voters 1 and 3 (compare the first preferences of the voters in table 1.1), it would appear that platform xy represents the strongest set of positions for a candidate.

But this conclusion is erroneous in the example here. Despite the fact that a majority prefers positions x and y were the issues voted on separately, platform $x'y'$ defeats platform xy

34. This example is taken from Claude Hillinger, "Voting on Issues and on Platforms," *Behavioral Science* 16, no. 6 (November 1971): 564–66. See also Joseph B. Kadane, "On Division of the Question," *Public Choice* 13 (Fall 1972): 47–54, for an analysis of the effects of combining different alternatives.

since it is preferred by a majority (voters 2 and 3). Thus, a platform whose positions, when considered separately, are both favored by a majority may be defeated by a platform containing positions that only minorities favor. A recognition that a majority platform may be constituted from minority positions is what Downs argued may make it rational for candidates to construct platforms that appeal to "coalitions of minorities."[35]

The divergence between less-preferred individual positions and a more-preferred platform that combines them depends on the existence of a *paradox of voting*.[36] In this example, this means that there is no platform that can defeat all others in a series of pairwise contests. As shown by the arrows in figure 1.11, which indicate majority preferences between pairs of platforms, every platform that receives majority support in one contest can be defeated by another majority in another contest. For this reason, the majorities that prefer each platform are referred to as *cyclical majorities*.

The main conclusion derived from the simple example in this section is that there may be no set of positions that a candidate can adopt on two (or more) issues that is invulnerable: any set of positions that one candidate takes can be defeated by a different set adopted by another candidate. This means that, without any shift in the preferences of voters, a candidate running on a given platform could win an election in one year and lose it in the next, depending on the positions his opponent took.[37] This fact helps to explain the importance that candidates attach to anticipating an oppo-

---

35. Downs, *Economic Theory of Democracy*, chap. 4.

36. Hillinger, "Voting on Issues and on Platforms," p. 565, claims this is not the case, but this is refuted in Nicholas R. Miller, "Logrolling and the Arrow Paradox: A Note," *Public Choice* 21 (Spring 1975): 110. A paradox of voting also underlies what has been called the "Ostrogorski paradox," which is essentially the same as that illustrated in the text. See Douglas W. Rae and Hans Daudt, "The Ostrogorski Paradox: A Peculiarity of Compound Majority Decision," *European Journal of Political Research* 4 (September 1976): 391–98. For a description and review of the literature on the paradox of voting, see Brams, *Paradoxes in Politics*, chap. 2.

37. Norman Frohlich and Joe A. Oppenheimer, *Modern Political Economy* (Englewood Cliffs, N.J.: Prentice-Hall, 1978), p. 135.

Figure 1.11
Cyclical Majorities for Platform Voting

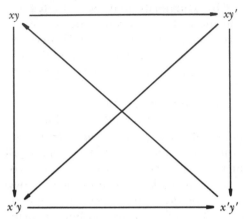

nent's positions so that they can respond with a set that is more appealing to the voters.

Of course, some candidates try to avoid this problem by being intentionally vague about their positions in the first place, as Downs pointed out.[38] But this strategy of ambiguity may lead to its own problems, as I showed in section 1.7.

By now it should be evident why primaries so often seem to yield topsy-turvy outcomes. The strongest theoretical result discussed in this chapter—the stability and optimality of the median in a two-candidate election—can be undermined if there is more than one issue on which candidates take positions. Indeed, no set of positions will be stable if there exists a paradox of voting, nor will any set be optimal in the sense of guaranteeing a particular outcome whatever the positions of one's opponent. In fact, contrary to expectations, one's best set of positions on issues in a race may be the minority positions on the issues considered separately, depending on the positions of one's opponent.

These findings do not depend on the exact nature of the underlying distributions of attitudes of voters or the precise

38. Downs, *Economic Theory of Democracy,* chaps. 8 and 9.

location of candidates with respect to these distributions. They depend only on qualitative distinctions (dichotomous positions of candidates, ordinal preferences of voters) and are, therefore, of rather general theoretical significance whatever the quantitative characteristics of a race are.

Probably the best advice to take from the analysis in this section is negative: avoid reading too much into spatial analysis based on a single issue if there may be other issues of significance in a campaign. Multiple issues greatly complicate—and may ultimately confound—single-issue spatial analysis, as the paradoxical findings in this section illustrate. Nevertheless, it is important to try to link candidate positions and voter attitudes, and spatial analysis provides a useful framework within which to relate these characteristics in both single elections and a series of primaries.

1.9. Conclusions

In this chapter I assumed the principal goal of a candidate is to avoid elimination in state primaries so that he may enter the second phase of the nomination game—the national party convention—as a serious contender, if not an outright winner. If it is winning—and not one's policy position on an issue—that counts most for candidates, however, the tables are reversed for the voter in the spatial model: he wants to maximize his satisfaction on the issue by choosing the candidate whose position is closest to his. The spatial games candidates play to try to maximize their appeal to voters were the focus of most of the analysis.

I would conclude that the evidence presented in this chapter offers general support for the proposition that candidates play these games. In some cases, candidates seem to hew to the median, in other cases to take more extremist positions, but both strategies may be rational depending on the number and positions of other candidates in the race.[39] Perhaps the

39. Even in two-candidate races the median voter result has recently been challenged. See Melvin J. Hinich, "Equilibrium in Spatial Voting: The Median Voter Result is an Artifact," *Journal of Economic Theory*, 16, no. 2 (December 1977): 208–19, where probabilistic voting is analyzed.

most surprising conclusion that emerges from the analysis is that a moderate candidate will not maximize his support by positioning himself midway between two opponents on the left and right but instead by taking a position closer to his less extreme opponent, given a symmetric, unimodal distribution of voter attitudes.

Yet, such findings derived from one-dimensional spatial models must be treated with caution if there is more than one issue in a campaign on which the positions of candidates determine the behavior of voters. To complicate matters further, in chapter 4 I shall introduce the activist support of party extremists into the calculations of candidates, which will lead to rather different conclusions about optimal positions in campaigns wherein the resources of candidates may be a significant factor.

The second phase in the presidential election game—the contest for a party's nomination in its national convention now held during the summer of a presidential election year—will be considered in chapter 2. I shall focus on contested nominations, not already decided by the results of the primaries or pre-convention maneuvers, that have required more than one ballot in the national party convention.

2 Party Conventions: Who Wins the Nomination?

2.1. Introduction

"Winning is everything" probably applies as well to politics as it does to professional sports. As William H. Riker put it,

> What the rational political man wants, I believe, is to win, a much more specific and specifiable motive than the desire for power. . . . The man who wants to win also wants to make other people do things they would not otherwise do, he wants to exploit each situation to his advantage, and he wants to succeed in a given situation.[1]

Because it helps him to achieve these things in elections, wars, and other arenas of political conflict, it is not surprising that the rational actor places a high value on winning. Moreover, as a concept that connotes the means for realizing a whole panoply of ends, the notion of winning offers the political theorist a generalized goal for political actors that conveniently subsumes particular goals which are often difficult to know or specify in actual situations. The consequences that Riker has derived from this postulated goal and other assumptions of his game-theoretic model—in particular, his well-known "size principle" that coalitions tend toward minimal winning size under specified conditions—have served as a powerful stimulus to a growing body of theory that I shall discuss in chapter 4.

Yet, when there are more than two actors, none of whom

This chapter is based largely on Steven J. Brams and G. William Sensiba, "The Win/Share Principle in National Party Conventions" (mimeographed, New York University, September 1971). I wish to thank the National Science Foundation for its generous financial support of this research under Grant GS-2798.

1. William H. Riker, *The Theory of Political Coalitions* (New Haven, Conn.: Yale University Press, 1962), p. 22.

can command sufficient resources to win in a political contest, winning may not be everything. This is fundamentally a coalition situation in which the winner is not a single actor but necessarily a coalition of actors, and the *share* of the payoff that each actor in the coalition can expect to receive if his coalition wins becomes a crucial consideration. An individual actor must concern himself not only with maximizing his probability of being a member of a winning coalition but also with maximizing his share of the total benefits that redound to all members of the winning coalition.

Typically, of course, the more "important" an actor is to a coalition's victory, the more he can expect to share in its benefits if it should win. In this chapter I shall operationally define the "importance" of an actor's contribution to a coalition and combine it with the probability that the coalition indeed becomes winning. Thereby I shall show how the goal of maximizing both one's share of the benefits and the probability of being a member of a winning coalition can be used to retrodict (i.e., predict a past state of affairs), and from its assumptions explain, the voting behavior of delegates in those multiballot national party nominations that have ended in narrow victories (with respect to the decision rule) for one side.

The marriage of the share-of-benefits notion with the concept of winning will lead to the formulation of what I shall call the "win/share principle." Like Riker's size principle, it is a theoretical statement about coalition outcomes, but unlike the size principle, it is based not only on the goal of winning in concert with others but also on the goal of simultaneously obtaining as large a portion of the benefits of victory as possible. In the context of national party conventions, the most important consequence of this dual goal is that a front-runner is less favored the larger the proportion of uncommitted delegates in a convention.

2.2. *The Need for Explanatory Models of National Party Convention Nominations*

Is a scientific explanation of the historical forces and human passions that have shaped national party convention nominations possible? This would appear not to be the case from Ralph G. Martin's dramatic description of the *bandwagon effect*, that peculiar phenomenon in politics where the momentum generated by a front-running candidate sweeps him on to victory:

> The bandwagon is a fever that takes statistics out of the definition of politics. It's a thing of chemistry that boils blood, jumps feet, waves hands, shouts voices, bangs fists, and heightens hangovers. It parts from reason in the same way that love does or hate does. It is a mass orgy feeling that sweeps with the fervor of a religious revival. It is the Fourth of July on Christmas morning.[2]

Others, however, see a rationale for this mystical force that grips delegates in the frenzy of political combat. Not quite so mystically, Gerald Pomper observes the sweet hand of reason at work:

> Delegates wish to be on bandwagons because support of the nominee at the convention will be a basic criterion for the later distribution of Presidential favors and patronage.[3]

And while delegates may be calculating individuals, Nelson Polsby sees the spread of information as a basic factor in such emotional upsurges:

2. Ralph G. Martin, *Ballots & Bandwagons* (Chicago: Rand McNally, 1964). p. 444. The drama of the nomination process is also highlighted in Herbert Eaton, *Presidential Timber: A History of Nominating Conventions, 1868–1960* (Glencoe, Ill.: Free Press of Glencoe, 1964), a personalized account that relies heavily on anecdotes and vignettes. For other colorful characterizations of party conventions by various analysts, see Judith H. Parris, *The Convention Problem: Issues in Reform of Presidential Nominating Procedures* (Washington, D.C.: Brookings Institution, 1972), chap. 1. On party choices before the nominating conventions, see James S. Chase, *Emergence of the Presidential Nominating Convention, 1798–1832* (Urbana: University of Illinois Press, 1973).

3. Gerald Pomper, *Nominating the President: The Politics of Convention Choice* (Evanston, Ill.: Northwestern University Press, 1963), p. 144.

How news travels in conventions may determine the direction and force of stampedes.[4]

Alternatively, the voting behavior of delegates may be such a complex tangle of forces that it may simply not be possible to untangle its mysteries:

> Voting behavior is only the end product of many factors of difference, each one of which may involve both a consciously planned decision and an unplanned motivation that may never reach the level of conscious perception. Convention voting behavior is essentially a summation of these factors as mirrored in the decisions of the individual delegates.[5]

Other descriptions and purported explanations of delegate behavior could be cited, but none seems to offer a parsimonious and rigorous model of decision making whose concepts can be operationalized and systematically applied to the test of empirical propositions about convention processes. What seems particularly lacking is a model that accounts for why convention delegates on some occasions favor the front-runner (i.e., a bandwagon effect develops) and on others a nonfront-runner (i.e., an underdog effect develops).[6] In one experimental study, the appeal of the underdog was shown to be stronger than the appeal of the front-runner, but no reasons why this should be the case were offered except that "common folklore holds that Americans are inclined to come to the aid of the underdog is an unequal fray between two antagonists."[7]

4. Nelson Polsby, "Decision-Making at the National Conventions," *Western Political Quarterly* 13, no. 3 (September 1960): 618.

5. Paul T. David, Ralph M. Goldman, and Richard C. Bain, *The Politics of National Party Conventions*, rev. ed. (New York: Vintage, 1964), pp. 258–59. This is a condensation of the original Brookings study, cited in note 13, which is now out of print.

6. This question is not directly addressed in a recent statistical study of bandwagons in conventions and other arenas. See Donald Collat, Stanley Kelley, Jr., and Ronald Rogowski, "Presidential Bandwagons" (paper delivered at the 1976 Annual Meeting of the American Political Science Association, Chicago, September 2–5).

7. Daniel W. Fleitas, "Bandwagon and Underdog Effects in Minimal-

Although the models described in this chapter can be applied to any two successive ballots in a multiballot nomination, the main analysis will be limited to only the final two ballots of a set of nominations. (As I shall argue later, however, the *logic* of the analysis is applicable to nominations in which there are no multiple ballots.) Since one of the great guessing games in American politics concerns who will carry each party's standard in the national election, it does not seem a trivial problem to try to isolate the factors at the penultimate stage in the nomination process that bear on who will be chosen.

Emphatically, however, the models as I shall apply them to empirical data are not predictive in the sense of being useful in determining in advance who will be nominated. (This could hardly be the case when some data utilized in the calculations are taken from the final ballot that determines the outcome!) Logical consequences derived from the assumptions of the models, however, may prove useful for purposes of prediction.

Just as important as the predictive power of a model is its ability to explain relationships among a set of phenomena, which in this case will be why individuals support a particular candidate in a convention as the final choice looms ahead. Earlier in the proceedings of a convention it seems that factors peculiar to the time, place, and setting are most prominent, such as the candidacy of favorite sons. As the final stage approaches, however, it seems likely that considerations related to winning and increasing one's share of the benefits predominate. If this is the case, it should be possible to demonstrate the utility of these concepts as indicators of political

Information Elections," *American Political Science Review* 65, no. 2 (June 1971): 438; see also Robert Navazio, "An Experimental Approach to Bandwagon Research," *Public Opinion Quarterly* 41, no. 2 (Summer 1977): 217–25. For an interesting analysis of the strategic effect of these countervailing forces in the prediction of election outcomes, see Herbert A. Simon, "Bandwagon and Underdog Effects of Election Predictions," *Public Opinion Quarterly* 18, no. 3 (Fall 1954): 245–53, which is also discussed in Steven J. Brams, *Paradoxes in Politics: An Introduction to the Nonobvious in Political Science* (New York: Free Press, 1976), pp. 65–77. For further analysis of bandwagon effects, see section 4.9.

behavior that transcend the peculiar circumstances and unique historical features of different conventions.

Unlike the assumptions of the spatial analysis in chapter 1, I assume in this analysis that the behavior of convention delegates is independent not only of the personalities of the candidates involved in a particular race but the positions of the candidates on the issues in the race as well. Like the analysis in chapter 1, however, this approach to the explanation of the choices that convention delegates make will facilitate the derivation of consequences from a set of assumptions that can be tested against real-world behavior. To the extent that these consequences are consistent with this observed behavior, the assumptions from which they are derived can be said to offer reasons for believing in relationships among the phenomena studied.

The consequences may also enable one to specify a mechanism that leads to the discovery of new relationships that would not have previously been suspected. By way of contrast, a set of empirical generalizations or "tested" hindsights, unmoored to the assumptions of a model, offers the analyst disconnected findings but no theoretical structure from which they can be derived.

The theoretical structure employed here, like that in chapter 1, starts from the assumption of individual rationality: people behave *as if* they order their alternative courses of action and choose that which is most preferred. If a person does not actually make, or is not able to understand, the rationalistic calculations imputed to him, the rationality assumption may still satisfactorily account for his (or a group's) behavior. I shall elaborate on this point at the conclusion of the empirical analysis, which demonstrates more vividly than can be suggested here some of the intellectual dividends offered by a rational-choice model of collective decision making.

In the analysis that follows, I assume that delegates in national party conventions act rationally to achieve certain goals. I measure their achievement by assuming they are acting as if to maximize their *expected utility*, which is the sum of the utility (or value) they associate with every possible outcome times the probability that it will occur. This value may be based on attaining such selfish ends as income, power, or prestige.

Certainly one of the most important avenues for attaining such ends in political life is through winning elections. Instrumental to winning the presidency and vice presidency in the United States is winning the nomination of one's party in quadrennial national party conventions. Given that this decision is still open after the conclusion of the first phase of the nomination game—the state primaries—what circumstances favor which candidates in conventions?

2.3. Calculating the Probabilistic Contribution of a Shift of Delegates in National Party Conventions

National party conventions, which began with the 1832 presidential campaign, provide an unusually good arena for the study of coalition-formation processes. In conventions with multiballot presidential and vice-presidential nominations, in particular, the shift of coalitions from roll call to roll call can be observed as each candidate tries to accumulate the number of votes necessary for nomination—or perhaps the number necessary to block another candidate. As John McDonald put it,

> The political conventions . . . are coalition games. Each candidate goes in generally with a number of votes short of a nominating majority. The "game" is for each candidate to secure that majority through coalitions with other-candidate groups and at the same time to break up or prevent competing coalitions.[8]

8. John McDonald, *Strategy in Poker, Business and War* (New York: Norton, 1950), p. 116; cited in William A. Gamson, "Coalition Formation at Presidential Nominating Conventions," *American Journal of Sociology* 68, no. 2 (September 1962): 157. Using such attributes of candidates as their personal characteristics, fame, interest-group support, electoral record, ideological orientation, and the size and party composition of states from which they came—as well as the proportion of votes each received on convention ballots—Gamson retrodicts with reasonable accuracy those coalitions of can-

Just as important as the contest in which the few major candidates participate, however, is the guessing game in which the many more delegates (now over 2,000 in the Republican convention, 3,000 in the Democratic convention) are engaged in the course of choosing their party's nominee. If, as Nelson W. Polsby and Aaron B. Wildavsky assert, "delegates to national conventions are expected to behave in a way that will maximize their political power,"[9] it is fair to ask what would be a reasonable measure of "political power" in conventions. From their assertion that delegates must support the eventual winner before he achieves a majority to gain the access necessary to press for future claims,[10] it seems reason-

didates that formed in several conventions since 1900. By contrast, I shall not attempt to retrodict the *composition* of coalitions, using many behavioral variables, but shall instead show regularities in the *formation* of coalitions by analyzing only the distribution of votes on the final ballots. For an attempt to retrodict the likelihood of coalitional alignments and vote totals in the 1968 Republican presidential nomination using a computer-simulation model, see James P. Zais and John H. Kessel, "A Theory of Presidential Nominations, with a 1968 Illustration," in *Perspectives on Presidential Selection*, ed. Donald R. Matthews (Washington, D.C.: Brookings Institution, 1973), chap. 5.

9. Nelson W. Polsby and Aaron B. Wildavsky, "Uncertainty and Decision-Making at the National Conventions," in *Politics and Social Life: An Introduction to Political Behavior*, ed. Nelson W. Polsby, Robert A. Dentler, and Paul A. Smith (Boston: Houghton Mifflin, 1963), p. 375.

10. Polsby and Wildavsky, "Uncertainty and Decision-Making at the National Conventions," p. 376. Polsby and Wildavsky also make this point in the latest edition of their book, *Presidential Elections: Strategies of American Electoral Politics*, 4th ed. (New York: Scribner's, 1976), p. 140, although they point out that ideological "purists," especially evident in the 1964 Republican and 1972 Democratic conventions, have generally been innocent of power aspirations—ultimately to the detriment of their party's chances in the general election. For a discussion of purism and professionalism in recent Democratic conventions, see Denis G. Sullivan, Jeffrey L. Pressman, Benjamin I. Page, and John J. Lyons, *The Politics of Representation: The Democratic Convention 1972* (New York: St. Martin's, 1974), pp. 116–34; and Denis G. Sullivan, Jeffrey L. Pressman, and F. Christopher Arterton, *Explorations in Convention Decision Making: The Democratic Party in the 1970s* (San Francisco: W. H. Freeman, 1976), pp. 103–06. It should be pointed out that amateurs in presidential politics are not invariably purists, as the candidacy of Jimmy Carter in 1976 demonstrated. For an analysis of the 1976 Democratic convention, see Denis G. Sullivan, Jeffrey L. Pressman, F. Christopher Arterton,

able to infer that the delegates' success in realizing these claims will be a function of their contributions to the candidate's victory.

To capture this notion of delegate contributions, define the *probabilistic contribution* that a set of delegates makes to a candidate's chances of achieving victory as the amount by which they increment a candidate's probability of winning from one ballot to the next. To measure this amount, the probability that a candidate becomes winning on two successive ballots must first be defined.

In the analysis that follows, I shall develop two probabilistic measures, one based on a "minimal winning" coalition model and the other on an "any winning" coalition model. However, for reasons to be indicated later, the measure based on the minimal winning model seems more suited to the data to be analyzed.

To illustrate the calculations, consider the numbers of votes received by each of the two leading candidates and all others in balloting for the vice-presidential nomination in the 1956 Democratic convention shown in table 2.1. This is the most recent presidential or vice-presidential nomination of either major party which has gone more than one ballot. In this race, which pitted Estes Kefauver against John Kennedy, Kefauver, after leading on the first ballot, lost the lead to Kennedy on the second ballot only to regain it and win the nomination (receiving more than a simple majority of 687 out of 1,372 votes necessary to win) after a "shift" of delegate votes from the initial second-ballot tally was recorded.

I shall treat the second ballot after the shift as in effect a third and final ballot since delegates in each state delegation were allowed to change their votes after the initial tally. Such

Robert T. Nakamura, and Martha Wagner Weinberg, "Candidates, Caucuses, and Issues: The Democratic Convention, 1976," in *The Impact of the Electoral Process*, ed. Louis Maisel and Joseph Cooper (Beverly Hills, Calif.: Sage Publications, 1977), pp. 81–132. In the discussion of party coalitions in chapter 4, I shall distinguish three different sets of interests in a political party and indicate how candidates try to reconcile these by the "compromise" positions they take in the primaries and general election.

Table 2.1

Votes Received by Two Leading Candidates, and All
Others, in Balloting for Vice-Presidential
Nomination in 1956 Democratic Convention

	1st ballot	2d ballot (before shift)	2d ballot (after shift)
Kefauver	466	551	755
Kennedy	294	618	589
Other	612	203	28

Source: Richard C. Bain, *Convention Decisions and Voting Records* (Washington, D.C.: Brookings Institution, 1960), appendix D. Fractional votes of one-half received by the two leading candidates have not been included in their vote totals but instead assigned to the "other" category to simplify the combinatorial calculations described in the text.

shifts have occurred quite frequently on final ballots in national party conventions and, though not officially classified as new ballots, would seem to qualify practically since a new round of voting occurred.

Consider only the second ballot, before and after the shift. The first step in the analysis is to calculate the probability that each candidate becomes *minimal winning* with exactly a simple majority of 687 votes.

At the conclusion of the second ballot before the shift, Kefauver, with 551 votes, needed 136 votes to win with exactly 687 votes. Assuming that he could obtain these only from defections by the 203 "other" delegates voting for lesser candidates—and not from delegates voting for Kennedy—we can count the number of ways in which it is theoretically possible to obtain 136 commitments from the pool of 203 "other" delegates. After doing the same for Kennedy, we can then calculate the probability that each candidate will attain a simple majority of 687 votes necessary to win.

To illustrate the logic of these calculations with a simple example, suppose that we wanted to know the number of ways of choosing three voters from a pool of four, designated by the set $\{a, b, c, d\}$. Clearly, any of the four voters may be excluded from the three chosen, yielding four different sets of three voters: $\{a, b, c\}$, $\{a, b, d\}$, $\{a, c, d\}$, and $\{b, c, d\}$.

The same logic governs the choice of 136 voters from a pool of 203 voters, but the calculations, though straightforward, are a good deal more complicated because of the larger numbers involved. Some notation from combinatorial mathematics will facilitate these calculations. The standard notation for combinations, $\binom{m}{n}$, will be used to denote the number of combinations that can be formed from m objects taken n at a time, or $\dfrac{m!}{n!(m-n)!}$. The exclamation point indicates a factorial; the number it follows is multiplied by every positive integer smaller than itself (e.g., $4! = 4 \cdot 3 \cdot 2 \cdot 1 = 24$).[11]

In this simple example, the number of ways of choosing three voters from a pool of four is

$$\binom{4}{3} = \frac{4!}{3!1!} = \frac{(4 \cdot 3 \cdot 2 \cdot 1)}{(3 \cdot 2 \cdot 1)(1)} = 4,$$

which coincides with the number of ways for choosing three different voters from the set of four by complete enumeration of all the possibilities. For the vice-presidential contenders on the second ballot before the shift, Kefauver could attract the 136 delegates necessary to win minimally in $\binom{203}{136}$ ways. Since Kennedy, with 618 votes, needed 69 of the 203 "other" delegates to win with a bare majority, he could attract the 69 delegates he needed to win minimally in $\binom{203}{69}$ ways.

Now calculate the probabilities that the two leading candidates could offer those "other" delegates not committed to either leading candidate of being in a minimal winning coalition. Although these delegates surely may have had preferences for one or the other of the leading candidates, in the absence of such information as-

11. For an elementary treatment of the counting and probabilistic concepts employed here, see John G. Kemeny, J. Laurie Snell, and Gerald H. Thompson, *Introduction to Finite Mathematics*, 3d ed. (Englewood Cliffs, N.J.: Prentice-Hall, 1974), chaps. 2 and 3.

sume that all combinations of the delegates committed to "other" lesser candidates, and necessary for the leading candidates to attract to achieve a simple majority, are equally likely.[12] Given this assumption, the probability that Kefauver eventually becomes *minimal winning* (P_{min}) is equal to the number of ways $\left[\binom{203}{136}\right]$ he can attract the necessary delegates to win with a simple majority divided by the total number of ways $\left[\binom{203}{136} + \binom{203}{69}\right]$ both he and Kennedy can attract the number each respectively needs:

$$P_{min}(\text{Kefauver}) = \frac{\binom{203}{136}}{\binom{203}{136} + \binom{203}{69}} = \frac{\frac{203!}{136!67!}}{\frac{203!}{136!67!} + \frac{203!}{69!134!}}$$

$$= \frac{69 \cdot 68}{69 \cdot 68 + 136 \cdot 135} = 0.20.$$

Kennedy's complementary probability of eventually putting together a minimal winning coalition is

$$P_{min}(\text{Kennedy}) = \frac{\binom{203}{69}}{\binom{203}{69} + \binom{203}{136}} = 0.80.$$

12. Other assumptions are, of course, possible. In a Markovian analysis of opinion change, for example, Germain Kreweras postulated that the probability that an uncommitted actor will commit himself to a candidate is a direct function of the number of supporters the candidate already has. See Germain Kreweras, "A Model for Opinion Change during Repeated Balloting," in *Readings in Mathematical Social Science*, ed. Paul F. Lazarsfeld and Neil W. Henry (Cambridge, Mass.: MIT Press, 1968), pp. 174–91; other bandwagon models are described in Robert M. May and Brian Martin, "Voting Models Incorporating Interactions between Voters," *Public Choice* 22 (Summer 1975): 37–53; Manfred Gartner, "Endogenous Bandwagon and Underdog Effects in a Rational Choice Model," *Public Choice* 25 (Spring 1976): 83–89; and Philip D. Straffin Jr., "The Bandwagon Curve," *American Journal of Political Science* 21, no. 4 (November 1977): 695–709. I shall describe Straffin's model, which he also applied to the Kennedy-Kefauver race, in section 4.9.

Since Kefauver went on to win on the second ballot after the shift, I *define* his probability of "becoming" minimal winning on this final ballot to be 1.00 (though, of course, he had already won, even if not quite minimally!), and Kennedy's complementary probability to be 0. Thus, the probabilistic advantage which the delegates shifting to Kefauver brought to his candidacy on the final ballot—some of whom were defectors from Kennedy, though Kennedy's delegates were considered unswitchable in making the previous calculation[13]—is the difference between the probability that Kefauver becomes minimal winning before (0.20) and after (1.00) the shift on the second ballot: $1.00 - 0.20 = 0.80$. This is the amount by which the shifting delegates augmented Kefauver's probability of becoming minimal winning.

If the candidates take into account not only the number of ways of becoming minimal winning but also the number of ways of winning with more than a simple majority, then the calculation of the probabilistic contribution of a shift of the "other" delegates is somewhat more complicated. Before the shift, the number of ways that Kefauver could attract not only the minimally sufficient 136 "other" delegates to win with exactly a simple majority of 687 votes, but also the 137 or 138

---

13. If all but Kefauver's delegates (i.e., those of all other candidates, including Kennedy) were considered as the potential "uncommitted" members (casting $1,372 - 551 = 821$ votes) who might defect to Kefauver on the final ballot, and the same done for Kennedy, then Kefauver's probability of becoming minimal winning (to two decimal places) would be

$$\frac{\binom{821}{136}}{\binom{821}{136} + \binom{754}{69}} = 1.00,$$

and Kennedy's complementary probability would be 0. Given Kennedy's lead on the second ballot before the shift, this result is absurd and I therefore stick with the assumption in the text that only those delegates not voting for the two front-runners constitute the potential defectors. For empirical evidence supporting this assumption, see Paul T. David, Ralph M. Goldman, and Richard C. Bain, *The Politics of National Party Conventions* (Washington, D.C.: Brookings Institution, 1960), pp. 376–80.

or 139 . . . up to all 203 "other" delegates sufficient to win with a coalition larger than minimal winning (i.e., an any winning coalition) is

$$n(\text{Kefauver}) = \binom{203}{136} + \binom{203}{137} + \cdots + \binom{203}{203}.$$

Similarly, the number of ways that Kennedy could construct an any winning coalition by securing commitments from at least the minimally sufficient 69 "other" delegates he needed to win is

$$n(\text{Kennedy}) = \binom{203}{69} + \binom{203}{70} + \cdots + \binom{203}{203}.$$

Analogous to the previous calculation of Kefauver's probability of becoming minimal winning on the next-to-final ballot, Kefauver's probability of becoming *any winning* (P_{any}) is

$$P_{\text{any}}(\text{Kefauver}) = \frac{n(\text{Kefauver})}{n(\text{Kefauver}) + n(\text{Kennedy})} = 0,$$

and Kennedy's complementary probability of becoming any winning is 1.00.

It is evident that when *all* possible ways that the two leading candidates can form winning coalitions with "other" delegates are assumed to be equally likely, the minimal winning probabilities favoring (or not favoring) each candidate on the next-to-final ballot become transformed in such a way as to magnify the odds favoring the front-runner against the nonfront-runner. The nonfront-runner (Kefauver) therefore receives a bigger boost on the final ballot when the "other" delegates swing in his favor, catapulting his probability of becoming any winning from 0 to 1.00 (when he has in fact won on the final ballot). The probabilistic contribution of 1.00 (1.00 − 0) produced by this shift in delegates between the next-to-final and final ballots based on the any winning model compares with a probabilistic contribution of 0.80 produced by this shift based on the previous minimal winning model.

Using two different models based on different assumptions about the set of outcomes considered to be possible, I have defined and illustrated the concept of the probabilistic contribution that a shift of delegates brings to the winning candidate between the next-to-final and final ballots. I shall next define the probabilistic contribution of a hypothetical "reverse shift" of votes from the winning candidate to the second-leading candidate, and vice versa, on the final ballot. Based on what the outcome *would have been*, I shall determine whether the shifting delegates acted rationally.

2.4. The Consequences of a Hypothetical Reverse Shift

As table 2.1 shows, between the next-to-final and final ballots (i.e., before and after the shift on the second ballot), Kefauver gained

$$755 - 551 = 204 \text{ votes,}$$

and Kennedy lost

$$618 - 589 = 29 \text{ votes.}$$

If the shifting delegates had reversed themselves, and Kefauver's gain had gone to Kennedy, Kennedy would have won the nomination with

$$618 + 204 = 822 \text{ votes;}$$

likewise, if Kennedy's loss had been Kefauver's, Kefauver would have lost the nomination with

$$551 - 29 = 522 \text{ votes.}[14]$$

Recall that Kennedy's probability of becoming minimal winning on the next-to-final ballot was 0.80. Since Kennedy's probability of becoming minimal winning would have been 1.00 if the reverse shift had occurred (i.e., he would have

14. It is possible, of course, for there to be a shift of delegates from one candidate to another and vice versa that preserves the vote totals of the two candidates. In the accounting here, however, a shift is defined in terms of the actual changes in vote *totals* from one ballot to the next; this definition of a shift does not require ascertaining how each individual voted on two successive ballots, which is information generally not available since votes are usually aggregated and recorded by states.

won, even if not minimally), the probabilistic contribution which delegates would have brought to his candidacy would have been $1.00 - 0.80 = 0.20$, which is less than what Kefauver's candidacy offered to those "other" delegates who ensured his nomination ($1.00 - 0.20 = 0.80$). Thus, it was rational, by this calculation, for those delegates who shifted on the final ballot to vote for the eventual winner (Kefauver, bringing a probabilistic contribution of 0.80 to his candidacy) rather than the front-runner on the next-to-final ballot (Kennedy, to whom the shifting delegates would have brought only a probabilistic contribution of 0.20).

This difference is even more striking when applied to the probabilities based on the any winning model. In this case, I previously showed that the probabilistic contribution of the shifting delegates to Kefauver's candidacy was the maximal probabilistic difference, $1.00 - 0 = 1.00$ (versus a 0.80 contribution using the minimal winning model). Had there been a reverse shift and had Kennedy won, the difference between his probability of becoming any winning between the next-to-final and final ballots would have been $1.00 - 1.00 = 0$, so the shifting delegates would have made no probabilistic contribution (versus a 0.20 contribution using the minimal winning model).

More formally, define the difference between the actual probabilistic contribution (PC_a) of a shift in votes from one ballot to the next, and the hypothetical probabilistic contribution (PC_h) had there been a reverse shift, as the *probabilistic contribution difference* (ΔPC):

$$\Delta PC = PC_a - PC_h, \qquad \text{where} - 1 \leqslant \Delta PC \leqslant 1.$$

When $\Delta PC > 0$, the behavior of the shifting delegates is considered rational. This is clearly the case for the final two ballots of the vice-presidential nomination in the 1956 Democratic convention, where for the minimal winning model,

$$\Delta PC_{\min} = 0.80 - 0.20 = 0.60,[15]$$

15. Actually, to three decimal places,
$$PC_{\min} = 0.796 - 0.204 = 0.592,$$
which rounds off to 0.59.

and for the any winning model,

$$\Delta PC_{any} = 1.00 - 0 = 1.00.$$

Later I shall discuss some of the implications of this concept of rationality. First, however, I shall suggest a refinement in the probabilistic contribution difference (ΔPC) calculation which will connect the concept of probabilistic contribution to the concept of winning.

2.5. Calculating the Share of Spoils

In section 2.1 I suggested that a basic factor motivating rational actors to form coalitions is the desire to win, which they cannot achieve in most political situations without enlisting the support of other actors. But more than just obtaining the benefits that a winning coalition offers, I suggested that a rational actor would also seek to maximize his individual portion of the benefits derived from winning. This will depend on how "important" he is to a coalition's victory; in section 2.4, the "importance" of the shifting delegates' contribution (their "political power," in the terminology of Polsby and Wildavsky) was operationalized as the increment they added to a candidate's probability of becoming minimal or any winning.

I shall now refine this incremental concept to take account of the probability that this contribution is likely to pay off—that is, that the candidate to whom the contribution is made will actually go on to win. After all, there is not much sense in augmenting a candidate's probability of becoming minimal or any winning if, even after one's contribution, his chances remain slim.[16]

16. For this reason it may on occasion be rational for a person to vote for a candidate other than the one he most prefers, which is a strategic calculation developed in Steven J. Brams, *Game Theory and Politics* (New York: Free Press, 1975), chap. 2; and Brams, *Paradoxes in Politics*, chap. 1. It may also be rational not to hold out too long for a candidate who is close to winning. Thus, in the 1960 campaign, Governor Robert Meyner of New Jersey, who was then very important, held out to extract as big a share as possible from John Kennedy. Unfortunately for Meyner, Kennedy got all he needed before Meyner came in; nobody ever heard of Meyner again. For an optimal commitment rule in such situations, see Steven J. Brams and José E. Garriga-Picó,

To discount the importance of such contributions to an unpromising candidate, consider again the probabilities of becoming minimal and any winning on the actual and hypothetical *final* ballots, which were used previously in defining the actual and hypothetical probabilistic contributions produced by delegate shifts between the next-to-final and final ballots. These probabilities of becoming minimal and any winning *after* the probabilistic contributions of the shifting delegates have been made will now be used to scale down the "present value"—before a candidate has won—of the actual and hypothetical probabilistic contributions. If these contributions have made a candidate winning, however, then their value is left unchanged.

More precisely, define the *share of spoils* (SS) as

$$SS = (PC)(P_{2d}),$$

or the probabilistic contribution (*PC*) of the shifting delegates (actual or hypothetical) times the probability (P_{2d}) that, with this contribution, the candidate becomes (minimal or any) winning on the second of the two successive ballots.[17] This may be thought of as the payoff from winning that the shifting delegates will on the average realize. This payoff may take the form of not only material and divisible benefits like patronage or even graft (with which the word "spoils" has often been linked) but also less divisible benefits that flow from policies and actions that have repercussions on all members of a political system. Whether private or public, symbolic or concrete, payoffs (and spoils) depend on the utility calculations of rational individuals, who can best achieve their

"Bandwagons in Coalition Formation: The 2/3's Rule," *American Behavioral Scientist* 18, no. 4 (March/April 1975): 472–96. This article is reprinted in *Coalitions and Time: Cross-Disciplinary Studies,* ed. Barbara Hinckley (Beverly Hills, Calif.: Sage Publications, 1976), pp. 34–58. I am indebted to William H. Riker for the Meyner example.

17. A similar expected-utility calculation is suggested in Norman Frohlich, Joe A. Oppenheimer, and Oran R. Young, *Political Leadership and Collective Goods* (Princeton, N.J.: Princeton University Press, 1971), p. 89. See also Anthony Downs, *An Economic Theory of Democracy* (New York: Harper & Row, 1957), pp. 47–50, 159.

ends—whatever they may be—by being members of a winning coalition.

In the vice-presidential nomination of the 1956 Democratic convention, because the second ballot is the final (decisive) ballot, P_{2d} in the actual case is equal to 1.00. When there is a hypothetical reverse shift, P_{2d} is also equal to 1.00 since Kennedy wins when this occurs. (As will be seen in a later example, however, a reverse shift may not be sufficient to turn an actual loser on the final ballot into a hypothetical winner, as occurs in this example.) Hence, for both the minimal winning and any winning models, the actual (a) and hypothetical (h) share of spoils in this race are equal to the actual and hypothetical probabilistic contributions:

$$SS_a = (PC_a)(1.00) = PC_a,$$

$$SS_h = (PC_h)(1.00) = PC_h.$$

This means that the difference between the actual and hypothetical share of spoils, or *share of spoils difference* (ΔSS),

$$\Delta SS = SS_a - SS_h, \qquad \text{where } -1 \leq \Delta SS \leq 1,$$

has the same value as ΔPC in this example. Since in this race $\Delta SS = \Delta PC$ is positive for both the minimal winning (0.60) and any winning (1.00) models, it can be concluded as before that it was rational for the shifting delegates to opt for the nonfront-runner (Kefauver) on the final ballot: their probabilistic contribution to Kefauver that ensured his nomination—and the share of spoils they might expect from their support—was greater than it would have been to Kennedy had they reversed themselves and ensured his nomination.

On some occasions, when a reverse shift is not sufficient to put a nonfront-runner over the top on the final ballot (as it was for Kefauver), it will pay for the shifting delegates to stick with the candidate who is the front-runner on the next-to-final ballot. In such an instance, because the *nonfront-runner's* probability of becoming (minimal or any) winning on the final ballot is less than certainty ($P_{2d} < 1.00$), his share of spoils,

$$SS = (PC)(P_{2d}),$$

will be less than his probabilistic contribution (PC). But since $P_{2d} = 1.00$ for the *front-runner* who is nominated on the final ballot, his SS will not be depreciated by P_{2d} and instead will be exactly equal to his PC. Even if the probabilistic contribution of the shifting delegates is greater to the nonfront-runner than the front-runner, the nonfront-runner's P_{2d} on the final ballot may deflate his larger PC to such an extent that the share of spoils which the delegates would derive from a reverse shift for him would be less than they would get by supporting the front-runner.

The vice-presidential race in the 1844 Whig convention, one of the earliest conventions for which ballot-by-ballot voting data are available, is a good illustration of a nomination in which it was rational for the delegates shifting after the next-to-final ballot to support the front-runner. As can be seen from table 2.2, Theodore Frelinghuysen held the lead on all three ballots, but I shall consider only the rationality of the shift of "other" votes on the final two ballots.

Table 2.3 summarizes the various calculations, developed in detail for the 1956 Democratic vice-presidential nomination, that lead to determining whether the actual probabilistic contribution (PC_a) is greater than the hypothetical probabilistic contribution (PC_h), i.e., $\Delta PC > 0$, or whether the actual share of spoils (SS_a) is greater than the hypothetical share of spoils (SS_h), i.e., $\Delta SS > 0$. The calculations are shown for both the minimal winning and any winning models, though I be-

Table 2.2
Votes Received by Two Leading Candidates, and All
Others, in Balloting for Vice-Presidential
Nomination in 1844 Whig Convention

	1st ballot	2d ballot	3d ballot
Frelinghuysen	101	118	154
Davis	83	75	79
Other	91	82	42

Source: Richard C. Bain, *Convention Decision and Voting Records* (Washington, D.C.: Brookings Institution, 1960), appendix D.

Table 2.3
Calculations for Final Two Ballots (2d and 3d) of Vice-Presidential Nomination in 1844 Whig Convention

Shift to	Minimal winning	Any winning
Frelinghuysen (actual)	$P_{1st} = 0.75 \quad P_{2d} = 1.00$ $PC_A = 1.00 - 0.75 = 0.25$ $SS_A = (0.25)(1.00) = 0.25$	$P_{1st} = 1.00 \quad P_{2d} = 1.00$ $PC_A = 1.00 - 1.00 = 0$ $SS_A = (0)(1.00) = 0$
Davis (hypothetical)	$P_{1st} = 0.25 \quad P_{2d} = 0.37$ $PC_H = 0.37 - 0.25 = 0.13$ $SS_H = (0.13)(0.37) = 0.05$	$P_{1st} = 0 \quad P_{2d} = 0.04$ $PC_H = 0.04 - 0 = 0.04$ $SS_H = (0.04)(0.04) = 0$
Summary values	$\Delta PC = 0.25 - 0.13 = 0.12$ $\Delta SS = 0.25 - 0.05 = 0.20$	$\Delta PC = 0 - 0.04 = -0.04$ $\Delta SS = 0 - 0 = 0$

lieve the minimal winning calculations are intuitively more reasonable for two reasons.

First, especially in close races, candidates probably think principally in terms of just winning (i.e., forming minimal winning coalitions) and only secondarily in terms of building up large pluralities. If this is the case, then in making probabilistic calculations they would consider as most likely those outcomes that give one side a minimal or small majority, for which the minimal winning model serves as the better approximation.

Second, a consequence of the any winning model, which was noted earlier, is that it tends to transform a relatively small numerical advantage on the part of one candidate into an overwhelming probabilistic advantage. For example, even though John Davis had almost two-thirds as many votes as Frelinghuysen on the second ballot of the 1844 Whig convention (see table 2.2), and Frelinghuysen was still twenty votes shy of a simple majority (138), Frelinghuysen's probability of becoming any winning was 1.00 on the next-to-final ballot (versus 0.75 based on the minimal winning model). As a consequence, the actual probabilistic contribution (PC_a) of the shifting delegates is 0, which seems an implausibly low contribution of these delegates to Frelinghuysen's victory.

The share-of-spoils calculation (SS_a) gives the same 0 value, but since it is matched by a hypothetical spoils value (SS_h) also equal to 0 (to two decimal places), one would predict on the basis of this model that the shifting delegates would be indifferent between the choice of one or the other of the leading candidates. For some situations (described in section 2.7), the any winning model might be preferable to the minimal winning model, but for the close races that I shall analyze later the minimal winning model seems more appropriate.

The two previous examples demonstrated that on some occasions it is rational for the shifting delegates to back the front-runner (1844 Whig vice-presidential nomination) and on other occasions a nonfront-runner (1956 Democratic vice-presidential nomination). Before applying the minimal winning model to a broader range of cases, however, it is important to indicate what it does *not* explain.

2.6. What the Model Does Not Explain

The model does not offer any insight into why a particular number of delegates decide to shift their support to different candidates from one ballot to the next. Since the number who shifted on the final ballot toward or away from either candidate swings the nomination to one or the other candidate, it is often desirable to know why fewer or more delegates decide to join, or disattach themselves from, each candidate. Unfortunately, the reasons a particular shift occurs are probably intimately related to the politics of each nomination and cannot, therefore, be derived from the assumptions of a model. The size of the total shift is treated as a parameter in the previously described model from which the consequence of what candidate the shift will favor is derived.

In the analysis, then, although which of the two candidates the "other" delegates will favor (if they are rational) depends on the number shifting, I make no attempt to specify a general mechanism which gives rise to a shift of a particular size in the first place. Whereas inquiry into the origins of goals has been a characteristic concern in both sociology and psychology, which emphasize the study of socialization processes, roles, values, beliefs, and so forth, my approach is to take goals as given and focus exclusively on the logical implications that their satisfaction has on the choices that actors make.[18] This approach makes goals and choices the "facts," and I try to explain them by relating them in a logically coherent structure.

Basic to the structure I have built is the assumption of individual rationality—that individuals maximize their expected utility by choosing the most preferred of their alternatives. To channel this rather amorphous assumption along

18. For an elaboration of these differences in approach, and the implications they have for the construction of more general and inclusive frameworks, see Mancur Olson, Jr., "The Relationship between Economics and the Other Social Sciences: The Province of a 'Social Report,' " in *Politics and the Social Sciences,* ed. Seymour Martin Lipset (New York: Oxford University Press, 1969), pp. 137–62; and Michael J. Shapiro, "Rational Political Man: A Synthesis of Rational and Social-Psychological Perspectives," *American Political Science Review* 63, no. 4 (December 1969): 1106–19.

particular paths, I have in addition postulated two goals for a rational actor.[19] He desires first to maximize his probability of being in a winning coalition and second to maximize the portion of the benefits he derives from that winning coalition.

As Anthony Downs has shown, however, a benefit-maximizing strategy on the part of individuals may not be consistent with their acting together as a group to form a winning coalition,[20] so it is convenient to combine these two goals in an expected-value calculation, as I have done in the share-of-spoils concept. When delegates maximize their share of spoils, they are not necessarily choosing the candidate with the greatest probability of winning or the candidate to whom they can make the largest probabilistic contribution—and from whom, presumably, they can derive the greatest benefits if he should win. Instead, they are choosing that combination of "winningness" and "benefits" that on the average gives them the greatest "spoils." It is this bundle of goods that delegates, acting rationally, seek to maximize.[21] This model of collective choice will now be tested.

2.7. How Rational Are Delegates in National Party Conventions?

To apply the model to voting data in national party conventions, it is first necessary to select those nominations which

19. For a comparison of different goals and their implications in coalition theory, see Steven J. Brams, "Positive Coalition Theory: The Relationship between Postulated Goals and Derived Behavior," in *Political Science Annual, IV: An International Review*, ed. Cornelius P. Cotter (Indianapolis: Bobbs-Merrill, 1972), pp. 101–24. See also Joseph A. Schlesinger, "The Primary Goals of Political Parties: A Clarification of Positive Theory," *American Political Science Review* 69, no. 3 (September 1975): 840–49.

20. Downs, *Economic Theory of Democracy*, p. 159.

21. For other conceptions of "rationality" in electoral politics—besides that discussed here and in chapter 1—see William H. Riker and Peter C. Ordeshook, "A Theory of the Calculus of Voting," *American Political Science Review* 62, no. 1 (March 1968): 25–42; and Shapiro, "Rational Political Man." A discussion of various meanings of rationality, and an assessment of the extent to which behavior is rational in experimental games, is given in William H. Riker and William James Zavoina, "Rational Behavior in Politics: Evidence from a Three-Person Game," *American Political Science Review* 64, no. 1 (March 1970): 48–60. More generally, see William H. Riker and Peter C. Ordeshook, *An Introduction to Positive Political Theory* (Englewood Cliffs, N.J.: Prentice-Hall, 1973), chap. 2.

most closely approximate the conditions of the model. Since, as I showed earlier, the any winning model tends to give an unrealistically high probabilistic advantage to a front-running candidate—at least in the close races (to be operationally defined presently) in the previous examples—I shall not apply this model to convention data to be analyzed subsequently.

It is worth pointing out that the assumption on which this model is based seems most applicable to nominations in which one candidate has a substantial enough early lead that all coalition outcomes with himself as the coalition leader— from minimal winning to unanimous—seem possible. This is so because a front-runner with an overwhelming lead from the beginning would seem a priori more capable of fashioning a victory of major proportions than a lesser candidate whose expectations center on putting together a coalition that is just sufficient to win. Since nominations with strong front-runners are frequently decided after only one ballot (as has been true of all major party nominations since the vice-presidential race in the 1956 Democratic convention), the any winning model, which—like the minimal winning model— requires voting data on two successive ballots, could not even be applied to the study of these nominations, for which its underlying rationale seems best suited.

For those nominations which required at least two ballots, there would appear to be prima facie evidence of the lack of dominance by a single candidate. One might therefore expect that, for these nominations, the calculations of the candidates and delegates would tend to center around forming minimal winning coalitions.

Yet even in multiballot nominations, one candidate is often dominant, and the first ballot (and sometimes subsequent ones) merely ritualizes the elimination of nonserious candidates such as favorite sons. One plausible criterion that might be applied to the selection of the close multiballot nominations would be to include only those that remained close to the end.

I have in fact adopted this criterion and analyzed only those nominations in majority-rule conventions where the combined votes of all opponents of the winning candidate on the final ballot were not less than 40 percent of the total number of convention votes (i.e., the winner won with not more than a 60 percent majority). In the analysis of voting data from conventions with a two-thirds decision rule (all Democratic conventions prior to 1936), the 40 percent combined-opposition criterion will be lowered to 20 percent as an operational definition of a *close race*.

To be sure, a race may be regarded as hard-fought and close despite the fact that the winner emerged with a large majority on the final ballot. An extreme example of this situation is the presidential nomination in the 1948 Republican convention, which was closely contested between Thomas Dewey and Robert Taft, with Harold Stassen running a strong third, on the first two ballots. On the third ballot, however, Dewey received the unanimous endorsement of the convention delegates.

Clearly, on the final ballot of such a nomination the delegates and candidates are no longer thinking in terms of forming minimal winning coalitions but simply in affirming an outcome already agreed to. For this reason, the rationale on which the calculations of the minimal winning model is based would be inapplicable. On the other hand, the calculations may be applicable to the prior two ballots of such a race, when a real contest *was* reflected in the voting totals. The delegates who shifted from the first ballot to the second presumably may have sought to maximize their share of spoils, even if they could not anticipate that the second ballot would not be decisive. I shall return to this point later.

For majority-rule conventions, I have applied the minimal winning model to the next-to-final and final ballots of *all* multiballot nominations with outcomes in which the combined opposition was at least 40 percent on the final ballot (see table 2.4). Since the analysis is based on all nominations that satisfy the specified criteria, the conclusions to be drawn extend to that entire class of events (i.e., close races) that meets the criteria and not just some selectively chosen events that happen to agree with the calculations of the model. Presum-

Table 2.4

Seven Multiballot Nominations in Majority-Rule Conventions
Where Combined Opposition on Final Ballot Was at
Least 40 Percent of Convention Vote

Nomination	Winner	2d-leading candidate	Final ballot	Takeover?	% Combined opposition	ΔSS_{min}
1956 Dem. VP	Kefauver	Kennedy	2d[a]	Yes	45%	0.59
1952 Dem. P	Stevenson	Kefauver	3d	Yes	50%	0.14
1880 Rep. P	Garfield	Grant	36th	Yes	47%	0.92
1876 Rep. P	Hayes	Blaine	7th	Yes	49%	0.87
1872 Rep. VP	Wilson	Colfax	1st[a]	No	47%	−0.29
1852 Whig P	Scott	Fillmore	53d	No	46%	0
1844 Whig VP	Frelinghuysen	Davis	3d	No	44%	0.20

Source: Richard C. Bain, *Convention Decisions and Voting Records* (Washington, D.C.: Brookings Institution, 1960, appendix D.

a. Ballot after "shifts" were made in the numbers of votes cast for each candidate, though not officially classified as a new ballot.

ably, the logic on which it (or the any winning model) is based may also apply to nominations decided by a single ballot, but other kinds of data would be required to test the model. This is a question that I shall consider in section 2.9.

For the minimal winning model, the difference (ΔSS_{min}) between the *actual* share of spoils which accrued to the shifting delegates, and the *hypothetical* share that they would have received from a reverse shift on the final ballot, is given in the last column of table 2.4. When the rationality of the delegates' shift between the next-to-final and final ballots is measured in terms of this difference, in only one case, where $\Delta SS_{min} < 0$ (the 1872 Republican vice-presidential nomination), would the shifting delegates have received a greater share of spoils by transferring their support to the second-leading candidate (Colfax) on the final ballot.

Since the vice-presidential nomination in this convention was swung to Wilson because of the shift of only one state delegation (Virginia) after the first ballot,[22] it is questionable whether all "other" delegates voting for lesser candidates can properly be considered to be potential defectors in the calculations of the minimal winning model. If only Virginia's delegates are treated as the potential defectors, they would have been indifferent ($\Delta SS_{min} = 0$) between the choice of either candidate after the first ballot. In opting for the front-runner (Wilson), they put him over the top, whereas their votes alone would not have been sufficient to ensure the second-leading candidate's (Colfax's) victory.

With the exception of this anomalous case, it was rational for the shifting delegates in all the nominations to choose

---

22. Richard C. Bain, *Convention Decisions and Voting Records* (Washington, D.C.: Brookings Institution, 1960), p. 98 and appendix D. This work is an indispensable sourcebook for voting data on most conventions; a new edition of this work covers conventions through 1972. See Richard C. Bain and Judith H. Parris, *Convention Decisions and Voting Records*, 2d ed. (Washington, D.C.: Brookings Institution, 1973). A more limited source of documentary material on earlier conventions is Thomas Hudson McKee, *The National Conventions and Platforms of All Political Parties, 1789–1905: Convention, Popular, and Electoral Vote* (Baltimore: Friedenwald, 1906).

the winning candidate whom they did, or in the case of the presidential nomination in the 1852 Whig convention to be indifferent between the choice of either leading candidate. It can be seen from table 2.4 that four of the seven nominations involve takeovers of the lead (and nomination) on the final ballot by a nonfront-runner on the previous ballot, while the remaining three nominations involve the front-runner's holding onto his lead on the final two ballots.

Probably the most dramatic example of a takeover by a dark-horse candidate was James Garfield's presidential nomination in the 1880 Republican convention, which also has the highest ΔSS_{min} value (0.92) in table 2.4. From fourth-leading candidate on the thirty-fifth ballot, he shot past Ulysses Grant on the thirty-sixth ballot to win the nomination. In the three other cases of takeover on the final ballot by an earlier nonfront runner, the winner who came from behind was always the second-leading candidate on the next-to-final ballot.

It is interesting to note that the 1948 Republican presidential nomination, for which Dewey was the unanimous choice on the final ballot, is the only majority-rule nomination in which there were at least two (contested) ballots preceding the final unanimous ballot. Applying the actual and hypothetical share-of-spoils calculations to these two ballots, it was rational ($\Delta SS_{min} = 0.10$) for the shifting delegates to favor Dewey on the second ballot (both Dewey and Taft increased their vote totals, but Dewey by the greater amount), giving him 47 percent of the convention votes prior to the final ballot. No presidential candidate, incidentally, has ever captured more than 41 percent of the votes on *any* ballot in a majority-rule convention and then gone on to lose.[23]

23. Ulysses Grant just missed this threshold (which he set) when he polled 41 percent of the votes on the thirty-fifth ballot of the 1880 Republican convention and went on to lose to James Garfield on the thirty-sixth ballot. In Democratic conventions prior to 1936, where the decision rule was a two-thirds majority, the threshold based on past conventions is a figure exceeding 55 percent; Martin Van Buren polled 55 percent of the votes on the first ballot of the 1844 convention, with James Polk eventually emerging as the

Turning to the Democratic nominations in conventions before 1936 in which a two-thirds majority was required for nomination, I have operationally defined close races to be those where the combined opposition on the final ballot was not less than 20 percent of the total number of convention votes (i.e., the winner won with not more than an 80 percent majority). Admittedly, this threshold is no less arbitrary than the 40 percent combined-opposition threshold for the majority-rule conventions. But by comparison with the majority-rule conventions, it seemed reasonable that since a two-thirds decision rule means that the winner must have at least twice as many votes as the vote total of all losers (versus only one more vote in majority-rule conventions), it would not be inappropriate to cut the combined-opposition threshold in half for the two-thirds conventions. A more practical justification is that the application of the 20 percent combined-opposition threshold to nominations in two-thirds conventions permits the inclusion of about the same number of cases (eight) as were included in the analysis of nominations in majority-rule conventions (seven).

In the analysis of the two-thirds nominations, I have made one alteration in the calculation of the probabilities that each candidate becomes minimal winning on the two final ballots (P_{1st} and P_{2d}). Since these probabilities are used in the calculation of the actual and hypothetical probabilistic contributions (PC_a and PC_h), and the actual and hypothetical share of spoils (SS_a and SS_h), they naturally affect our measure of the rationality of the shifting delegates' choosing the candidate who was actually nominated (ΔSS_{min}).

Instead of calculating the probability that each of the two candidates becomes minimal winning (with exactly, or as exactly as possible, two-thirds of the total vote) on two successive ballots, I instead make this calculation only for the front-

winner on the ninth ballot. See Bain, *Convention Decisions and Voting Records*, appendix D. The strong residual support commanded by both Grant and Van Buren might in part be a function of the fact that both had previously served as president but had not been reelected (Grant did not run for a third term in 1876) in the term prior to being rejected by their parties.

runner on the next-to-final ballot. For the other candidate I assume that his highest-priority strategy is first to block the front-runner, so I calculate his probability of becoming minimal blocking (with exactly, or as exactly as possible, one-third of the total vote plus one) on the next-to-final ballot.

I repeat the same calculations for each candidate on the final ballot, when, of course, one candidate has won, giving him a minimal winning probability of 1.00, and the other candidate has lost, giving him a minimal blocking probability of 0. Just as the probabilities that each candidate becomes minimal winning in majority-rule conventions are complementary (i.e., they add up to 1.00), so the probabilities that one candidate becomes minimal winning and the other candidate becomes minimal blocking are also complementary on the next-to-final and final ballots in the two-thirds conventions.

After calculating these winning and blocking probabilities from the actual vote totals on two successive ballots, I then assume as before that there is a hypothetical reverse shift on the final ballot and recalculate the probability that the early front-runner again becomes minimal winning and the other candidate again becomes minimal blocking. I thus assume that even if there were a reverse shift, the candidates' strategies on the final ballot (that of becoming minimal winning for the initial front-runner, that of becoming minimal blocking for the other candidate) remain the same as on the next-to-final ballot.

To determine whether the shifting delegates could have augmented their share of spoils had they reversed themselves—either by pushing the initial front-runner over the top or by blocking him (and, on the final ballot, giving the nomination to the other candidate)—I calculate the share-of-spoils difference (ΔSS_{min}) with the new minimal winning and minimal blocking probabilities. This seems a realistic calculation for the candidates and delegates in two-thirds conventions, in which calculations underlying a blocking strategy would appear to differ significantly from those underlying a winning strategy.

Granted, there is no way of knowing how the size of a candidate's vote total on a ballot—relative to that of others—will affect the precise strategy he pursues. For lack of better information, I therefore make the simplifying assumption that the front-runner desires to win and the nonfront-runner to block.

Ultimately, one or both of the leading candidates may have some positive probability of becoming minimal winning, as was assumed in the majority-rule conventions. But since I assume that the most a nonfront-runner aspires to is to block in the two-thirds conventions, it is perhaps not surprising that when he does violate this assumption and goes on to win, the model works less well. Indeed, the single nomination in the two-thirds conventions given in table 2.5 that produced the highest negative ΔSS_{min} (-0.57, in the 1924 Democratic vice-presidential race) was that in which a takeover of the lead (and nomination) by the initial second-leading candidate occurred on the final ballot.

In six of the seven remaining nominations, ΔSS_{min} is positive, indicating that the shifting delegates for the most part supported the candidate (in these cases, the initial front-runner) who—based on the revised calculations—could most increase their share of spoils. The fact that the only case of a takeover by a nonfront-runner gives a strongly negative ΔSS_{min}, however, casts some doubt on the ability of the revised model to yield a measure of rationality that is consistent with the shifting delegates' observed behavior on takeover as well as nontakeover nominations. It is possible, of course, that these delegates are not rational with respect to the postulated goal of maximizing their share of spoils, but more cases seem necessary to establish this conclusion.

To expand the population of instances in which a front-runner was displaced in two-thirds conventions, all cases of multiballot nominations have been examined in which the eventual winner took over the lead from an earlier front-runner *prior to* the point of nomination. The four instances in which the takeover did not occur on the final ballot in these conventions (including three nominations that also met the 20

Table 2.5

Eight Multiballot Nominations in Two-Thirds Conventions Where Combined Opposition on Final Ballot Was at Least 20 Percent of Convention Vote

Nomination	Winner	2d-leading candidate	Final ballot	Takeover?	% Combined opposition	ΔSS_{min}
1924 Dem. P	Davis	Underwood	103d[a]	No	23%	0.15
1924 Dem. VP	Bryan	Berry	1st[a]	Yes	33%	−0.57
1920 Dem. P	Cox	McAdoo	44th	No	36%[b]	0.57
1904 Dem. P	Parker	Hearst	1st[a]	No	32%	0.04
1896 Dem. P	Bryan	Bland[c]	5th	No	30%	0.66
1892 Dem. VP	Stevenson	Gray	1st[a]	No	28%	1.00
1876 Dem. P	Tilden	Hendricks	2d	No	28%	−0.08
1848 Dem. P	Cass	Woodbury	4th	No	30%[d]	0.26

Source: Richard C. Bain, *Convention Decisions and Voting Records* (Washington, D.C.: Brookings Institution, 1960), appendix D.

a. Ballot after "shifts" were made in the numbers of votes cast for each candidate, though not officially classified as a new ballot.

b. Although short of a two-thirds majority, Cox was declared the unanimous nominee of the convention on the forty-fourth ballot.

c. Third-leading candidate on final ballot, but since second-leading candidate on next-to-final ballot, probabilistic calculations are based on his vote totals on final two ballots.

d. Figure based on two-thirds of those *present and voting* on the final ballot, which was used as the decision rule for this nomination.

percent combined-opposition criterion on the final ballot presented in table 2.5) are given in table 2.6. Although ΔSS_{min} is 0 in two of these four instances, indicating indifference for the choice between the two candidates, none of the four takeovers yields a negative ΔSS_{min}, which gives additional support to the proposition that the shifting delegates have generally acted to maximize their share of spoils, whether it involves supporting the front-runner or a nonfront-runner.

2.8. The Percent Shift in Strength

Although the shifting delegates in general appear to act rationally on both takeover and nontakeover nominations, one remarkable difference distinguishes a takeover nomination from a nontakeover nomination. In the majority-rule nominations in table 2.4, there are four instances when a takeover occurred and three instances when it did not. For both cases, by summing (or subtracting) the percentage of delegates who shifted to the winner and the percentage who defected from (or joined) the second-leading candidate on the final ballot, the *percent shift in strength* produced by the defecting delegates can be calculated.

(This measure can also be described as the percentage by

Table 2.6

Four Multiballot Nominations in Two-Thirds Conventions
Where Early Front-Runner Lost His Lead to Eventual
Winner Prior to Final Ballot

Nomination	Eventual winner	Front-runner preceding winner	Takeover (and final) ballots	ΔSS_{min}
1924 Dem. P	Davis	Smith	101st (103d[a])	0.03
1920 Dem. P	Cox	McAdoo	39th (44th)	0
1912 Dem. P	Wilson	Clark	30th (46th)	0
1896 Dem. P	Bryan	Bland	4th (5th)	0.09

Source: Richard C. Bain, *Convention Decisions and Voting Records* (Washington, D.C.: Brookings Institution, 1960), appendix D.
a. Ballot after "shifts" were made in the numbers of votes cast for each candidate, though not officially classified as a new ballot.

which the spread in votes between the winner and nonfront-runner changed between the next-to-final and final ballots. In majority-rule conventions, its minimum value can approach 0 percent and its maximum value 150 percent, the latter occurring when the votes of a nonwinning candidate with 50 percent of the total votes, and all "other" votes [50 percent], are transferred to a new candidate on the final ballot, who gains from a 100 percent shift to himself plus a 50 percent shift away from the second-leading candidate. With a 40 percent combined-opposition requirement on the final ballot, the upper limit is reduced to 110 percent.)

For the four *takeover* nominations in the majority-rule conventions, the average shift in strength is 36 percent (ranging from a low of 17 percent to a high of 47 percent), while for the three *nontakeover* nominations the average shift in strength is only 8 percent (ranging from a low of 6 percent to a high of 12 percent). It thus seems that the larger the percent shift in strength, the more a nonfront-runner will be favored.[24] I would expect the same to hold for nominations in the two-thirds conventions, but only one instance of a final-ballot takeover nomination does not provide sufficient data to make a meaningful comparison between takeover and non-takeover nominations.

It might be argued that since a greater percent shift in

24. Experimental studies of convention-type situations have shown a tendency of coalitions to form which exclude the largest actor (i.e., a nonfront-runner usually wins, whatever the circumstances), but this divergence in findings from the results here seems largely due to a difference in initial conditions assumed in the experimental studies (three factions rather than two). For a review of the experimental studies, see Lawrence H. Nitz and James L. Phillips, "The Effects of Divisibility of Payoff on Confederative Behavior," *Journal of Conflict Resolution* 13, no. 3 (September 1969): 381–87; more recently, see Lawrence H. Nitz, "Resource Theory and Ameliorative Strategy in a Minimal Information Political Convention," *Behavioral Science* 21, no. 3 (May 1976): 161–72. See also William H. Riker, "Bargaining in a Three-Person Game," *American Political Science Review* 61, no. 3 (September 1967): 642–56. On the role of neutral actors in coalition-building games, see Robert C. Ziller, Harmon Zeigler, Gary L. Gregor, and Wayne Peak, "The Neutral in a Communication Network under Conditions of Conflict," *American Behavioral Scientist* 13, no. 2 (November-December 1969): 265–82.

strength is required to put a nonfront-runner over the top than a front-runner, these percentages on the takeover nominations would on the average naturally be expected to exceed the percentage on the nontakeover nominations. Yet this will *necessarily* be the case only when delegates seek to maximize their share of spoils. If being on the winning side were their only concern, irrespective of the payoff they could expect to receive from abetting a candidate's chances, then it would always be to the delegates' advantage to join the front-runner. For no matter how much they swell his plurality, this is the choice that maximizes their probability of being on the winning side.

Only the additional consideration of how much the shifting delegates are likely to get from their contribution will stop such a bandwagon from inexorably developing for the expected winner—and make big shifts in his favor an unprofitable choice. For this commonsensical reason, big shifts will tend to favor a nonfront-runner when the delegates act rationally with respect to the postulated goal of maximizing their share of spoils. In other words, the proposition that big shifts favor a nonfront-runner is a *consequence* of this goal. In providing empirical support for this consequence, the data at the same time confirm the plausibility and usefulness of this goal as the cornerstone of the rational-choice model of convention decision making used here.

I have not attempted in this chapter to specify, except in rather imprecise terms (e.g., "big shift"), under what specific conditions front-runners and nonfront-runners will be favored in coalition situations. More precise and specific conclusions which can be drawn from such situations will depend on a number of parameters, some of which have been incorporated in various models of coalition-formation processes.[25]

25. Steven J. Brams and William H. Riker, "Models of Coalition Formation in Voting Bodies," in *Mathematical Applications in Political Science, VI,* ed. James F. Herndon and Joseph L. Bernd (Charlottesville: University Press of Virginia, 1972), pp. 79–124, in which calculations of "takeoff points" suggested by the models are applied to voting data in four conventions; Steven J. Brams, "A Cost/Benefit Analysis of Coalition Formation in Voting Bodies," in *Probability Models of Collective Decision Making,* ed. Richard G. Niemi and Herbert F. Weisberg (Columbus, Ohio: Charles E. Merrill, 1972), pp. 101–

Applications of these and related models to other coalition situations in presidential election politics will be discussed in chapter 4.

2.9. Conclusions

In section 2.1 I mentioned but did not explain what is meant by the win/share principle. First, it is based on the assumption that rational actors seek simultaneously to win and maximize their share of the benefits that accrue to the winning coalition. I operationalized this dual goal in terms of a concept called the share of spoils, which measures what on the average an actor or set of actors contributes to the probability that a candidate becomes minimal or any winning, discounted by the probability that, with this contribution, the candidate will indeed become minimal or any winning. In making this calculation, an equivalence was assumed between the size of the discounted contribution made by these actors and the payoff they could expect to receive should the candidate they support win.

If the shifting delegates are rational with respect to maximizing their share of spoils, one consequence is that the larger their numbers, the more they will tend to favor a nonfront-runner, as I showed for the majority-rule conventions. This finding suggests that the *win/share principle* might not only be stated in terms of the operational form given its *assumptions*—rational actors seek to maximize their share of spoils—but also in terms of a *consequence* of these assumptions on outcomes: *when there are two major competing candidates in a convention, the larger the bloc of uncommitted delegates that considers joining a candidate, the more likely it will join the nonfront-runner to augment his probability of becoming minimal winning and its (the bloc's) own share of spoils.*

An important caveat must be appended to these results. In the preceding analysis, the implicit assumption was that information is perfect—specifically, that the shifting delegates

24; Steven J. Brams and John G. Heilman, "When to Join a Coalition, and with How Many Others, Depends on What You Expect the Outcome to Be," *Public Choice* 16 (Spring 1974): 11–25; and Brams and Garriga-Picó, "Bandwagons in Coalition Formation: The 2/3's Rule."

have full knowledge, or at least have a very good idea, of how others like themselves will act at each stage in the proceedings. If there is anything that emerges from the descriptive studies of national party conventions that I criticized earlier, however, it is that reliable information is very much at a premium in most conventions, even when pandemonium does not reign supreme (as it sometimes does). As Polsby and Wildavsky put it, delegates "may have to search frantically for clues as to the best time to make the jump [onto a bandwagon] and gain the greatest bargaining advantages for themselves."[26] It is precisely in those situations where information is most imperfect that I would expect that its scarcity would retard rational strategic calculations and act as a major limiting condition on the applicability of the model and the truth of the win/share principle.

An inability of actors to make the complex calculations of our model may also vitiate its usefulness. Yet it seems that even if delegates to a national party convention are not able to *make* such calculations, they may still somehow "sense" the *results* of the calculations with more or less clarity. That I treat what calculations delegates *actually* make as a "black box" does not detract from the fact that I have suggested a way in which the data from two successive ballots can be transformed into the quantitative concept of share-of-spoils difference, whose values, when interpreted, are largely consistent with the coalition-forming behavior of the delegates to national party conventions.

26. Polsby and Wildavsky, "Uncertainty and Decision-Making at the National Conventions," p. 380. For amusing evidence on this point at the preballot stage, see Aaron Wildavsky, " 'What Can I Do?': Ohio Delegates View the Democratic Convention," in *Inside Politics: The National Conventions, 1960,* ed. Paul Tillet (Dobbs Ferry, N.Y.: Oceana, 1962), pp. 112–31. For studies of when delegates make commitments, see Eugene B. McGregor, Jr., "Predicting the Outcomes of National Nominating Conventions: Assumptions of Rationality and Uncertainty Applied to Data," *Journal of Politics,* 35, no. 2 (May 1973): 439–58; Barbara Hinckley, "The Initially Strongest Player: Coalition Games and Presidential Nominations," *American Behavioral Scientist* 18, no. 4 (March/April 1975): 497–512; and Eugene B. McGregor, Jr., "The Uncertainty Principle and National Nominating Conventions," *Journal of Politics* (forthcoming, 1978).

With the decline in multiballot nominations in recent years, this behavior has become more difficult to analyze. Perhaps one reason why no presidential or vice-presidential nomination has taken more than one ballot in over twenty years is because of the widespread use of polls and the rapid dissemination of information through the media today, which means that calculations can more readily be made prior to the balloting. This fact, of course, does not invalidate the logic of the models but does make it more difficult to obtain information that could be used to test the rationality of the choice process in, or prior to, conventions. More indirect forms of evidence, like preballot polls—even if they fail to capture the complex and subtle psychological determinants of convention behavior and are only an imperfect reflection of delegate preferences—may provide useful surrogate data (see section 4.9).

The analyst must live with these difficulties and use ingenuity to overcome them—instead of labeling nomination processes as "irrational" and by their very nature inexplicable in terms of a mechanism based on the motivations of the actors involved. This kind of thinking, which has been prevalent in the past, leads to the denial of explanation. It is hardly better than looking for empirical correlations in a mass of data with no model to guide one's search, an approach that has been unfortunately common in much behavioral political science.

It is useful to bear in mind that the nomination processes I have analyzed in this chapter are but one manifestation of more general coalition-formation processes that occur in, among other places, legislative and judicial bodies, electoral systems, and the international system.[27] In chapter 4 I shall look at party and electoral coalitions and develop models that seem relevant to understanding their rise and fall in American politics. First, however, I turn to the third and final phase of the presidential election game.

27. For studies of coalition behavior in different political arenas, see *The Study of Coalition Behavior: Theoretical Perspectives and Cases from Four Continents*, ed. Sven Groennings, E. W. Kelley, and Michael Leiserson (New York: Holt, Rinehart and Winston, 1970).

3 The General Election: How to Run the Final Stretch

3.1. Introduction

After the conclusion of the national party conventions in the summer of a presidential election year, the party nominees enjoy a short breathing spell before the fall general election campaign gets into full swing in early September. Then, for the next two months before Election Day in early November, the candidates usually barnstorm across the country in simultaneous attempts to persuade undecided voters that they are the best qualified candidates and to retain the allegiance of their previous supporters.

At the start of the fall campaign, the main issues that distinguish the Democratic and Republican nominees have usually been pretty well defined by previous statements of the candidates. The party platforms approved at the conventions also provide a backdrop to the campaign debate, although the ambiguous wording of particular planks of the platform often allows each candidate leeway to define his positions more precisely.[1] Some candidates exercise this privilege and some do not, for reasons given in section 1.7.

Much of the analysis in chapter 1 is in fact applicable to the general election as well as the primaries, though typically the mobility of the candidates on issues in the general election is more restricted than in the primaries because of pledges they have already made. Indeed, a recurring problem party nominees face is how best to retreat strategically from the

1. Platforms, however, are not as vague as is generally thought. One study found that only about one out of six statements in the twelve platforms of both major parties between 1944 and 1964 were "rhetoric and fact," the remainder being statements of "evaluation" or "future policy." See Gerald M. Pomper, *Elections in America: Control and Influence in Democratic Politics* (New York: Dodd, Mead, 1970), p. 159.

more extreme positions they took in the primaries, which may have been tactically sound then but have less broad-gauged appeal later among the entire electorate. This particular problem for candidates is a manifestation of a more general problem for political actors—how to play by the rules of more than one game—on which little formal work has been done.[2]

In this chapter I shall assume, as in chapter 2, that the positions of candidates on issues have already been chosen, based on, perhaps, the analysis described in chapter 1. In contrast to the analysis in chapter 2, however, I do not assume that undecided voters, like uncommitted delegates in national party conventions, desire to maximize their share of spoils. Instead, I assume that they are responsive to the way in which candidates allocate their resources in the general election, given that they do not favor—or are not able to distinguish— the positions of one candidate from another.

By viewing the general election as a problem in resource allocation, with the positions of the candidates on issues fixed, I obviously abstract a great deal from the drama and emotion of presidential campaigns. But so did the theoretical perspectives offered in chapters 1 and 2, which ignored—among other things—the resources available to the candidates to publicize their positions in primaries and attract convention votes. Clearly, primaries are not decided exclusively on the issues, and convention nominations are not determined solely by the calculations of uncommitted delegates.

Insofar as any theoretical perspective neglects manifold possible influences on electoral outcomes, it is, in a manner of speaking, "narrow." Yet, to say something nonobvious and significant in politics—or, for that matter, most other

2. Two attempts have been made, however, to model and deduce optimal strategies in a two-stage game that comprises first nomination by one's party and then a general election for a political office. See Peter H. Aranson and Peter C. Ordeshook, "Spatial Strategies for Sequential Elections," and James S. Coleman, "The Positions of Political Parties in Elections," both in *Probability Models of Collective Decision Making*, ed. Richard G. Niemi and Herbert F. Weisberg (Columbus, Ohio: Charles E. Merrill, 1972), pp. 298–331 and 332–57. This problem in state primaries is discussed in V. O. Key, Jr., *American State Politics: An Introduction* (New York: Knopf, 1956), pp. 153 ff.

fields—one must usually drastically simplify its reality. Full descriptions of political phenomena as complicated as presidential elections are generally quite unmanageable theoretically.

If the models do not tell the whole story, they may provide insight into important questions that less rigorous analysis has failed to resolve. One such question in the case of presidential elections concerns the effects of the Electoral College on campaign strategies and outcomes.

These effects, I shall demonstrate, are far from negligible, both in theory and in practice. Moreover, they seem egregiously out of line with certain principles of representative democracy. They would be eliminated, I shall show, if the Electoral College were abolished and the popular-vote election of a president substituted in its place.

In this chapter, then, I shall attempt not only to describe the consequences that extant rules have on the campaign behavior of presidential candidates but also will suggest how they should be changed to avoid these consequences. In this manner, I shall illustrate how models can be used for both explanatory and normative purposes—the latter being served when one recommends, on the basis of the consequences uncovered by the models, what kind of system would be desirable.

3.2.   Two Models of Resource Allocation in Presidential Campaigns

To make a cogent argument for the reform of a system, it is not enough to demonstrate that its present consequences are distasteful. One must also compare these consequences with those that would be engendered were the reform made.

In the case of the Electoral College, this comparison requires the development of two different but related models for analyzing resource-allocation strategies of presidential candidates in the general election. The first model to be developed excludes, and the second model includes, the Electoral College in the strategic calculations of the candidates.[3]

_____

3. Material in the remainder of this chapter is based largely on Steven J.

In the first model, I assume that the goal of a candidate is to maximize his popular vote (or more accurately, expected popular vote, since a probabilistic decision rule on the part of each voter is assumed), and the candidate who receives the greatest number of popular votes wins the election. In the second model, I assume that a candidate desires to maximize his expected electoral vote, which takes account of the fact that under the rules of the Electoral College the popular-vote winner in each state wins all the electoral votes of that state.

In both models, I assume that a presidential campaign influences only the voting behavior of voters uncommitted to a candidate prior to the start of the campaign. For these uncommitted voters, the amount of resources (e.g., time, money, and media advertising) that a candidate allocates to each state—relative to that allocated by his opponent(s)—determines the probability that an uncommitted voter will cast his vote for him in the election. Since the total resources of each candidate are assumed to be fixed, the question of how to allocate these resources to each state in a campaign assumes great importance in close races that may be decided by the choices of relatively few uncommitted voters.

In the initial development of the models, it is assumed that there are only two candidates (a Republican and a Democrat), and that the numbers of voters committed to each candidate prior to the general election campaign are evenly divided between the two candidates in each state. The choices of the uncommitted voters will therefore be decisive to both the collective choice of a majority of voters in each state and to the collective choice of a majority of voters nationwide. However, the resource-allocation strategy that maximizes a candidate's

Brams and Morton D. Davis, "Models of Resource Allocation in Presidential Campaigning. Implications for Democratic Representation," *Annals of the New York Academy of Sciences (Conference on Democratic Representation and Apportionment: Quantitative Methods, Measures and Criteria*, ed. L. Papayanopoulos), vol. 219 (New York: New York Academy of Sciences, 1973), pp. 105–23; and Steven J. Brams and Morton D. Davis, "The 3/2's Rule in Presidential Campaigning," *American Political Science Review* 68, no. 1 (March 1974): 113–34; the permission of the American Political Science Association to adapt material from the latter article is gratefully acknowledged.

expected electoral vote, which is based on the probabilities that majorities of voters in each state favor a particular candidate, differs markedly from the strategy that maximizes a candidate's expected popular vote, which depends only on the probabilities that individual voters in each state favor a particular candidate and not on the majority choice in each state.

The main conclusion drawn from this analysis is that the winner-take-all feature of the Electoral College induces candidates to allocate campaign resources roughly in proportion to the 3/2's power of the electoral votes of each state. This creates a peculiar bias in presidential campaigns that makes the largest states the most attractive campaign targets of the candidates—even out of proportion to their size—which would not be the case if the Electoral College were abolished and presidents were elected by direct popular vote. On the basis of the 1970 census and the electoral votes of each state through the 1980 election, a presidential candidate's "optimal" expenditures of resources in all fifty states and the District of Columbia will be indicated under both the Electoral College system and the popular-vote alternative. In the case of the Electoral College, the optimum is unstable: any allocation of resources can be "beaten" under this system. This is not the case for the popular-vote alternative, which, because of the stability of its optimum, would tend to relieve the candidates of the necessity of making some of the manipulative strategic calculations that are endemic to the present system.

I shall conclude the analysis by comparing the ability of the two different systems to translate the attention (in time, money, and other resources) that presidential candidates—and after the election, incumbent presidents looking to the next election—pay to their state constituencies as a function of their size. This comparison will reveal that the nonegalitarian bias of the Electoral College, which makes a voter living in one state as much as three times more attractive a campaign target as a voter living in another state, would be eliminated if the president were elected by direct popular vote.

3.3. The Need for Models to Assess the Consequences of Electoral Reform

Probably the most important reason that the structural reform of major political institutions is so controversial is because reforms often produce shifts in the distribution of power among political actors. When the precise effects of these shifts are uncertain, confusion tends to beset and compound controversy. As Senator Birch Bayh of Indiana said on the floor of the U.S. Senate on September 8, 1970, about hearings that had been held on the reform of the Electoral College:

> I must say, sitting through two or three volumes of hearings over the last 4 or 5 years was not at all times an inspirational experience. Some of the testimony was repetitive. Nevertheless, as chairman of the Subcommittee on Constitutional Amendments, I sat there. I thought it amusing, if not ironic, that on the last day—and I am not going to name individuals or organizations—and after 4 years of study, the last two witnesses appeared before our committee. One witness came before our committee suggesting the present [electoral] system should be maintained because it gave an advantage to the large States and the next witness suggested the present system should be maintained because it gave an advantage to the small States.[4]

After several thousand pages of testimony before both Senate and House committees and subcommittees in the past few years,[5] there remains today a good deal of confusion and

4. *Congressional Record*, September 8, 1970, p. 30813.

5. The most recent hearings were *The Electoral College and Direct Election of the President and Vice President*, Hearings (with Supplement) before the Committee on the Judiciary, United States Senate, 95th Congress, First Session (1977). Hearings that preceded the most recent congressional action (see text) were *Electoral College Reform*, Hearings before the Committee on the Judiciary, United States Senate, 91st Congress, Second Session (1970); *Electoral College Reform*, Hearings before the Committee on the Judiciary, United States House of Representatives, 91st Congress, First Session (1969).

controversy about the possible effects of various proposed changes in the Constitution—relating to the election of a president—on the creation of new parties and minor candidates, the political influence of small and large states and groups and individuals within these states, governmental stability, and a host of other aspects of the electoral process. This is true despite the plethora of proposals for electoral reform that have been extensively discussed, if not analyzed, in congressional hearings and in numerous books and articles.

This discussion and analysis has in many cases been shallow, however, producing controversy based not on genuine differences of opinion but rather on a confused understanding on the part of different analysts of what consequences would follow from various changes in the electoral system. The main reason for this confusion seems not to stem from any paucity of factual information on national elections. Rather, there has been a lack of rigorous deductive models which can be used to explore the logical and quantitative consequences of different electoral systems, particularly as manifested in their effects on competition among candidates.

Such models not only can aid one in deducing consequences from a limited set of assumptions but also can help one to clarify the kinds of evidence appropriate to testing the empirical validity of these consequences, as the case of state primaries and party conventions in chapters 1 and 2 illustrated. In addition, models can be used to lay the groundwork for the construction of better democratic theory, as I shall try to show in this chapter.

The consequences that would flow from electoral reform cannot be assessed simply by asking how hypothetical changes in the present system—specifically, in procedures for aggregating popular votes that produce a winner in presidential elections—would have affected previous election outcomes, as has been frequently done in the past. When an alternative procedure would be likely to have changed the campaign strategies of candidates in these elections to produce returns in states different from those that actually occurred, it is evident that the past returns cannot be held constant, with only the hypothetical procedure for aggregating them being allowed to vary, for estimating what consequences alternative aggregation procedures *would have had* on previous outcomes. As Alexander M. Bickel argued, "Any [major] change in the system . . . may induce subtle shifts in electoral strategies, rendering prediction based on past experience hazardous."[6] Curiously, it is just such "hazardous" predictions that Bickel conjured up to support his argument for retention of the Electoral College.[7]

Toward improving this state of affairs, I shall outline and report on tests of some game-theoretic models of the presidential campaign process that help one to assess the consequences produced by the present electoral system and its most prominent alternative, direct popular-vote election of the president.[8] I have focused on the direct popular-vote alterna-

---

6. Alexander M. Bickel, *Reform and Continuity: The Electoral College, the Convention, and the Party System* (New York: Harper & Row, 1971), p. 35.

7. This problem also characterizes the reconstruction of 1972 Democratic primary outcomes, based on three different rules for allocating delegates (winner-take-all, proportional, and districted), in James I. Lengle and Byron Shafer, "Primary Rules, Political Power, and Social Change," *American Political Science Review* 70, no. 1 (March 1976): 25–40. Lengle and Shafer recognize that "if the rules had been changed, the strategic decisions of some participants would surely have changed, too, with some (changed) electoral outcomes," but they argue that "only massive strategic shifts . . . could have altered the general thrust of each primary plan." See also Richard A. Joslyn, "The Impact of Decision Rules in Multi-Candidate Campaigns: The Case of the 1972 Democratic Presidential Nomination," *Public Choice* 25 (Spring 1976): 1–18; and Louis Maisel and Gerald J. Lieberman, "The Impact of Electoral Rules on Primary Elections: The Democratic Presidential Primaries in 1976," in *The Impact of the Electoral Process*, ed. Louis Maisel and Joseph Cooper (Beverly Hills, Calif.: Sage Publications, 1977), pp. 39–80.

8. From a critical review of literature on campaigning, Gerald Pomper concludes that "in future research, more attention needs to be directed to the effects, rather than the characteristics, of campaigns." See Gerald M. Pomper, "Campaigning: The Art and Science of Politics," *Polity* 2, no. 4 (Summer 1970): 539. Toward this end, mathematical models of the campaign process are developed in John A. Ferejohn and Roger G. Noll, "Uncertainty and the Formal Theory of Political Campaigns," *American Political Science Review* (forthcoming, 1978); Harold D. Shane, "Mathematical Models for Economic and Political Advertising," *Operations Research* 25, no. 1 (January-February

tive, and not proportional, district, and other plans for electing a president, because it has been the most widely discussed
of the proposed alternatives to the Electoral College.[9] With a

1977): 1–14; John Blydenburgh, "An Application of Game Theory to Political Campaign Decision Making," *American Journal of Political Science* 20, no. 1
(February 1976): 51–66; Joel D. Barkan and James E. Bruno, "Operations
Research in Planning Political Campaign Strategies," *Operations Research* 20
no. 5 (September-October 1972): 925–41; and Gerald H. Kramer, "A
Decision-Theoretic Analysis of a Problem in Political Campaigning," in *Mathematical Applications in Political Science, II*, ed. Joseph L. Bernd (Dallas: Southern Methodist University Press, 1966), pp. 137–60. In the Kramer article, a
resource-allocation model is used to analyze the effects of different canvassing techniques on turnout and voting from the vantage point of one
candidate—and not his opponent(s) directly, whose possible strategies the
later game-theoretic models explicitly take into account; for an empirical test
of the effects of canvassing in recent elections, see Gerald H. Kramer, "The
Effects of Precinct-Level Canvassing on Voter Behavior," *Public Opinion Quarterly* 34, no. 4 (Winter 1970–71): 560–72. Empirical data on political advertising in the 1968 presidential campaign are analyzed in Phillip Nelson, "Political Information," *Journal of Law and Economics* 19 (August 1976): 315–36.
The most complete treatment of different strategic factors in a presidential
campaign, developed from a coalition-theoretic perspective, is John H. Kessel, *The Goldwater Coalition: Republican Strategies in 1964* (Indianapolis:
Bobbs-Merrill, 1968). Useful compilations of material on techniques of campaign management and communication and their effects on the electorate
can be found in Robert Agranoff, *The Management of Election Campaigns*
(Boston: Holbrook Press, 1976); Arnold Steinberg, *The Political Campaign
Handbook: A Systems Approach* (Lexington, Mass.: Lexington Books, 1976);
and Arnold Steinberg, *Political Campaign Management* (Lexington, Mass.:
Lexington Books, 1976); for a collection of articles on new campaign methods, see *The New Style in Election Campaigns*, 2d ed., ed. Robert Agranoff
(Boston: Holbrook Press, 1976). A study of the use of electoral propaganda
in Great Britain, whose practices are compared with those of the United
States, is given in Richard Rose, *Influencing Voters: A Study of Campaign Rationality* (London: Faber & Faber, 1967).
    9. A summary of different proposals, and a biased assessment (in favor of
the present Electoral College) of their likely impact, considered especially in
light of the three-way presidential contest in 1968, is given in Wallace S. Sayre
and Judith H. Parris, *Voting for President: The Electoral College and the American
Political System* (Washington, D.C.: Brookings Institution, 1970). In view of
the controversial aspects of Electoral College reform alluded to in the text,
Sayre and Parris's belief that "the political effects of the electoral college
system are as clear as any in the nonexact science of American politics" (p. 43)
is difficult to accept, their "nonexact science" qualification notwithstanding.

provision for a runoff election between the top two candidates if neither secures as much as 40 percent of the popular
vote in the initial election, this alternative was approved by the
U.S. House of Representatives on September 18, 1969, by a
vote of 338 to 70, considerably more than the two-thirds
majority required for the proposal of constitutional amendments.[10] This plan fared less well in the U.S. Senate and
eventually became the victim of a filibuster by southern and
(strangely, as will be shown) small-state senators; cloture mo-
tions on September 17 and 29, 1970, won the approval of a
majority of senators but failed to receive the required two-
thirds endorsement needed to cut off debate.[11] This plan,
nevertheless, has been strongly supported by the American
public, receiving 66 to 19 percent approval (15 percent undecided) prior to the three-way 1968 presidential election and

Other summaries that reflect a similar bias in favor of the Electoral College
include Bickel, *Reform and Continuity*, pp. 4–36; Nelson W. Polsby and Aaron
Wildavsky, *Presidential Elections: Strategies of American Electoral Politics*, 4th ed.
(New York: Scribner's, 1976), pp. 242–53; and Judith Best, *The Case Against
Direct Election of the President: A Defense of the Electoral College* (Ithaca, N.Y.:
Cornell University Press, 1975). On the other side, a report by the American
Bar Association's Commission on Electoral College Reform has called the
popular-vote plan "the most direct and democratic way of electing a Presi-
dent." See American Bar Association (ABA), *Electing the President: A Report of
the Commission on Electoral College Reform* (Chicago: ABA, 1967). Also suppor-
tive of the direct-vote plan is Neal R. Pierce, *The People's President: The
Electoral College in American History and the Direct-Vote Alternative* (New York:
Simon and Schuster, 1968); Harvey Zeidenstein, *Direct Election of the President*
(Lexington, Mass.: Lexington Books, 1973); and Lawrence D. Longley and
Alan G. Braun, *The Politics of Electoral College Reform*, 2d ed. (New Haven,
Conn.: Yale University Press, 1975). See also John H. Yunger and Lawrence
D. Longley, "The Biases of the Electoral College: Who is Really Advan-
taged?" and Max S. Power, "Logic and Legitimacy: On Understanding the
Electoral College Controversy," both in *Perspectives on Presidential Selection*, ed.
Donald R. Matthews (Washington, D.C.: Brookings Institution, 1973), pp.
172–203 and 204–37.

10. *Congressional Record*, September 18, 1969, pp. 26007–08.

11. *Congressional Quarterly Almanac*, vol. 26, 91st Congress, Second Session
(Washington, D.C.: Congressional Quarterly, 1971), p. 840. For further
details, see Alan P. Sindler, "Basic Change Aborted: The Failure to Secure
Direct Popular Election of the President, 1969–1970," in *Policy and Politics in
America*, ed. Alan P. Sindler (Boston: Little, Brown, 1973), pp. 30–80.

81 to 12 percent approval (7 percent undecided) after that election.[12]

3.4. Presidential Campaigns and Voting Behavior

If anything has emerged from research on electoral behavior over the past forty years, it is that most people make up their minds about whom they will vote for in a presidential election well before the onset of the general election campaign that commences at the beginning of September in a presidential election year. Yet, although the campaign changes few minds, it does serve the important function of reinforcing choices already made, as many studies have documented.

On the other hand, for the typically 20 to 40 percent of the electorate undecided about their choice of a candidate at the start of a presidential campaign,[13] the campaign will not only be decisive to their individual voting decisions but also will often prove decisive to the choice of a candidate by a majority or a plurality of the electorate. This 20 to 40 percent minority of the electorate is usually more than sufficient to change the outcome of almost all presidential elections, which is why most campaigns are waged to make only marginal changes in the distribution of voter choices. Indeed, when a presidential candidate does succeed in capturing as much as 55 percent or more of the popular vote, his victory is considered a landslide.

If presidential campaigns are decisive principally for the minority of undecided or uncommitted voters who will be crucial in determining the election outcome, then a candidate's ability to project favorably his personality and positions on issues during the campaign assumes great importance. To determine how he should allocate his total resources among the fifty states and the District of Columbia to convey as favorable an image as possible to the voters, I take his positions and personality as given in the models in this chapter.

12. Sayre and Parris, *Voting for President*, p. 15.
13. Herbert B. Asher, *Presidential Elections and American Politics: Voters, Candidates, and Campaigns since 1952* (Homewood, Ill.: Dorsey Press, 1976), p. 270, table 10.1.

An optimal strategy in these models is a set of resource allocations to each state, not, as in chapter 1, a specification of issue positions of candidates. (As indicated in section 3.1, the spatial analysis in chapter 1 is obviously relevant to the general election campaign as well as primaries; it will be pursued further in chapter 4.) These allocations, it will be shown, can be derived from the maximization of different functions that embody different goals of candidates.

Although expenditures beyond a certain point in some campaigns may become counterproductive, I assume that a positive correlation in general exists between the amount of resources a candidate spends in a state—in relationship to that spent by his opponent—and the favorableness of the image he projects to voters in that state. Moreover, the more favorable a candidate's image, the more likely previously uncommitted voters will be to vote for him.

Given this connection between campaign spending and voting behavior, the major strategic problem a candidate faces is how best to allocate his total resources among the states to win over the decisive portion of the electorate—the uncommitted voters—without alienating voters already predisposed to his candidacy. His problem is rendered even more difficult by the fact that his opponent(s) will tend to allocate his (their) resources in such a way as to exploit any mistakes he might make in his allocations. It is this competitive aspect of presidential campaigns that the mathematics of game theory proves helpful in illuminating.

I shall not consider here second-order strategic and tactical questions relating to how a candidate should spend his campaign resources *within* each state (e.g., on mass media advertising versus canvassing). Neither shall I consider the question of what portion of a candidate's resources should be devoted to *nonstate*-oriented campaign activities (e.g., nationwide television broadcasting).

3.5. *The Goals of Candidates*

The underlying assumption of this analysis is that both voters and candidates are rational individuals who seek to maximize the attainment of certain goals. To be sure, these goals may be the products of sociological, psychological, and other conditioning forces in their lives, but this does not invalidate the assumption that, whatever their goals, candidates and voters seek the most rational means to achieve them. In the 1964 presidential election, for example, there is strong evidence to support the contention that the Republican nominee, Barry Goldwater, did not so much desire to win as to present voters with "a choice, not an echo." If this is true, then his apparently aberrant campaign behavior, at least as measured against the normal canons of presidential campaigning, may have been quite rational, given his principal goal of espousal of a conservative ideology rather than winning.[14] Provided that plausible—if not totally realistic—goals can be imputed to presidential candidates and voters, the test of rationality involves determining whether their behavior comports with these goals (compare section 2.2).

A goal one might postulate initially for voters in each state is that they vote for a presidential candidate solely on the basis of how much time (and, in principle, other resources) he spends in each state, as compared with that spent by his opponent. Clearly, this assumption is wildly unrealistic for the

14. As another possible goal, Stanley Kelley, Jr., has suggested that "at least some of the Goldwater inner circle set control of the Republican party—not winning the Presidency—as their principal objective in 1964. That is the implication, certainly, of Senator Goldwater's statement that the conservative cause would be strengthened if he could win as much as 45 percent of the vote." Stanley Kelley, Jr., "The Presidential Campaign," in *The National Election of 1964*, ed. Milton C. Cummings, Jr. (Washington, D.C.: Brookings Institution, 1966), p. 58. Furthermore, there is evidence that Goldwater, who was well aware of his impending defeat from polls commissioned by the Republican National Committee, did little to try to stem its magnitude in the latter half of his campaign (which would be consistent with the goal of winning) but instead tried to rationalize the conduct of his campaign and the anticipated action of the voters. See Stephen C. Shadegg, *What Happened to Goldwater?* (New York: Holt, Rinehart and Winston, 1965), p. 241. In chapter 4 I shall consider the question of how a Goldwater (or McGovern) was able to engineer a first-ballot convention victory and then lose the general election so decisively, paying particular attention to the implications of such nominations for the stability of national coalitions in American politics.

majority of voters already predisposed to one candidate before the start of a campaign. It is even a radical simplification for uncommitted voters, whom I argued earlier are usually decisive to the outcome of most presidential elections. Yet this assumption, which I *shall* apply to uncommitted voters in the models, does offer a means for capturing one salient aspect of the campaign—how candidates view the relationship between their expenditures and the potential voting behavior of uncommitted voters in each state—from which prescriptions of how much time the candidates should allocate to each state can be derived. Whether in fact this assumption is plausible is an empirical proposition that I shall test indirectly through corroboration of the consequence deducible from it of how much time the candidates would spend in each state if their goals were to maximize their expected electoral or popular vote.

Maximizing one's expected electoral vote under the present system, and one's expected popular vote under a system allowing for popular-vote election of a president, seem plausible goals to ascribe to most presidential candidates, the case of Senator Goldwater notwithstanding. Both goals, based on probabilistic calculations, incorporate the idea that presidential campaigning is shot full of uncertainties and that there is no surefire campaign strategy that can guarantee victory. For the models I develop here, the goal of maximizing one's expected popular vote will always be synonymous with maximizing one's probability of winning under the popular-vote system, though under the Electoral College system maximization of one's expected electoral vote may under certain circumstances be inconsistent with maximizing one's probability of winning. I shall point out some implications of these different maximization goals for the Electoral College in the later analysis.

3.6. The Popular-Vote Model

To point up the need for models of the campaign process, consider first Richard Goodwin's testimony before the Judiciary Committee of the Senate:

Today, nearly every State has a swing vote which, even though very small, might win that State's electoral vote. Thus, nearly every State is worth some attention. If the focus shifts to numbers alone [under a system of direct popular vote], then the candidate will have to concentrate almost exclusively on the larger States. That is where the people are, and where the most volative [*sic*] vote is to be found. . . . What does this mean? It means that direct election would greatly intensify the attention given to the largest States.[15]

Now compare Goodwin's statement to Senator Bayh's response:

The record will show that the major party candidates spend considerably more time [under the Electoral College system] in States that have large blocks of electoral votes. . . . It seems to me you have to be rather naive to overlook the fact that today the whole emphasis of the campaign is in . . . major states.[16]

If these contrary assertions are perplexing, what can be said after several further pages of testimony—interspersed with inconclusive evidence presumably supporting each of these diametrically opposed viewpoints—about which system will force candidates to spend a disproportionally large portion of their time in the largest states? A recognition that the rules of politics are not neutral does not necessarily produce an immediate understanding of what biases they create and which contestants they favor.

To develop models that may help resolve such a question as that discussed above, consider first the popular-vote plan. Assume that the probability that a randomly selected *uncommitted voter* in state i votes for the Republican candidate is

$$p_i = \frac{r_i}{r_i + d_i},$$

15. Senate Hearings, *Electoral College Reform* (1970), p. 82.
16. Senate Hearings, *Electoral College Reform* (1970), pp. 82–83.

where r_i is the amount of time, money, or other resources spent by the Republican candidate in state i and d_i is the amount spent by the Democratic candidate over the course of the campaign. In addition, assume that all uncommitted voters vote. (These are the same assumptions which will be made in the case of the electoral-vote model.)

If n_i is the number of uncommitted voters in state i, then to maximize his *expected-popular vote* among the uncommitted voters in all fifty states, the Republican candidate should maximize the quantity W_p, which is defined below:[17]

$$W_p = \sum_{i=1}^{50} n_i p_i \qquad r_i, d_i, n_i > 0,$$

where

$$\sum_{i=1}^{50} r_i - R, \ \sum_{i=1}^{50} d_i = D, \text{ and } \sum_{i=1}^{50} n_i - N.$$

The term "expected" is used to signify the fact that W_p, the sum of the number of uncommitted voters in each state times the probability of their voting Republican, is not a certain quantity but instead the *average* Republican share of the total uncommitted vote for given allocations r_i and d_i by both candidates in all states.

Given that neither candidate has any information about the allocations made by his opponent(s), one can show that the optimal strategy for each candidate consists of allocating

17. This model leads to the same results as one in which the quantity maximized is the *expected plurality* of uncommitted voters:

$$\sum_{i=1}^{50} n_i \left(\frac{r_i - d_i}{r_i + d_i} \right) = \sum_{i=1}^{50} n_i \left(\frac{2r_i}{r_i + d_i} - 1 \right) = 2 \sum_{i=1}^{50} n_i p_i - N.$$

See Richard A. Epstein, *The Theory of Gambling and Statistical Logic* (New York: Academic Press, 1967), pp. 121–23; for a generalization of this model, see Shane, "Mathematical Models for Economic and Political Advertising." Note that the summations which follow range only over the fifty states, though in presidential elections beginning in 1964 the District of Columbia must also be included.

funds in proportion to the number of uncommitted voters in each state.[18] That is,

$$r_i = \left(\frac{n_i}{N}\right)R, \tag{3.1}$$

and

$$d_i = \left(\frac{n_i}{N}\right)D, \tag{3.2}$$

for all states i. For these allocations, the expected number of uncommitted voters that the Republican candidate can assure himself of from the entire pool of uncommitted voters is

$$W_p = \left(\frac{R}{R + D}\right)N.$$

If $R = D$ (i.e., the total resources of the Republican and Democratic candidates are equal), then

$$W_p = \frac{N}{2}.$$

That is, the two candidates would split the total uncommitted vote.

To this vote, of course, must be added the votes of previously committed Republican and Democratic voters—on whom it is assumed the campaign has no effect—to get the total number of votes that each candidate receives. (I shall show later how these committed voters can be incorporated directly into the resource-allocation calculations.) For now it will be convenient to assume that there are only two candidates (or parties) in each state, though this assumption will later be abandoned. Also, assume that the committed voters are split evenly between the parties in each state so that the winner of the uncommitted vote in each state captures a majority of popular votes in that state.

18. Because the mathematical derivation of this result and others described in subsequent sections involve more advanced methods than are assumed in this book, they will not be given here. For derivations and proofs of this and subsequent mathematical results, see Brams and Davis, "Models of Resource Allocation in Presidential Campaigning."

The allocations just specified are optimal in the sense that if either candidate adopts the proportional-allocation strategy, the other cannot gain by deviating from such a strategy. Since neither candidate has an incentive to depart from this strategy because he might fare worse if he did, the strategies are in equilibrium (see section 1.3).

Any departure from an equilibrium strategy by one candidate can be exploited by his opponent. If the Republican candidate, for example, were able to obtain information about deviations by the Democratic candidate from his equilibrium strategy, he could act on this information (i.e., the nonoptimal allocations of the Democratic candidate) in distributing his own resources so as to capitalize on his opponent's mistakes. It can readily be demonstrated that, *knowing* the d_i, the Republican candidate can maximize his expected popular vote among the uncommitted voters by allocating his own resources in the following way:

$$r_i = \frac{\sqrt{n_i d_i}}{\sum_{i=1}^{50} \sqrt{n_i d_i}} (R + D) - d_i. \qquad (3.3)$$

Similarly, for the Democratic candidate,

$$d_i = \frac{\sqrt{n_i r_i}}{\sum_{i=1}^{50} \sqrt{n_i r_i}} (R + D) - r_i. \qquad (3.4)$$

If the Democratic candidate pursues an optimal strategy of proportional allocations according to equation 3.2, then for the Republican candidate equation 3.3 reduces to equation 3.1—that is, his best response is to allocate his resources proportionally, too, which is the minimax solution in pure strategies for both candidates in this two-person, constant-sum, infinite game.

The game is *constant-sum* because what uncommitted votes one candidate wins the other candidate necessarily loses (the game is *zero-sum* if it is conceptualized as a plurality maximization game; see note 17), and it is *infinite* because each player has a choice among infinitely many possible expenditure levels in each state. The outcome is a *minimax*, or *saddlepoint*, when the *pure strategies* (i.e., sets of resource allocations to the states) prescribed by equations 3.1 and 3.2 are played, for if either candidate plays his optimal strategy, his opponent can do no better than play his own.[19]

To see how the Republican candidate could do better than his optimal strategy, given nonoptimal allocations by his Democratic opponent, consider the nonoptimal allocations d_i of the Democratic candidate shown in table 3.1 (which are assumed for convenience to total ten times the total number of voters). Note that the Democrat's allocations are less than the (proportional) minimax allocations for the two smallest states (states 1 and 2) and greater than these minimax allocations for the two largest states (states 4 and 5). Assuming that the Republican candidate is privy in advance to these (planned) allocations by his Democratic opponent, his best response according to equation 3.3 is to outspend his opponent in the three smallest states and underspend him in the two largest states, as shown in table 3.1.

It can be observed that the Republican candidate, knowing the Democratic candidate's allocations, usually responds with an allocation somewhere between his opponent's allocations and the minimax allocations. Yet of 190 votes, this best response garners the Republican candidate only 0.6 votes (95.3 for Republican to 94.7 for Democrat) more than his opponent when their total resources are equal, illustrating the relative insensitivity of the popular-vote model to nonoptimal allocations. In sharp contrast, allocations under the Electoral College system are extremely sensitive in the range where the two candidates about match each other's expenditures in states (i.e., $p_i \approx 0.50$ for voters in state i), as will be seen.

3.7.   *The Electoral-Vote Model*

Under the present Electoral College system, the geographic origin of the vote is salient. Because all the electoral votes of

19. For an elaboration of these concepts, with examples, see Steven J. Brams, *Game Theory and Politics* (New York: Free Press, 1975), chap. 1.

Table 3.1
Allocation of Resources

State i	Number of voters n_i	Nonoptimal Democratic allocations d_i	Optimal Republican allocations r_i	Expected vote W_{p_i}	Minimax allocations r_i and d_i
1	20	100	143	11.8	200
2	30	200	247	16.6	300
3	40	400	404	20.1	400
4	50	600	553	23.4	500
5	50	600	553	23.4	500
Sum	190	1900	1900	95.3	1900

Source: Steven J. Brams and Morton D. Davis, "The 3/2's Rule in Presidential Campaigning," *American Political Science Review* 68, no. 1 (March 1974): 119, table 1; reprinted with permission.

each state—equal to the total number of its senators plus representatives—are awarded to the majority (or plurality) winner in that state, such a winner-take-all decision rule is often referred to as "unit rule." In this section I shall outline some of the difficulties connected with the concept and interpretation of "optimal strategy" under this system, and in section 3.8 I shall develop an intriguing, though somewhat fragile, solution to the resource-allocation problem for this system.

For purposes of comparison with the popular-vote model, assume that v_i is the number of electoral votes of state i, where $\sum_{i=1}^{50} v_i = V$. Then, to maximize his *expected electoral vote* among the uncommitted voters in all fifty states, the Republican candidate should maximize the quantity W_e:

$$W_e = \sum_{i=1}^{50} v_i \pi_i, \tag{3.5}$$

where, assuming for convenience an even number of voters n_i,

$$\pi_i = \sum_{k=\frac{n_i}{2}+1}^{n_i} \binom{n_i}{k} p_i^k (1 - p_i)^{n_i-k} \tag{3.6}$$

is the probability that the Republican candidate obtains *more* than 50 percent of the uncommitted voters in state i—that is, the probability that state i goes Republican if the committed voters are split fifty-fifty. I assume that the voting of uncommitted voters *within* each state is statistically independent.[20]

---

20. For the reader unfamiliar with the binomial distribution, equation 3.6 simply sums the probabilities that the Republican candidate obtains exactly

$$\frac{n_i}{2} + 1 \quad \text{or} \quad \frac{n_i}{2} + 2 \quad \text{or} \quad \ldots n_i$$

uncommitted votes in state i and thereby wins the state. To use the binomial distribution in this case requires the assumption that the votes cast by each

Unfortunately, unlike the maximization of W_p in the popular-vote model according to equation 3.3, the maximization of W_e in the electoral-vote model does not yield a closed-form solution for the optimal values of r_i (or d_i) when the d_i (r_i) are known.[21] This makes problematic comparisons with the explicit solution to the popular-vote model (equations 3.3 and 3.4).

When the allocations of an opponent are not known, the minimax solution to the optimization problem in general does not take the form of pure strategies in a two-person, constant-sum, infinite game, where the players are the two candidates. Like the popular-vote model, the contest is a game because it depends on the strategy choice of the other player (i.e., an interdependent decision situation exists). Unlike the popular-vote model, this game has no saddlepoint, which means that the choice by a candidate of a best strategy will depend on his opponent's choice. To keep his opponent from discovering his choice, each candidate will leave his choice to chance by choosing from a set of pure strategies at random, with only the probabilities determined. That is, he will use a *mixed strategy*, or a probability distribution over a set of pure strategies.

(Only under special circumstances does such a game have a pure-strategy solution. To wit, when one candidate has more than twice the resources of the other candidate, it is easy to show that the richer candidate can assure himself, at least with a high probability, of a majority in the Electoral College. He can accomplish this by pursuing the pure strategy of distributing his greater campaign resources among the various states in proportion to their electoral votes v_i, which is analogous to the pure minimax strategy of both candidates in the popular-vote model. Since this is a pure strategy, the poorer candidate will know what this strategy is, and in particular will

---

uncommitted voter have no effect on (i.e., are statistically independent of) the votes cast by other uncommitted voters in state i.

21. Roughly speaking, a closed-form (or analytic) solution is one in which an explicit expression, or formula, can be given for the unknowns (i.e., r_i and d_i) in terms of the other variables.

know the richer candidate's expenditure levels in various states. But even if the poorer candidate spends only slightly more than the richer candidate in several states, the electoral votes of these states can never equal a majority because the resources of the poorer candidate are less than half those of the richer candidate. More specifically, if the poorer candidate concentrates all his resources on a set of states with a bare majority of electoral votes, he may capture most of these states by spending just a little more than the richer candidate spends in them, but the richer candidate will still be able to outspend him in at least one state, which will deny the poorer candidate his majority with almost certainty.)

In the more plausible case in which the two candidates' campaign resources are more evenly balanced, the richer candidate cannot use a pure strategy because this would enable the poorer candidate to outspend him in a sufficient number of states to achieve a majority in the Electoral College. In other words, the richer candidate must keep secret how much he is going to spend in each state, and so, for similar reasons, must the poorer candidate. (In game-theoretic language, neither candidate has a pure minimax strategy since such a strategy on the part of either candidate would be known and could be "beaten" by the other candidate.) The solution for both candidates, therefore, will be in mixed strategies, but the mixed-strategy solution to this game is not known.[22]

22. In so-called Colonel Blotto games—where the candidate who outspends his opponent in a state by whatever amount wins that state with certainty, in contrast to the probabilistic relationship that is assumed here between expenditures and winning—a minimax solution in mixed strategies has been found when all states have the same number of electoral votes. See David Sankoff and Koula Mellos, "The Swing Ratio and Game Theory," *American Political Science Review* 66, no. 2 (June 1972): 551–54. For a discussion of related Colonel Blotto games, see Lawrence Friedman, "Game Theory Models in the Allocation of Advertising Expenditures," *Operations Research* 6, no. 5 (September-October 1958): 699–709; for an extension to games in which the candidates cannot freely allocate all their resources (i.e., in which some proportion have already been allocated), see David Sankoff, "Party

It can be shown that if

$$p_i = \frac{r_i}{r_i + d_i}$$

is *defined* to be the probability that a majority of uncommitted voters (rather than a randomly selected uncommitted voter) in state i votes Republican—i.e., if $\pi_i = p_i$—then the game will have a solution in ˋpure strategies for both candidates. Analogous to the solution in the popular-vote model (with v_i and V now substituted for n_i and N, respectively), the (pure) minimax strategy of each candidate is to allocate resources in proportion to the number of electoral votes of each state:

$$r_i = \left(\frac{v_i}{V}\right)R; \quad \text{and} \quad d_i = \left(\frac{v_i}{V}\right)D.$$

Because this consequence is derived from the assumption that resource expenditures under the Electoral College system affect directly a majority—and not single individuals—in each state, it is not directly comparable to the proportional-allocation rule in the popular-vote model, which is derived from the individualistic assumption. Although it is hard to entertain the belief that aggregates, rather than individuals, respond to the actions of the candidates, I shall nonetheless compare the empirical correspondence of the proportional-allocation strategy under the Electoral College with an allocation strategy based on the voting behavior of individuals (described in section 3.8).

3.8.   The 3/2's Allocation Rule

Whatever its exact form, a mixed-strategy solution to the electoral-vote model based on the individualistic assumption will be difficult to interpret, let alone to verify empirically. To exorcise this strategy of its random element, an additional assumption can be made that invests optimal strategies under the Electoral College system with greater determinateness.

Strategy and the Relationship between Votes and Seats," *Theory and Decision* 5 (October 1974): 289–94.

The assumption is that the two presidential candidates match each other's resource expenditures in each state. This assumption seems reasonable in light of the fact that the candidates tend to agree on which states (usually large and heterogeneous) are the most attractive campaign targets. Even Senator Goldwater decided to abandon early plans in 1964 to write off the big industrial northeastern states and instead "go shooting where the ducks are." Of the seven states he visited most frequently, and which collectively claimed more than half his time, three (New Jersey, New York, and Pennsylvania) were in the Northeast.[23]

As further support for the matching assumption, the product-moment correlation coefficients between the combined appearances (to be defined later) of the Republican and Democratic presidential and vice-presidential candidates in all fifty states are 0.92 in the 1960 campaign, 0.83 in the 1964 campaign, 0.90 in the 1968 campaign, and 0.74 in the 1972 campaign. Such strong empirical relationships between appearances of the two slates lend support to the proposition that the postulated goal of maximizing one's expected electoral vote is generally consistent, at least in four recent presidential campaigns, with concentrating one's time in the same set of states.

In the statement of the Electoral College model, this matching assumption can be incorporated by assuming that $r_i = d_i$ (and necessarily $R = D$) for all states i in solving equation 3.5 for a maximum. This assumption makes it possible to obtain an explicit expression for r_i that maximizes the Republican's expected electoral vote:

$$r_i = \left(\frac{v_i \sqrt{n_i}}{\sum_{i=1}^{50} v_i \sqrt{n_i}} \right) R. \qquad (3.7)$$

Since it was assumed that $d_i = r_i$ (and $D = R$) for all i, the Democrat's optimal resource allocation,

23. Kelley, "The Presidential Campaign," pp. 50–51, 75.

$$d_i = \left(\frac{v_i\sqrt{n_i}}{\displaystyle\sum_{i=1}^{50} v_i\sqrt{n_i}} \right) D, \qquad (3.8)$$

is the same as his Republican opponent's.

It can be shown that these allocations are in equilibrium: any *arbitrarily small* (but finite) deviation from these strategies on the part of either candidate will be nonoptimal. A *sufficiently large* deviation by one candidate could, however, prove profitable. If, for example, the Republican candidate reallocated all the resources he spends in one state, as prescribed by equation 3.7, to a larger state, he would lose the smaller state with certainty but almost surely win a majority of popular votes (and all the electoral votes) in the larger state. Thus, instead of exactly splitting his expected electoral vote with his opponent—by matching expenditures with him in all states according to equations 3.7 and 3.8—he could, by such a unilateral deviation, easily win a majority of the electoral votes, holding constant his total expenditures.

It cannot be readily specified *how small* the deviation must be so as to be nonoptimal for a candidate. As I have shown by the previous example, however, the equilibrium is only *local* and not a minimax solution, for *some* unilateral deviation can secure a candidate a more preferred outcome (i.e., a higher expected electoral vote). The matching strategies prescribed by equations 3.7 and 3.8 are therefore not optimal in a *global* sense. To be optimal in this sense, the strategies would have to be such that, whenever the candidates spend the same amount in all states, there would be an incentive for both to move toward the particular matching expenditures defined by equations 3.7 and 3.8. There is, however, no such incentive. Only when the candidates' expenditures are near or at this point is there an incentive *not to deviate* from these expenditures by a small amount.

Because the allocations defined by equations 3.7 and 3.8 constitute only a local equilibrium point, it is unstable.[24] Yet,

24. Whenever the term *unstable* is used, it means "globally unstable," for this point is stable locally (i.e., impervious to small deviations).

despite its instability, it is suggestive of a possible reference point in the calculations of candidates that does have an interesting interpretation. This interpretation can most easily be grasped by making the simplifying assumption that the electoral votes of state i, v_i, are proportional to the number of uncommitted voters, n_i, in that state. Given this assumption, the terms in parentheses in the numerator, and in the summation of the denominator, of equations 3.7 and 3.8, $v_i\sqrt{n_i}$, will be proportional to $v_i\sqrt{v_i} = v_i^{3/2}$. The (local) equilibrium strategies of the Republican and Democratic candidates who match each other's resource expenditures in each state will then be, respectively,

$$r_i = \left(\frac{v_i^{3/2}}{\sum\limits_{i=1}^{50} v_i^{3/2}}\right) R,$$

and

$$d_i = \left(\frac{v_i^{3/2}}{\sum\limits_{i=1}^{50} v_i^{3/2}}\right) D.$$

In other words, to maximize his expected electoral vote, each candidate should allocate his total resources, which were assumed to be the same for the Republican and Democratic candidates ($R = D$) in making the matching assumption ($r_i = d_i$ for all i), in proportion to the 3/2's power of the number of electoral votes of each state.

This is what is meant by the "3/2's allocation rule" in the heading of this section. It implies that both candidates, in matching each other's resource expenditures, should not simply allocate on the basis of the electoral votes of each state but rather should allocate decidedly more than proportionally to large states than to small states. For example, if one state has four electoral votes, and another state has sixteen electoral votes, even though they differ in size only by a factor of four, the candidates should allocate eight times as much in resources to the larger state because

$$\frac{16^{3/2}}{4^{3/2}} = \frac{64}{8} = 8.$$

This allocation rule thus favors large states with more electoral votes, even out of proportion to their size. It is a strikingly simple and nonobvious consequence of the postulated goal that candidates seek to maximize their expected electoral vote, given that they match each other's resource expenditures.[25] Although simple in form, however, it is not immediately obvious why large states are so advantaged, apart from the commonsensical observation that voters in large states have greater potential influence over the disposition of large blocs of electoral votes.

3.9.   Why the Large States Are Favored

To give greater insight into the quantitative dimensions of this potential influence, it is useful to calculate the "expected minimum number of voters sufficient to change the outcome" in a state. This quantity is simply the sum of the probability of an exactly even split (i.e., a tie, assuming an even number of voters) times 1 (one "swing voter" is minimally sufficient to change the outcome—a deadlock—by changing his vote), the probability of a one-vote victory by either candidate ($k = +1$ or $k = -1$ below) times 2 (two "swing voters" are minimally sufficient to change the outcome by changing their votes), and so on. If we assume for convenience that there are $2n$ voters (i.e., an even number) in a state, then this expected minimum number, which I shall refer to as the *expected number of decisive voters*, is

$$N(D) = \sum_{k=-n}^{n} \binom{2n}{n+k} p^{n+k}(1-p)^{n-k}(|k|+1),$$

25. If the total resources of the candidates are not equal (i.e., $R \neq D$), it is not difficult to show that a "proportional matching" of expenditures, wherein the candidates spend the same proportion (or percentage) of their total resources in each state, yields a somewhat more complicated expression for a local maximum.

where p is equal to the probability that a randomly selected uncommitted voter in the state votes for one candidate and $(1 - p)$ the complementary probability that such an uncommitted voter votes for the other candidate. When $p = (1 - p) = 1/2$, it can be shown that

$$N(D) = \left(\frac{1}{2}\right)^{2n}\left[n\binom{2n}{n} + 2^{2n}\right].$$

Since

$$\left(\frac{1}{2}\right)^{2n}\binom{2n}{n} \approx \sqrt{\frac{1}{\pi n}},$$

the central term of the binomial distribution,[26]

$$N(D) = \sqrt{\frac{n}{\pi}} + 1. \tag{3.9}$$

That is, when the probability is fifty-fifty that the voters will vote for one candidate or the other—and thereby enhance the likelihood of a close outcome—the expected number of decisive voters in a state varies with the square root of its size, the first term on the right-hand side of equation 3.9.

The number of decisive voters *per voter* in a state, or what might be called the *decisiveness* of an average voter, is found by dividing $N(D)$ by $2n$:

$$D(2n) = \frac{1}{2\sqrt{\pi n}} + \frac{1}{2n}.$$

To illustrate this measure of decisiveness, in a state with $2n = 100$ voters,

$$D(100) = 0.040 + 0.010 = 0.050,$$

---

26. James S. Coleman has developed a measure of power based on this term, which here gives the probability of an exactly even split of the uncommitted voters in a state. (Note that π in the expression in this section refers to the number 3.14159, not the probability defined earlier.) See James S. Coleman, "Loss of Power," *American Sociological Review* 38, no. 1 (February 1973): 1–17.

whereas in a state with $2n = 400$ voters,

$$D(400) = 0.020 + 0.003 = 0.023.$$

Although the larger state has four times as many voters as the smaller state, the decisiveness of an individual voter in the larger state decreases only by a factor of about two (from 0.050 to 0.023). Thus, even though an individual voter has a reduced chance of influencing the outcome in a large state because of the greater number of people voting, this reduction is more than offset by the larger number of electoral votes he can potentially influence. Hence, despite the apparent dilution of his vote under a winner-take-all system like the Electoral College, a voter in a large state has on balance greater potential voting power to affect the outcome of a presidential election than a voter in a small state.[27]

It is precisely this greater potential voting power of voters in large states which makes them more attractive as campaign targets to the candidates. Is it any wonder why, then, the candidates view the large states as more deserving of their attention—even on a per capita basis—than small states?

27. Compare the similar findings in John P. Banzhaf III, "One Man, 3.312 Votes: A Mathematical Analysis of the Electoral College," *Villanova Law Review* 13, no. 2 (Winter 1968): 304–32. Banzhaf's analysis of the voting power of voters in a state is based on the concept of a "critical vote," which can occur only if there is a fifty-fifty split and is similar to that used in Coleman, "Loss of Power." By contrast, the concept of "decisiveness" given in the text takes into account other possible divisions of the vote. It should be noted that Banzhaf combines the concept of a critical vote of a voter in a state with his index of voting power applied to states in the Electoral College to obtain a composite measure of the power of a voter in each state to affect the outcome in the Electoral College; this measure is rigorously developed and calculated for the Electoral College in Guillermo Owen, "Multilinear Extensions and the Banzhaf Value," *Naval Research Logistics Quarterly* 22, no. 4 (December 1975): 741–50. A similar measure, based on the Shapley-Shubik index, is calculated in Guillermo Owen, "Evaluation of a Presidential Election Game," *American Political Science Review* 69, no. 3 (September 1975): 947–53; see also the exchange between Owen and Chester Spatt in "Communications," *American Political Science Review* 70, no. 4 (December 1976): 1221–24. (An application of the Shapley-Shubik index is given in section 4.9.) Both Banzhaf and Owen conclude that citizens in the largest states are considerably advantaged, which accords pretty much with the conclusions presented later in this chapter.

This result, though not directly tied to the earlier resource-allocation models, sheds considerable light on the
strategic advantage of voters in large states. Yet, because the
3/2's rule that favors large states is only a local equilibrium
point when candidates match each other's resource allocations, it is highly vulnerable when the matching assumption is
discarded. In fact, it can be shown that when a candidate
knows the allocations of his opponent under the Electoral
College system, the most devastating strategy he can generally
use against him is to spend nothing in the smallest state and
instead use these extra resources (assuming the total resources of both candidates are equal) to outspend his opponent in each of the other states.

In general, adaptive strategies which exploit the commitments of an opponent demand a flexibility in responding to
an opponent's allocations and recommitting one's own resources that does not seem to accord with such campaign
realities as the need for advance scheduling or the purchase
of future broadcast time. It is for this reason that the 3/2's
rule, despite its instability, may better reflect a fixed, if intui-
tive and not well understood, point of reference for the major
candidates than do allocation strategies directed only to responding to an opponent's commitments. Although admittedly most candidates, and especially successful ones, are
probably incrementalists in the way they define and quickly
respond to issues in a campaign,[28] it nevertheless appears that
decisions about resource allocations are inherently less fluid.

Having already justified the assumptions and logic that
generate the 3/2's rule, and posted warnings about its fragile
nature, I shall report in section 3.10 on its empirical validity.
Since by election time the candidates necessarily have made a
set of choices that fixes their allocations, one can check these
against the 3/2's and other rules without inquiring into what
determines each and every choice. In this analysis, the 3/2's
rule is refined by assuming that the number of uncommitted

28. See Karl A. Lamb and Paul A. Smith, *Campaign Decision-Making: The
Presidential Election of 1964* (Belmont, Calif.: Wadsworth, 1968).

voters in each state is directly proportional to the population, and not to the number of electoral votes, of that state. Especially in small states, where the two-senator bonus in the Electoral College greatly magnifies their per capita electoral-vote representation, there is no reason to assume that the proportion of uncommitted voters will be so magnified. It seems far more reasonable to tie estimates of uncommitted voters directly to the population, thus retaining the original form of the 3/2's rule, $v_i\sqrt{n_i}$, where n_i is assumed proportional to the population.[29]

3.10. Testing the Models

Political campaigns in the United States have grown enormously expensive in recent years. Herbert E. Alexander, director of the Citizens' Research Foundation, estimated that political spending on all levels during the 1968 campaign ran to $300 million—up 50 percent from the total cost of campaigns in 1964—and that it cost $100 million to elect a president that year.[30] The New York Times estimated that a total of $400 million was spent on political campaigns in 1972.[31]

Legislation enacted in 1974, however, promises some relief from the spiraling costs of presidential campaigns by limiting the campaign spending of presidential candidates to $10 million in the primaries (up to $5 million of this total may be provided by matching public funds), and the major parties to $20 million in the general election (the entire amount may be provided by public funds), with adjustments in these totals made for inflation. However, the Supreme Court held on January 30, 1976, that these limits do not apply if candidates

29. The population of a state, of course, is not an exact reflection of the proportion of the voting-age population who are registered and actually do vote in a presidential election. Since it is not at all clear whether and how the proportion of uncommitted voters in a state is related to differences in registration and turnout among the states, I have taken the simplest course of using population as a first-approximation estimate of the proportion of voters likely to be uncommitted at the start of a campaign. This assumption can, of course, be modified at a later time if found to be deficient.

30. The New York Times, January 31, 1972, p. 48.

31. The New York Times, November 19, 1972, p. 1.

finance their campaigns exclusively with private contributions.[32]

Unfortunately, up until recently reliable data on the financial expenditures of the presidential candidates in each state have not been generally available. Although the Federal Communications Commission has published data on the campaign expenditures of the major political parties for radio and television advertising in recent presidential election years, these figures are not disaggregated for presidential races.[33] Despite the wealth of data that has been collected on the financial contributions and expenditures of candidates,[34] their completeness and reliability have been hampered by unsystematic reporting and the lack of effective governmental controls on contributions and expenditures. The Federal Election Campaign Act of 1971 and the Federal Election Campaign Act Amendments of 1974 tighten up reporting procedures and should improve this situation.

In the absence of reliable state-by-state data on financial expenditures of presidential candidates, I have turned to the one resource which imposes the same implacable restraints on the campaign behavior of all candidates—time. With a finite amount of it to spend in a campaign, the crucial question for a candidate becomes how to apportion it most wisely so as to gain favorable and far-reaching exposure.

In the models, I assumed that the favorableness of a candidate's image in a state depends on his resource expenditures in that state as compared to those of his opponent. To test

32. "Campaign Finance: Congress Weighing New Law," *Congressional Quarterly Weekly Report* 34, no. 6 (February 7, 1976): 267–74.

33. Federal Communications Commission (FCC), *Survey of Political Broadcasting: 1960, 1964, 1968, 1972* (Washington, D.C.: FCC, 1961, 1965, 1969, 1973), which includes data on both primary and general-election campaigns. I learned recently, however, that disaggregated data are available in *Hearings* before a Subcommittee on Communication, Committee on Commerce, on S. 372, United States Senate, 93d Congress, First Session (1973), Serial Number 93–4, appendix A.

34. The most comprehensive source of this information for the 1972 election is Herbert E. Alexander, *Financing the 1972 Election* (Lexington, Mass.: Lexington Books, 1976).

these models, I operationalized expenditures of time in terms
of the total number of *campaign appearances* that a candidate
makes in a state, where campaign appearances are defined to
be events at which a candidate either makes some public
address to an audience (whether the address takes the form of
a major speech or brief remarks, but excluding news confer-
ences) or participates in some public activity like a parade,
motorcade, or fair. To be sure, counting all campaign appearances in a state as equivalent ignores important differences among them (e.g., size of audience and extent of
news coverage), but the distribution of both politically "important" and "unimportant" appearances in each state visited
probably makes the aggregated data roughly comparable for
this analysis.

The campaign appearance data are based on news coverage
of the 1960, 1964, 1968, and 1972 presidential campaigns in
The New York Times, from September 1 to the day before
Election Day in November in each year, supplemented by
such other sources as congressional reports, *Congressional
Quarterly Weekly Reports*, and *Facts on File*.[35] Although these

35. For other data on the itineraries of presidential candidates, see *Source
Book of American Presidential Campaign and Election Statistics: 1948–1968*, ed.
John H. Runyon, Jennefer Verdini, and Sally S. Runyon (New York: Fred-
erick Ungar, 1971), pp. 139–73. This work does not contain data on the
itineraries of vice-presidential candidates, whose campaign appearances were
combined with the appearances of presidential candidates in the analysis, for
reasons given in the text. State-by-state appearance data of the candidates in
the 1976 presidential campaign have recently been published and indicate, as
in the four previous campaigns, a large-state bias by both the Republican and
Democratic slates. See Senate Hearings (Supplement), *The Electoral College
and Direct Election of the President and Vice President* (1977), p. 29; and *Direct
Popular Election of the President and Vice President of the United States*, Report of
the Committee on the Judiciary, United States Senate, 95th Congress, First
Session (1977), p. 15. It is interesting to contrast these behavioral data with
planned "percent of effort" figures for the Carter-Mondale campaign in each
state, based on a scheduling formula devised by campaign director Hamilton
Jordan prior to the general-election campaign. These data are given in
Martin Schram, *Running for President: A Journal of the Carter Campaign* (New
York: Pocket Books, 1978), appendix 3. Jordan's planned percentages reveal
no large-state bias, but his figures were apparently disregarded by the Democratic candidates in the 1976 campaign. As shown in Steven J. Brams, "Re-

data on campaign appearances are only as accurate as coverage by the media, they are generally highly correlated with data collected by Stanley Kelley, Jr., on the number of hours spent by the presidential and vice-presidential candidates in each state in the 1960 and 1964 elections, which is based in part on the candidates' own personal schedules.[36]

For each party, the appearances made by both its presidential and vice-presidential candidates were combined, and this total was used as an indicator of the candidates' resource allocations to each state in the four campaigns studied. Combining the appearances of each party's two nominees seemed preferable to singling out the time expenditures of only the presidential candidate, since the two candidates often adopt complementary strategies. For example, in the 1960 race, Lyndon Johnson, the Democratic vice-presidential candidate, was assigned the task of holding the South for the Democrats, and he devoted more than twice as much time to this region as his running mate, John Kennedy, or either of the Republican candidates, Richard Nixon and Henry Cabot Lodge, Jr.[37] If Johnson's campaign appearances had not been added to Kennedy's, it would appear that the Democrats did not consider the southern states strategically important to their fashioning a victory, which was manifestly not the case.

Since a detailed analysis of the campaign appearance data has been reported elsewhere,[38] I shall summarize here only the conclusions of the analysis. Generally speaking, the 3/2's rule was found to fit the campaign appearance data somewhat better than the proportional rule, but Brams and Davis did not promulgate it as an "immutable law":

source Allocations in the 1976 Campaign" (mimeographed, New York University, 1978), the 3/2's rule held up reasonably well for both the Democratic and Republican slates.

36. These data are summarized in Stanley Kelley, Jr., "The Presidential Campaign," in *The Presidential Election and Transition*, ed. Paul T. David (Washington, D.C.: Brookings Institution, 1961), pp. 57–87; and Kelley, "The Presidential Campaign," in *National Election of 1964*, pp. 42–81.

37. Computed from data given in Kelley, "The Presidential Campaign," in *Presidential Election and Transition*, p. 72.

38. Brams and Davis, "The 3/2's Rule in Presidential Campaigning."

Like any theoretical consequence of a set of assumptions, its applicability will be limited to those situations that can be reasonably well characterized by these assumptions—particularly the postulated goal of maximizing one's expected electoral vote and the assumption that candidates match each other's campaign expenditures in each state—which are not easy to verify. Further, the instability of the 3/2's rule as an equilibrium point, which makes it vulnerable to only small deviations, may also limit its applicability, especially when candidates resort to adaptive strategies in response to each other's allocations. Finally, another potential source of slippage between the theoretical allocations and the actual campaign behavior of candidates occurs in the reconstruction of campaign itineraries, which is a task fraught with difficulties that certainly contributes to unreliability in the data.[39]

Brams and Davis nonetheless concluded:

Our data do make clear that the candidates generally make disproportionately large expenditures of time in the largest states. While one could always find a better-fitting function than the 3/2's rule for any particular campaign, it would not constitute an explanatory model unless one could derive it from assumptions that are both interpretable and plausible. Fitting a curve to empirical data may help one summarize repeated instances of a phenomenon, but in itself it does not impart a logic to the curve that we consider the hallmark of scientific explanation.[40]

In section 3.11, the allocations prescribed by the 3/2's rule will be given for each state from 1972 through 1980, when the next decennial census will be taken. (Population figures from this census will be used to reapportion electoral votes of the

39. Brams and Davis, "The 3/2's Rule in Presidential Campaigning," p. 126.
40. Brams and Davis, "The 3/2's Rule in Presidential Campaigning," p. 126.

states for the 1984 presidential election.) The calculations will reveal the extent to which the 3/2's rule favors the largest states, even on a per capita basis, despite the two-senator bonus that favors the smallest states.[41]

3.11. Campaign Allocations and Biases through 1980

Using data from the 1970 census and the electoral votes of each state through 1980, I have indicated in table 3.2 the percentages of time a candidate would spend in each state and the District of Columbia if he allocated his resources proportionally or if he allocated them according to the 3/2's rule. (These figures are also given for large, medium, and small states: large states have twenty or more electoral votes, medium states between ten and nineteen, and small states less than ten.) For example, a candidate's proportional allocation to California on the basis of its forty-five electoral votes represents about an 8 percent commitment of his resources, but the 3/2's rule nearly doubles this commitment to 15 percent. On the other hand, the 3/2's rule would slash a 0.56 percent commitment to Alaska by nearly a factor of five. According to this rule, then, California should receive about twice as much, and Alaska about one-fifth as much, resources *per electoral vote* as would be commensurate with their respective forty-five and three electoral votes.

This is what I call the *electoral bias* (EB) of the present system, which is simply the ratio of 3/2's allocations to proportional allocations for all states. These ratios are given in table 3.2 and show that the nine largest states, with 52 percent of the population, are advantaged by the 3/2's rule (EB > 1.00), the remaining forty-one disadvantaged (EB < 1.00).

The *individual bias* (IB) of the Electoral College is the concept most relevant to assessing the degree to which the 3/2's rule engenders campaign allocations in states that are incon-

41. In the following analysis I assume that Maine operates under the Electoral College system, though starting with the 1972 presidential election it adopted a "district plan," whereby its two senatorial electoral votes go to the winner of the state, but its two electoral votes based on population are decided on a district-by-district basis.

sistent with the egalitarian principle of one man, one vote. This bias is the ratio of each state's 3/2's percent allocation to its percent share of the total population.

In substantive terms, IB represents the relative proportion of resources a candidate would commit *per person* to each state if he made his allocations according to the 3/2's rule. These per capita allocation ratios are also given in table 3.2, along with the ranks (in parentheses) of these ratios from the highest to the lowest for the fifty states and the District of Columbia.

The ranking of states on the basis of their IB values, unlike their ranking on EB values, does not correspond perfectly to their ranking in terms of electoral votes. Thus, for example, whereas an individual voter in the largest state, California, ranks as the most attractive target for a candidate who allocates according to the 3/2's rule—receiving 50 percent more attention (IB = 1.50) than he would get if the candidate allocated his time strictly according to the population of each state—a voter in the smallest state, Alaska, with an IB of 0.81, is still comparatively well off based on Alaska's sixteenth position among the fifty states and the District of Columbia. Its IB is below the proportional norm of 1.00, but far from the bottom rung of the ladder that citizens who live in Washington, D.C., have the dubious distinction of occupying, with IBs equal to 0.51.

There are two reasons why the IB scores of states are only an imperfect reflection of their electoral votes. First, when two states have the same number of electoral votes, like Texas and Illinois with twenty-six each, citizens of the larger state (Texas) will be slightly disadvantaged, because the attention they receive from the candidates according to the 3/2's rule must be divided among more people.

The two-senator bonus accorded to all states more seriously upsets the generally positive relationship between IB scores and the electoral votes of a state. This bonus, naturally, is much more significant to a state like Alaska, with one representative, than a state like California, with forty-three representatives: in terms of percentages, the two-senator bonus

Table 3.2
Electoral and Individual Biases of 3/2's Campaign
Allocations in Fifty States and
District of Columbia

State	Electoral votes	Proportional allocation (%)	3/2's allocation (%)	Electoral bias (EB): 3/2's / Proportional	Individual bias (IB): 3/2's / Population
1. Calif.	45	8.36	14.69	1.76	1.50 (1)
2. N.Y.	41	7.62	12.78	1.68	1.43 (2)
3. Pa.	27	5.02	6.78	1.35	1.17 (3)
4. Texas	26	4.83	6.36	1.32	1.15 (5)
5. Ill.	26	4.83	6.34	1.31	1.16 (4)
6. Ohio	25	4.65	5.96	1.28	1.14 (6)
7. Mich.	21	3.90	4.57	1.17	1.05 (7)
Lge. States	211	39.22	57.48	1.47	1.27
8. N.J.	17	3.16	3.33	1.05	0.94 (9)
9. Fla.	17	3.16	3.24	1.02	0.97 (8)
10. Mass.	14	2.60	2.44	0.94	0.87 (10)
11. Ind.	13	2.42	2.17	0.90	0.85 (12)
12. N.C.	13	2.42	2.14	0.89	0.86 (11)
13. Mo.	12	2.23	1.90	0.85	0.82 (15)
14. Va.	12	2.23	1.89	0.85	0.83 (14)
15. Ga.	12	2.23	1.88	0.84	0.83 (13)
16. Wis.	11	2.04	1.69	0.83	0.78 (18)
17. Tenn.	10	1.86	1.45	0.78	0.75 (22)
18. Md.	10	1.86	1.45	0.78	0.75 (21)
19. Minn.	10	1.86	1.43	0.77	0.76 (20)
20. La.	10	1.86	1.40	0.75	0.78 (17)
Med. States	161	29.93	26.41	0.88	0.84
21. Ala.	9	1.67	1.22	0.73	0.72 (28)
22. Wash.	9	1.67	1.21	0.73	0.72 (27)
23. Ky.	9	1.67	1.18	0.71	0.75 (23)
24. Conn.	8	1.49	1.02	0.68	0.68 (36)

Table 3.2 Continued

	Electoral votes	Proportional allocation (%)	3/2's allocation (%)	Electoral bias (EB): 3/2's Proportional	Individual bias (IB): 3/2's Population
State					
25. Iowa	8	1.49	0.98	0.66	0.71 (30)
26. S.C.	8	1.49	0.94	0.63	0.74 (25)
27. Okla.	8	1.49	0.94	0.63	0.74 (24)
28. Kans.	7	1.30	0.77	0.59	0.69 (34)
29. Miss.	7	1.30	0.76	0.59	0.70 (33)
30. Colo.	7	1.30	0.76	0.58	0.70 (32)
31. Ore.	6	1.12	0.63	0.57	0.62 (43)
32. Ark.	6	1.12	0.61	0.55	0.64 (41)
33. Ariz.	6	1.12	0.58	0.52	0.67 (39)
34. W.Va.	6	1.12	0.58	0.52	0.67 (38)
35. Neb.	5	0.93	0.45	0.48	0.61 (44)
36. Utah	4	0.74	0.30	0.40	0.58 (49)
37. N.M.	4	0.74	0.29	0.40	0.59 (48)
38. Me.	4	0.74	0.29	0.39	0.60 (47)
39. R.I.	4	0.74	0.29	0.38	0.61 (45)
40. Haw.	4	0.74	0.26	0.35	0.68 (37)
41. N.H.	4	0.74	0.25	0.34	0.69 (35)
42. Idaho	4	0.74	0.25	0.33	0.70 (31)
43. Mont.	4	0.74	0.24	0.33	0.71 (29)
44. S.D.	4	0.74	0.24	0.32	0.73 (26)
45. D.C.	3	0.56	0.19	0.34	0.51 (51)
46. N.D.	3	0.56	0.17	0.31	0.57 (50)
47. Del.	3	0.56	0.16	0.29	0.60 (46)
48. Nev.	3	0.56	0.15	0.28	0.64 (42)
49. Vt.	3	0.56	0.15	0.26	0.67 (40)
50. Wyo.	3	0.56	0.13	0.23	0.77 (19)
51. Alas.	3	0.56	0.12	0.22	0.81 (16)
Sm. States	166	30.86	16.11	0.52	0.68

Source: Steven J. Brams and Morton D. Davis, "The 3/2's Rule in Presidential Campaigning," *American Political Science Review* 68, no. 1 (March 1974): 128, table 5; reprinted with permission.

inflates Alaska's per capita representation by 200 percent, California's by only about 5 percent.

Some critics of the Electoral College have charged that this bonus favors small states, which it obviously does on a proportional basis. On the other hand, proponents of the Electoral College have responded that this favoritism is counteracted by the fact that the large blocs of votes cast by large states in the Electoral College have a greater chance of being decisive, especially in close elections. To what extent do these opposing forces cancel each other out?

The balance between these forces, it turns out, is very one-sided: the large-state bias created by the 3/2's rule swamps the small-state bias resulting from the two-senator bonus, giving citizens of the fifteen most populous states the highest IB scores. This is not unexpected, since the 3/2's rule compels the candidates to make inordinately large expenditures of resources in the largest states, even out of proportion to their populations.

Yet not all citizens of even these fifteen large states are favored by the 3/2's rule. Only the citizens of the seven very largest states, which comprise less than a majority (45 percent) of the population, receive representation greater than in proportion to their numbers (IB > 1.00). Citizens in the remaining forty-three states, plus the District of Columbia (whose sad plight will be recounted subsequently), receive attention below the one-man, one-vote standard from candidates who adhere to the 3/2's allocation rule.

Only with Alaska's entry into the sixteenth position of the IB ranking does the two-senator bonus begin to help the very small states. Although Wyoming breaks into the IB ranking at the nineteenth position, none of the four other very small states with three electoral votes is successful in outdistancing the 3/2's rule by an amount sufficient to rank it above the fortieth position. In the cases of Alaska and Wyoming, the two-senator bonus gives each a per capita electoral-vote representation more than four times greater than that of California, which accounts for their ability to overcome to some degree the large-state bias of the 3/2's rule.

Although the states that the two-senator bonus helps most are among the smallest, small size alone is not the only factor that tends to counteract the 3/2's rule. The ability of a state just to meet the quota for a certain number of electoral votes is also important, for it gives the state higher per capita representation than that of larger states with the same number of electoral votes. Thus, the three smallest states with four electoral votes—Idaho, Montana, and South Dakota—succeed in raising their population rankings of forty-second, forty-third, and forty-fourth by eleven, fourteen, and seventeen notches (one more notch if the District of Columbia is included), respectively, on the IB scale. No other states besides these and Alaska and Wyoming are able to better their population rankings by as much as ten positions.

From the perspective of per capita representation, the most unfortunate citizens are those who live in Washington, D.C. The Twenty-third Amendment limits the District of Columbia to electoral representation no greater than the least populous state (Alaska), which has three electoral votes. This limitation is strangely inconsistent with the fact that the District's population is greater than that of four states that each have four electoral votes. With an IB of 0.51, its citizens rank below those of all fifty states in per capita representation.

Using Washington, D.C., as a basis for comparison, the ratios of the IBs of all states to the District's IB are ranked in table 3.3. Similarly, taking the lowest-ranking state on the EB scale (Alaska), the ratios of all states' EB scores to that of Alaska are also ranked. These ratios reveal that the largest state, California, has 2.92 times as great individual representation as Washington, D.C., and 8.13 times as great electoral representation as Alaska. This means that a candidate who campaigns according to the 3/2's rule would allocate to California more than eight times as many resources per electoral vote as he does to Alaska, and almost three times as many resources per person as he does to Washington, D.C. Although the District of Columbia has 1.76 times as many electoral votes per person as California, which is why its individual bias of 0.51 is greater than (i.e., deviates less from

Table 3.3

Rankings of EB and IB Ratios for Fifty States and District of Columbia

Rank	EB ratio: EB (state i) / EB (Alaska)	IB ratio: IB (state i) / IB (D.C.)	Rank	EB ratio: EB (state i) / EB (Alaska)	IB ratio: IB (state i) / IB (D.C.)
1	Calif. (8.13)	Calif. (2.92)	27	Okla. (2.91)	Wash. (1.41)
2	N.Y. (7.76)	N.Y. (2.79)	28	Kans. (2.73)	Ala. (1.41)
3	Pa. (6.25)	Pa. (2.28)	29	Miss. (2.71)	Mont. (1.39)
4	Texas (6.09)	Ill. (2.26)	30	Colo. (2.70)	Iowa (1.38)
5	Ill. (6.07)	Texas (2.25)	31	Ore. (2.63)	Idaho (1.37)
6	Ohio (5.94)	Ohio (2.22)	32	Ark. (2.52)	Colo. (1.37)
7	Mich. (5.42)	Mich. (2.04)	33	Ariz. (2.42)	Miss. (1.36)
8	N.J. (4.87)	Fla. (1.89)	34	W.Va. (2.40)	Kans. (1.35)
9	Fla. (4.74)	N.J. (1.84)	35	Neb. (2.22)	N.H. (1.35)
10	Mass. (4.34)	Mass. (1.70)	36	Utah (1.87)	Conn. (1.33)
11	Ind. (4.15)	N.C. (1.67)	37	N.M. (1.83)	Haw. (1.32)
12	N.C. (4.10)	Ind. (1.65)	38	Me. (1.81)	W.Va. (1.32)

13	Mo.	(3.94)	Ga.	(1.62)
14	Va.	(3.92)	Va.	(1.61)
15	Ga.	(3.90)	Mo.	(1.61)
16	Wis.	(3.82)	Alas.	(1.58)
17	Tenn.	(3.60)	La.	(1.52)
18	Md.	(3.60)	Wis.	(1.52)
19	Minn.	(3.55)	Wyo.	(1.51)
20	La.	(3.47)	Minn.	(1.49)
21	Ala.	(3.38)	Md.	(1.46)
22	Wash.	(3.36)	Tenn.	(1.46)
23	Ky.	(3.26)	Ky.	(1.45)
24	Conn.	(3.17)	Okla.	(1.45)
25	Iowa	(3.06)	S.C.	(1.44)
26	S.C.	(2.93)	S.D.	(1.42)

39	R.I.	(1.77)	Ariz.	(1.31)
40	Haw.	(1.60)	Vt.	(1.30)
41	D.C.	(1.58)	Ark.	(1.25)
42	N.H.	(1.56)	Nev.	(1.24)
43	Idaho	(1.54)	Ore.	(1.20)
44	Mont.	(1.52)	Neb.	(1.19)
45	S.D.	(1.49)	R.I.	(1.19)
46	N.D.	(1.43)	Del.	(1.18)
47	Del.	(1.35)	Me.	(1.16)
48	Nev.	(1.27)	N.M.	(1.15)
49	Vt.	(1.21)	Utah	(1.13)
50	Wyo.	(1.05)	N.D.	(1.11)
51	Alas.	(1.00)	D.C.	(1.00)

Source: Steven J. Brams and Morton D. Davis, "The 3/2's Rule in Presidential Campaigning," *American Political Science Review* 68, no. 1 (March 1974): 130, table 6; reprinted with permission.

the standard of 1.00) as its electoral bias of 0.34, it would still need about twice as many electoral votes as it has (six), holding all other states constant, to wipe out its individual bias (i.e., to make its IB ≈ 1.00).

To be sure, residents of Washington, D.C., probably do not suffer from any lack of exposure to presidential candidates. Yet for Alaska, whose electoral votes have only 12 percent of the drawing power of California's (EB of 0.22 for Alaska versus 1.76 for California), it may be more than distance that has kept away all presidential and vice-presidential candidates except Richard Nixon in his 1960 campaign. And for the citizens living in the small and medium states who together constitute 55 percent of the population of the United States, the average IB and EB scores given in table 3.2 indicate that these groups of states are generally disadvantaged, even if the inequities of the electoral system visited upon them do not match the injustice done to the citizens of Alaska (by the EB measure) and the District of Columbia (by the IB measure).

So far I have shown that the 3/2's rule greatly favors the large states and generally overwhelms what per capita electoral-vote advantage the small states do have. Of course, the relative neglect of some states by presidential candidates is not only a function of their electoral representation but also the degree to which candidates estimate that their campaigning or other expenditures of resources can make a difference in the probable outcome of the election in these states. If no feasible allocations of time, money, or other resources can possibly change the probable outcome, then a candidate would be foolish to give it anything more than token attention. Richard Nixon, who placed great stress on the symbolic value of visiting all fifty states in his 1960 presidential bid, despite an injury at the beginning of the campaign that kept him sidelined for several days, dumped this strategy in his 1968 and 1972 campaigns. There is no evidence that such "tokenism" brings any payoff in extra votes.

In an actual campaign, a candidate and his advisers would normally pare down the fifty states and the District of Columbia (for which 3/2's allocations are given in table 3.2) to a smaller list of states in which uncommitted voters are likely to have a decisive impact on the election outcome. The states a candidate should ignore by this criterion would include not only those in which his opponent is heavily favored but also those in which he has piled up big early leads prior to the campaign, for it makes as little sense to expend resources in states that seem invulnerable to one's opponent as it does to conduct forays into states that an opponent has virtually locked up.

In fact, candidates and their advisors seem to make precisely these calculations, which V. O. Key, Jr., reports also characterize the effects of unit rule in Georgia. There, in party nominations for statewide races, the candidate who wins a plurality in each of Georgia's 159 counties receives all the unit votes of that county (one, two, or three, depending on its population):

> . . . [a practical politician] classifies the counties into three groups: those in which he is sure of a plurality; those in which he has no chance of a plurality; those which are doubtful. He forgets about the first two groups except for routine campaign coverage. He concentrates his resources in the third group; expenditures, appearances by the candidate, negotiations, all the tricks of county politicking.[42]

42. V. O. Key, Jr., *Southern Politics in State and Nation* (New York: Knopf, 1949), p. 122. This citation is due to Melvin J. Hinich and Peter C. Ordeshook, "The Electoral College: A Spatial Analysis," *Political Methodology* 1, no. 3 (Summer 1974): 1–29, in which the effect of the Electoral College on equilibrium strategies, given different distributions of policy preferences of the electorate, is examined; see also Eric M. Uslaner, "Spatial Models of the Electoral College: Distribution Assumptions and Biases," *Political Methodology* 3, no. 3 (Summer 1976): 335–81. For related research on the Electoral College, see Melvin J. Hinich, Richard Mickelson, and Peter C. Ordeshook, "The Electoral College Vs. A Direct Vote: Policy Bias, Reversals, and Indeterminate Outcomes," *Journal of Mathematical Sociology* 4 (1975): 3–35; Seymour Spilerman and David Dickens, "Who Will Gain and Who Will Lose under Different Electoral Rules?" *American Journal of Sociology* 79, no. 2 (September 1974): 443–77; Douglas H. Blair, "Electoral College Reform and the Distribution of Voting Power" (mimeographed, University of Pennsyl-

In presidential campaigns today, the widespread use of public opinion polls makes it easier than ever before to weed out those states securely in the camp of one candidate and pinpoint the "toss-up" states likely to swing either way. Insofar as polls indicate the largest states to be the toss-up states, candidates who act on this information and concentrate almost all their resources in these states will magnify even the large-state bias of the 3/2's rule. This is so because the noncompetitive (small) states would be eliminated from consideration altogether, and allocations that would ordinarily go to them would be concentrated in the competitive (large) states. Indeed, the Democrats reportedly wrote off twenty-four states in 1968,[43] though the campaign appearance data indicate that one or both of the Democratic candidates made appearances in more than half these states. Apparently, even the best laid plans are not always followed.

3.12. Limitations and Extensions of the Models

The rationale of the 3/2's rule rests on the idea that states can be pinpointed like military targets and, independent of nearby and faraway other targets, captured with a high probability by a concentration of forces superior to that of one's opponent (given that his allocations are known or can be

vania, 1976); Samuel Merrill, III, "Citizen Voting Power under the Electoral College: A Stochastic Model Based on State Voting Patterns," *SIAM Journal on Applied Mathematics* 34, no. 2 (March 1978): 376–90; Merrill, "Empirical Estimates for the Likelihood of a Divided Verdict in a Presidential Election," *Public Choice* (forthcoming, 1978); and Claude S. Colantoni, Terrence J. Levesque, and Peter C. Ordeshook, "Campaign Resource Allocations under the Electoral College," *American Political Science Review* 69, no. 1 (March 1975): 141–54. In the latter article, the authors criticize some aspects of the empirical analysis in Brams and Davis, "The 3/2's Rule in Presidential Campaigning"; this article is followed by a "Comment" from Brams and Davis, pp. 155–56, and a "Rejoinder" by Colantoni, Levesque, and Ordeshook, pp. 157–61. See also H. P. Young, "The Allocation of Funds in Lobbying and Campaigning," *Behavioral Science* 23, no. 1 (January 1978): 21–31, who offers a different model of resource allocation that he applies to presidential campaigning; and Young, "Power, Prices, and Incomes in Voting Systems," *Mathematical Programming* 14, no. 2 (March 1978): 129–48.

43. Joseph Napolitan, *The Election Game and How to Win It* (Garden City, N.Y.: Doubleday, 1970), p. 62.

estimated). As Richard M. Scammon and Ben J. Wattenberg warn, however, this logic may be seriously flawed:

> It is extremely difficult, and probably impossible, to move 32,000 votes in a New Jersey Presidential election without moving thousands and tens of thousands of votes in each of the other forty-nine states. The day of the pinpoint sectional or statewide campaign is gone—if it ever existed—and the fact that votes cannot be garnered in bushels on specific street corners is of crucial significance when one looks at the arithmetic of the future.[44]

Scammon and Wattenberg go on to point out that political rallies usually draw mostly partisans already committed to a candidate. For this reason, relatively few uncommitted voters are likely to observe, much less be persuaded by, the speech a candidate makes at a rally in their state.[45] Their choices, Scammon and Wattenberg argue, will depend much more on national coverage of the campaign, particularly by television.[46]

Yet, these analysts do not dismiss campaigns as insignificant:

44. Richard M. Scammon and Ben J. Wattenberg, *The Real Majority: An Extraordinary Examination of the American Electorate* (New York: Coward, McCann and Geoghegan, 1970), p. 213.

45. According to a series of Gallup polls, less than 6 percent of all people saw any one of the presidential candidates in person in 1968. See Sara Davidson, "Advancing Backward with Muskie," *Harper's*, June 1972, p. 61.

46. Scammon and Wattenberg, *Real Majority*, pp. 214–16. Moreover, television news shows, documentaries, and other specials, which are generally beyond the direct control of candidates, rank far above television advertising as the most important media influences, at least for the split-ticket voter. See Walter De Vries and Lance Tarrance, Jr., *The Ticket-Splitter: A New Force in American Politics* (Grand Rapids, Mich.: William B. Erdemans, 1972), p. 78. Recent research on media effects in presidential elections is reported in Thomas E. Patterson and Robert D. McClure, *The Unseeing Eye: The Myth of Television Power in National Politics* (New York: Putnam's, 1976); and Herbert B. Asher, "The Media and the Presidential Selection Process," in *The Impact of the Electoral Process*, ed. Louis Maisel and Joseph Cooper (Beverly Hills, Calif.: Sage Publications, 1977), pp. 207–34.

[T]he campaign is important in providing the candidate with *something to do* that can be televised, photographed, and written about for national consumption. . . . Further, if a candidate does *not* campaign at all, his opposition will criticize him for "not taking his case to the people."

Beyond all that, however, is a certain extremely valuable symbolism that underlies all the flesh pressing, baby kissing, hurly-burly of a campaign. There is great value in a system that somehow demands that a candidate get sweaty and dirty and exhausted, his hands bleeding, his hair messed by the masses of people whom he wants to represent. The successful candidate in America must touch the people, figuratively and literally.[47]

How a candidate does this is not well understood, even if it is known that campaigns often decide the outcomes of elections.[48]

The thrust of this analysis, however, is not to show how the conduct of campaigns affects election outcomes.[49] Rather, it is to establish that candidates act *as if* they believe their conduct

47. Scammon and Wattenberg, *Real Majority*, p. 217; italics in original.

48. At the local level, party organization activities do appear to influence election results favorably, including the vote for president. See William J. Crotty, "Party Effort and Its Impact on the Vote," *American Political Science Review* 65, no. 2 (June 1971): 439–50, and references cited therein; also, Robert J. Huckshorn and Robert C. Spencer, in *The Politics of Defeat: Campaigning for Congress* (Amherst: University of Massachusetts Press, 1971), stress the importance of campaign organization on election results. At the national level, on the other hand, there is no clear-cut relationship between the campaign spending of each party and the outcome of presidential elections. See Twentieth Century Fund, *Voters' Time: Report of the Twentieth Century Fund Commission on Campaign Costs in the Electronic Era* (New York: Twentieth Century Fund, 1969), pp. 11–13; Congressional Quarterly, *Dollar Politics: The Issue of Campaign Spending* (Washington, D.C.: Congressional Quarterly, 1971), pp. 14, 19–31; and Delmer D. Dunn, *Financing Presidential Campaigns* (Washington, D.C.: Brookings Institution, 1972), p. 9. More opaque, still, is the relationship between major strategic decisions made by candidates, especially during the heat of a close race, and their effect on the vote. See Polsby and Wildavsky, *Presidential Elections*, pp. 184–91.

49. That the organization and planning of presidential campaigns is criti-

matters when it comes to making campaign allocations. Perhaps "the spectacle of seeing one's opponent run around the country at a furious pace without following suit is too nerve-racking to contemplate,"[50] but it also appears that the as-if assumption is rooted in the actual beliefs of candidates, who, at least at the state and local level, think their campaigns have an impact on the election outcome.[51] As evidence for the postulated goal that presidential candidates campaign as if they seek to maximize their expected electoral vote, I have already shown that the 3/2's rule that follows from this goal mirrors quite well the actual campaign allocations of candidates.

The increasing nationalization of presidential campaigns obviously limits the applicability of any resource-allocation model that makes states the units of analysis. It is worth noting, though, that in postulating that candidates maximize their expected electoral vote, I did *not* assume that voting by individuals in different states is statistically independent. If I had postulated for candidates the goal of maximizing their probability of winning a majority of electoral votes, the statistical-independence assumption would be convenient, and probably necessary, to obtain tractable results.

---

cal to a candidate's eventual success is stressed in Jerry Bruno and Jeff Greenfield, *The Advance Man* (New York: William Morrow, 1971). See also Xandra Kayden, *Campaign Organization* (Lexington, Mass.: D. C. Heath, 1978).

50. Polsby and Wildavsky, *Presidential Elections*, p. 170. If the steeliness of a candidate's nerves can be judged by this standard, Richard Nixon's nerves progressively hardened in his successive bids for the presidency: as an incumbent president in the 1972 campaign, he made only 18 campaign appearances, whereas as a nonincumbent in 1968 and 1960 he made 140 and 228 appearances, respectively. Yet, though he cut down the number of his appearances in successive campaigns, in all three races Nixon made disproportionally greater allocations to the large states than to the medium and small states.

51. John W. Kingdon, *Candidates for Office: Beliefs and Strategies* (New York: Random House, 1968), pp. 109–14. See also Robert A. Schoenberger, "Campaign Strategy and Party Loyalty: The Electoral Relevance of Candidate Decision-Making in the 1964 Congressional Elections," *American Political Science Review* 63, no. 2 (June 1969): 515–20.

The goal of maximizing one's expected electoral vote may not be equivalent to maximizing one's probability of winning the election. To illustrate, a candidate who concentrates his resources in states with a bare majority of electoral votes may win these states and the election with a high probability, but his expected number of electoral votes will be relatively small. On the other hand, if he spreads his resources somewhat thinner over more states, he may increase his expected number of electoral votes, but at the price of lowering the probability that he will win a majority of electoral votes. Thus, the two goals may be logically inconsistent—that is, they may lead to contradictory strategic choices on the part of rational candidates. It does not seem that the implications of these different goals will be seriously contradictory in most cases —at least in two-candidate races—but this question needs to be explored further.[52]

Finally, it should be pointed out that several restrictive assumptions made earlier in the development of the models can be relaxed. The minimax solution of the popular-vote model, and the (unstable) equilibrium solution of the elctoral-vote model, hold *mutatis mutandis* when three or more candidates compete in an election. Furthermore, it is not necessary to assume, as was done initially, that the committed voters in each state are evenly divided at the outset of a campaign. If a candidate's polls indicate, for example, that he is ahead by particular margins in some states and behind by particular margins in others, he can use this information to determine his optimal allocations to each state, given that he can estimate the probable allocations of his opponent.

This problem can be conceptualized as one in which a candidate tries to reduce the effect of an opponent's supporters in a state by matching them against his own. If at the start of a campaign one candidate has more supporters in a state

---

52. Consequences of the probability-of-winning goal have recently been obtained and are reported in Mark Lake, "A New Campaign Resource Allocation Model" (mimeographed, New York University, 1978).

than the other candidate, the lesser candidate faces the problem of winning over a sufficient number of uncommitted voters to neutralize both his opponent's extra supporters and those uncommitted voters his opponent is likely to pick up, assuming that commitments once made are not broken.

Given the allocations of the candidates for all states i that define p_i, and the distribution of supporters committed to each candidate in each state, the probability of neutralizing an opponent's support and then going on to win is given by Lanchester's Linear Law, for which Richard H. Brown has provided a useful approximate solution.[53] Optimal allocations can be obtained by maximizing the expected electoral vote based on these probabilities for all states. Holding size constant, it would appear that the most attractive targets by far for campaign allocations in the electoral-vote model are those states in which the committed voters are split roughly fifty-fifty.

Finally, it seems possible that the models developed here may be applicable to the analysis of resource-allocation decisions in other political arenas, particularly those involving the distribution of payoffs to members of a coalition. For example, the apportionment of foreign aid, the commitment of military forces, the granting of patronage and other favors, and even the assignment of priorities all involve decisions about how to allocate resources among actors (or programs) of different weight or importance. Moreover, these decisions are often influenced by the actions or probable responses of an opponent in an essentially zero-sum environment. Presumably, the extent to which decision making in such competitive situations is conditioned by the kinds of goals postulated in this chapter could be determined by comparing the resource expenditures actually made with the theoretical implications that these goals entail (e.g., the proportional or 3/2's rules).

53. Both a description of this law and an approximate solution are given in Richard H. Brown, "Theory of Combat: The Probability of Winning," *Operations Research* 11, no. 3 (May-June 1963): 418–25.

3.13. Conclusions

Unlike the spatial models discussed in chapter 1, which take
the positions of candidates on issues as their focus for analysis, in the models developed in this chapter I took these
positions as given and instead asked how a presidential candidate should allocate his resources to convey as favorable an
impression of his positions and personality as possible. I assumed that the favorableness of his image to uncommitted
voters in each state would be a function of the amount of
resources he allocated to each state, as compared with the
amount allocated by his opponent.

Probably the most compelling conclusion that emerges
from the analysis, at least for noncandidates, does not concern campaign strategy but rather concerns the severely un-
representative character of presidential campaigns under the
Electoral College. By forcing candidates—and after the election, incumbent presidents with an eye on their reelection—to
pay much greater attention in terms of their allocations of
time, money, and other resources to the largest states, the
Electoral College gives disproportionally greater weight to the
attitudes and opinions of voters in these states. On a per
capita basis, voters in California are 2.92 times as attractive
campaign targets as voters in Washington, D.C.; even greater
than this ratio of the most extreme individual biases is the
most extreme electoral-bias ratio, which makes California
8.13 times as attractive per electoral vote as Alaska.

Although no voter today is actually deprived of a vote by
the Electoral College, an aggregation procedure that works to
deflate the weight of some votes and inflate the weight of
others seems clearly in violation of the egalitarian principle of
one man, one vote. The reapportionment decisions of the
courts since 1962 have upheld this principle, with reapportionment itself obviating the need for an institution with a
large-state "urban bias" like the Electoral College to offset the
rapidly fading "rural bias" of the House of Representatives.
Furthermore, as a procedure that places a premium on gaining information and responding to an opponent's allocations

in each state, the Electoral College tends to encourage manipulative strategic calculations for outmaneuvering the opposition in each state, which may divert a candidate from seeking broad-based nationwide support.

From a normative viewpoint, this is the goal it seems desirable the electoral system should promote. The Electoral College subverts this goal by giving special dispensation to particular states and, additionally, fostering manipulative strategies in them.[54] As an alternative, direct popular-vote election of the president, which would render state boundaries irrelevant, would encourage candidates to maximize their nationwide appeal by tying their support directly to potential votes everywhere on a proportional basis.

54. If there is no majority winner in the Electoral College, a presidential election is resolved in the House of Representatives wherein each state casts one vote (for an example, see sections 4.7 and 4.8). This institution reverses the large-state bias and gives voters in states with only one representative, like Alaska, 7.98 times as much voting power (Banzhaf index) as voters in California. Since all presidential elections except two (1824 and 1876) have been decided in the Electoral College, the approximately 3:1 advantage voters in large states enjoy in the Electoral College has, over the long haul, more than offset the approximately 8:1 advantage voters in small states enjoy when the election is thrown into the House. Steven J. Brams and Mark Lake, "Power and Satisfaction in a Representative Democracy," *Game Theory and Political Science*, ed. Peter C. Ordeshook (New York: New York University Press, forthcoming, 1978).

4 Coalition Politics:
No Permanent Winners

4.1. Introduction

In analyzing different phases of the presidential-election game in chapters 1 through 3, I treated candidates and parties as "on their own," so to speak. To be sure, the models of voting in primaries (chapter 1) and national party conventions (chapter 2) allowed candidates to seek the support of uncommitted voters and delegates, but competing candidates were not allowed to form coalitions among themselves (e.g., to stop a front-runner).

I shall extend the analysis to coalitions in this chapter, with an emphasis on what coalitions will form, how large they will be, and individual motivations for joining them at a particular time. While the focus of the empirical analysis will be on the behavior of parties and candidates at the national level, the coalition models can also be applied to the analysis of political competition at other levels (e.g., state and local politics).

The first model to be described is closely related to the spatial-competition models developed in chapter 1 to analyze party primaries, but it allows for the expression of divergent interests *within* parties. The question asked is what coalition of party interests will form to meet competition from the outside.

This question is turned around in the second model, wherein parties—and the candidates who carry their banners—are assumed to be unitary actors. For these actors the question is not what coalition of interests will solidify internally but instead how large a coalition should be to ensure a winning outcome that is stable.

In still a third coalition model, maximization of one's share of spoils will be reintroduced as a goal of potential coalition members. I shall derive from this model conclusions about the optimal timing of one's actions that will help to shed light on the dynamics of coalition-formation processes in which individual actors (not blocs, as in chapter 2) desire not only to win but also to benefit individually in a winning coalition. In a related model, "bandwagon curves" will be developed and studied. Applications of each model to party and election politics in the United States will illustrate the fluidity of coalition politics—and the concomitant lack of permanent winners—when there is a genuine competition in the system.

4.2. Political Parties: Three-Headed Monsters

American political parties have a colorful history, and literally millions of words have been written about them and the candidates who have represented them.[1] Still, their images, and the way they function in the American political system, remain somewhat of a mystery, although there is general agreement that the major parties embrace a curious cast of characters.

In the first coalition model, I assume that parties contain three distinguishable sets of players: (1) professionals, (2) activists, and (3) voters. The *professionals* are elected officials and party employees who have an obvious material stake in the party's survival and well-being. The *activists* are amateurs—either voters or candidates—who volunteer their services or contribute other resources to the party, especially during elections.[2] The *voters*, who make up the great mass of the party, generally do not participate in party activities, except to vote or possibly make minimal contributions.

It is this mixture of players, each with their own diverse interests, that makes a party a "three-headed monster"—not so much because parties are terrifying creatures but rather

1. Material in this and the next three sections is based largely on Steven J. Brams, *Spatial Models of Election Competition*, Monograph in Undergraduate Mathematics and Its Applications Project (Newton, Mass.: Education Development Center, 1978), which also includes exercises and their solutions.

2. David Robertson also introduces activists in his model of party competition. See David Robertson, *A Theory of Party Competition* (London: Wiley, 1976), pp. 31–33.

because they are so hard to control. That is why it is useful to think of parties as coalitions of players whose members somehow must reach agreement among themselves if they are to be effective political forces.

What complicates the process of reaching agreement is that the activists *tend* to take more ideologically extreme positions than the professionals and ordinary voters. There are exceptions, of course, but I assume in the subsequent analysis that activists give their support because they believe in, or can gain from, the adoption of certain extremist policies.

Not only do these policies generally give them certain psychic or material rewards, but they also usually exclude others from similar benefits. Activists tend to be purists, and they are not generally satisfied by "something-for-everything" compromise solutions.

Professionals, on the other hand, are interested in the survival and well-being of their party, and they do not want to see its chances or their own future employment prospects jeopardized by the passions of the activists. Their positions generally correspond to those of the median voter, whom they do not want to alienate by acceding to the wishes of the activists.

Yet, by virtue of the large contributions the activists make to the party, activist interests cannot be ignored. The election outcome, I assume, would be imperiled if the professionals, who are mainly interested in winning, lost either the support of the activists or the support of the voters.

What is the outcome of such a medley of conflicting forces? Before possible outcomes can be analyzed, the goals of candidates—what they seek to optimize, given the conflicting interests of the various groups whose support they seek—must be specified.

4.3. *Reconciling the Conflicting Interests*

In chapter 1 I analyzed the positions of candidates in primaries that were both optimal and in equilibrium vis-à-vis one or more other primary candidates. After the nomination of one candidate by each of the major parties at its national convention, the presidential-election game is usually reduced to a contest between only two serious contenders. In chapter 3 I analyzed the resource-allocation strategies in this contest induced by the unit-rule feature of the Electoral College, but I did not try to account for the positions of candidates in the general election.

To generate financial support (primarily from activists) and electoral support (primarily from voters) in the general election, I assume that a candidate tries to stake out positions—within certain limits—that satisfy, or at least appease, both activists and voters. To model his decisions in the general election, I shall ignore for now the positions that the other major-party candidate may take. While the positions of a candidate's opponent will obviously determine in part his own positions as the campaign progresses, I assume in the subsequent analysis that a party nominee's top-priority goal after the convention is to consolidate his support within the ranks of his own party.

To satisfy this goal, I assume that a candidate cannot afford to ignore the concerns of either the activists or the voters. Without the support of the former, a candidate would lack the resources to run an effective campaign; without the support of the latter, his appeal would be severely limited even if his resources were not.

Consequently, I assume that a presidential candidate seeks to maximize both his resources and his appeal, the former by taking positions that increase his attractiveness to activists and the latter by taking positions that increase his probability of winning among voters.[3] Specifically, if resources (contributed by activists) are measured by the utility (U) activists derive

3. For other perspectives on goals, see Joseph A. Schlesinger, "The Primary Goals of Political Parties: A Clarification of Positive Theory," *American Political Science Review* 69, no. 3 (September 1975): 840–49; and Donald A. Wittman, "Parties as Utility Maximizers," *American Political Science Review* 67, no. 2 (June 1973): 490–98. On difficulties parties now face, see Gerald S. Pomper, "The Decline of Partisan Politics," in *The Impact of the Electoral Process*, ed. Louis Maisel and Joseph Cooper (Beverly Hills, Calif.: Sage Publications, 1977), pp. 13–38; and Austin Ranney, *Curing the Mischiefs of Faction* (Berkeley: University of California Press, 1975).

from his positions, and appeal (to voters) by the probability (P) that these positions—*given* sufficient resources to make them known—will win him the election, then the goal of a candidate is to take positions that maximize his expected utility (EU), or the product of U and P:

$$EU = U(\text{to activists})P(\text{of winning among voters}).$$

This calculation is similar in form to the share-of-spoils (SS) calculation I defined in section 2.5 for two-candidate contests in national party conventions. The SS calculation measured the average spoils uncommitted delegates would derive from supporting one of the two major candidates at a particular point in the convention balloting. (I shall redefine this concept in a different context later.) By comparison, the EU calculation by party nominees provides a measure of the combined activist and voter support the candidates can generate from taking particular positions in the general election.

Maximization of EU implies seeking a compromise satisfactory to both the activists and the voters. Normally, this compromise will be aided by professionals who seek to reconcile the conflicting interests of the two groups. In section 4.4 I shall show what form this reconciliation may take, depending on the nature of the conflicting interests that divide the activists and the voters.

4.4.   Optimal Positions in a Campaign

For simplicity, assume that the campaign involves a single issue, and the positions on this issue that a candidate of the left-oriented party may take range from the left extreme (LE) to the median (Md), as shown in figure 4.1. Assume further that the utility (measured along the vertical axis) that activists derive from the positions a candidate takes along the horizontal axis falls linearly from a high of 1 at LE to a low of 0 at Md. On the other hand, assume that the probability of winning (also measured along the vertical axis) varies in just the opposite fashion, starting from a low of 0 at LE and rising to a high of 1 at Md.[4]

4. If a candidate's opponent also adopts a position at Md, then the candi-

Figure 4.1
Utility and Probability of Candidate Positions

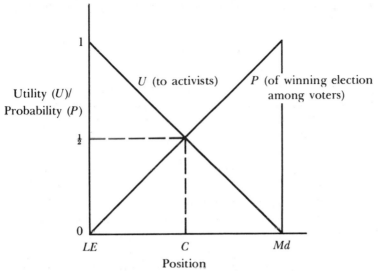

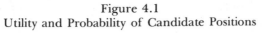

I assume that the maximum probability of winning cannot be attained, however, unless adequate resources are contributed by activists to publicize the nominee's positions. Since a left-oriented activist derives 0 utility from a candidate who takes the median position, it seems reasonable to assume that no resources will be contributed to a left-oriented candidate whose position is at Md.

A candidate increases his resources, but decreases his probability of winning, as he moves toward the left extreme. Clearly, if he moves all the way left to LE, $P = 0$, just as $U = 0$ at Md. Thus, a candidate who desires to maximize EU would never choose positions at LE or Md where $EU = 0$.

In fact, it is possible to show that the optimal position of a candidate is at the center (C) of figure 4.1—that is, the point

date's P at Md will be 0.5 instead of 1.0, assuming the activist support (resources) of both candidates are the same at Md. Although the actual value of a candidate's P at Md—dependent on his opponent's behavior—does not affect the maximization of EU (defined in the text below), it may affect strategy choices in a manner to be discussed later.

on the horizontal axis midway between LE and Md where the lines representing U and P intersect. Since this point is also midway between 0 and 1 on the vertical axis—at the point 1/2—

$$EU = \left(\frac{1}{2}\right)\left(\frac{1}{2}\right) = \frac{1}{4}.$$

There is no other point on the horizontal axis at which a candidate can derive greater EU. Consider, for example, the point midway between C and Md, where $U = 1/4$ and $P = 3/4$. At this position,

$$EU = \left(\frac{1}{4}\right)\left(\frac{3}{4}\right) = \frac{3}{16},$$

which is less than $EU = 1/4$ at C.

The optimality of position C in figure 4.1 may be upset if U and P are not linear functions of a candidate's position (i.e., functions that can be represented by straight lines) but instead are curves like those shown in figure 4.2. As in figure 4.1, the utility of a candidate's position decreases, and the probability of his position being winning increases, as the candidate moves from LE to Md. Now, however, since U and P are not linear functions of a candidate's position along the horizontal axis, the point of intersection of the P and U curves at C on the horizontal axis may no longer be optimal.

To illustrate this proposition, calculate EU at C and at points to the left and right of C. Clearly, at C in figure 4.2,

$$EU = \left(\frac{1}{3}\right)\left(\frac{1}{3}\right) = \frac{1}{9} = 0.111,$$

but at L (to the left of C),

$$EU = \left(\frac{1}{2}\right)\left(\frac{1}{4}\right) = \frac{1}{8} = 0.125,$$

and at R (to the right of C),

$$EU = \left(\frac{1}{4}\right)\left(\frac{1}{2}\right) = \frac{1}{8} = 0.125.$$

Figure 4.2
Nonlinear Utility and Probability Functions

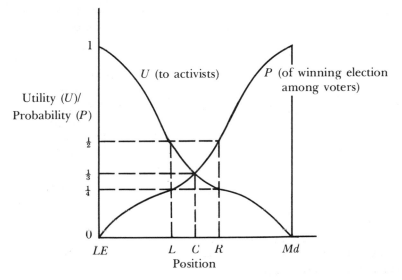

Hence, given the nonlinear utility and probability functions shown in figure 4.2, a candidate can do better by taking a position *either* to the left or to the right of *C*.

The exact positions along the horizontal axis which maximize *EU* for a candidate will depend on the shape of the *U* and *P* curves. These optimal positions can be determined from the equations that define the curves, but since there is no empirical basis for postulating particular functional relationships between candidate positions and *U* and *P*, I shall not pursue this matter further here.

The main qualitative conclusion derived from this analysis is that there is nothing sacrosanct about the center position *C*. Depending on the shape of the *U* and *P* functions, a candidate may do better—with respect to maximizing *EU*—by moving toward *LE*, toward *Md*, or in either direction.

Whatever the shape of the *U* and *P* functions, however, if *P* = 0 at *LE* and *U* = 0 at *Md*, the positions at *LE* and *Md* will never be optimal since *EU* = 0 in either case. But as long as *U* decreases monotonically from LE to Md (i.e., does not change direction by first decreasing and then increasing), and P increases monotonically from LE to Md, any points in between LE and Md may be optimal, depending on the shape of the U and P curves.

If these curves are symmetric (i.e., mirror images of each other, as in figure 4.2), there may be two optimal positions, one on each side of C. Yet symmetry is not a sufficient condition for there to be more than one optimal position: the straight lines in figure 4.1 are symmetric, but the only position along the horizontal axis where EU is maximized is at C.

What are the implications of this analysis? If activists prize "extremeness," and ordinary voters prize "moderation," then any position in between may be optimal for a candidate who desires to maximize some combination of his resources (from activists) and his electoral support (from voters). More surprising, there may be different optimal positions, one more favorable to the activists and one more favorable to the voters, as illustrated in figure 4.2.

4.5. Empirical Examples of Different Optimal Positions in Campaigns

So far I have shown how a model might offer an explanation—in terms of a candidate's desire to maximize EU—for the optimality of different positions in a campaign. The utility and probability functions that I postulated may, depending on their shape, push candidates toward an extreme position (left extreme in our example), the median position, or a center position somewhere in between.

In recent presidential campaigns, it is possible to observe a variety of positions that nominees of both major parties have adopted. Barry Goldwater, the 1964 Republican nominee, and George McGovern, the 1972 Democratic nominee, provide the best examples of candidates who took relatively extreme positions in their campaigns. Both candidates had strong activist support from the extremes of their parties in the primaries, which they almost surely would have lost had they tried to move too far toward the median voter in the general election. In addition, given the moderate opposition both candidates faced from relatively strong incumbents in the general election, neither Goldwater nor McGovern probably stood much chance of picking up many voters near the median had he tried to shift his early extremist positions very much.

If Goldwater had run against John Kennedy rather than Lyndon Johnson in 1964, however, he probably would have been a viable candidate. He could have carried all the South and West and some of the Midwest and, conceivably, might have won. Against Johnson, though, he was a loser because he and Johnson appealed in great part to the same interests, while the old Kennedy voters were stuck with Johnson. Goldwater planned his strategy with Kennedy alive and could not jettison it after Kennedy was assassinated.

By comparison, McGovern's early extremist positions were no match from the beginning against Nixon's middle-of-the-road positions. When, in desperation, McGovern attempted to moderate some of his early positions, he was accused of being "wishy-washy" and probably suffered a net loss in electoral and financial support (see section 1.7).

In general, if the utility for activists falls off rapidly, and the probability of winning increases only slowly, as a candidate moves toward the median, his optimal position will be near the extreme. Such a position gains him more in resources than he loses in probability of winning compared with a position near the median. With this trade-off in mind, both Goldwater and McGovern seem to have acted rationally with respect to the maximization of EU, though McGovern seems to have been more willing to sacrifice activist support to increase his chances of winning.

The incumbent presidents that Goldwater and McGovern faced, Lyndon Johnson and Richard Nixon, had more moderate activist supporters who were less disaffected by middle-of-the-road politics. Not only could these incumbents afford to move toward the median voter and still count on significant activist support, but, because of the extreme positions of their opponents, they could probably rapidly increase the number of their moderate supporters with such a strategy.

However, as James S. Coleman has pointed out, if an incumbent already has greater a priori strength than his opponent—and his opponent magnifies the discrepancy in strength by adopting an extremist position—the incumbent will *not* significantly improve his (already high) probability of winning by moving farther away from the *other* extremist position and toward the median.[5] Against such an opponent, therefore, an incumbent with a large built-in advantage from the start has little incentive to move toward him. Thus, extremist positions, especially when there is an a priori difference in electoral strength (e.g., when a nonincumbent runs against an incumbent), will tend to reinforce each other: *both* candidates will be motivated to adopt relatively extreme positions, because movement by one candidate toward the other decreases his activist support more than it increases his probability of winning.

The problem with this conclusion is that it seems to have little empirical support. The Goldwater-Johnson and McGovern-Nixon races did not produce extremists on both sides but only on one. If fact, if one candidate's position diverges sharply from the median, as did those of Goldwater and McGovern, his opponent tends to move toward that position rather than stay the same or move in the opposite direction.

This behavior is explained quite well by the earlier spatial models (see, in particular, section 1.3), but it is difficult to derive it from the goal of maximization of EU in which P is one factor. After all, if P is already high for a strong incumbent running against an opponent who adopts an extremist position (for reasons given earlier), why should the incumbent move toward his opponent if this movement has little effect on P and may lower U at the same time?

The answer seems to lie in the fact that some candidates

5. James S. Coleman, in "Communications," *American Political Science Review* 67, no. 2 (June 1973): 567–69.

seem to be as interested in the absolute size of their majorities as in winning. That is, they desire large majorities at least as much as victory itself. If this is the case, then movement toward an extremist opponent can be explained by the fact that this movement steadily increases a strong candidate's vote total even if it does not significantly alter his probability of winning.

Both Johnson and Nixon ran campaigns which strongly indicate that, even with victory virtually assured months before the election, they wanted more than victory: they desired to pile up huge majorities by whatever means they had at their disposal—including misrepresentation of their positions and those of their opponents. Although both incumbents succeeded in crushing their opponents in their respective elections, both were later driven from office by a welter of forces that I shall analyze later.

If the goals presidential candidates seek to maximize preclude *both* candidates from diverging from the median—and may encourage convergence, as in the 1960, 1968, and 1976 elections—then it is unlikely that one of the major parties can be written off the national political scene for very long. Indeed, in recent presidential elections, there has been a steady alternation of ins and outs: no party since World War II has held office for more than two consecutive terms.

This alternation of ins and outs was not so steady before the postwar era, with one or the other party on occasion holding sway for a generation or more. I shall examine cases of one-party dominance in presidential politics of an earlier era in section 4.7, but first I shall describe a principle, and a model of political coalitions from which it is derived, that has been developed to explain coalition outcomes.

4.6. The Size Principle

So far in this analysis I have assumed that political candidates seek to maximize both activist support and their probability of winning. I suggested that the latter objective could be modified to reflect the desire—apparently true of certain candidates—to maximize their vote totals, which may only marginally affect their probability of winning beyond a certain point.

In his model of political coalitions, William H. Riker divorces winning from other objectives and postulates it to be the *only* goal of political man (see the quotation at the beginning of chapter 2). He also says:

> The desire to win differentiates some men from others. Unquestionably there are guilt-ridden and shame-conscious men who do not desire to win, who in fact desire to lose. These are the irrational ones of politics. . . . Politically rational man is the man who would rather win than lose, regardless of the stakes.[6]

In one stroke, then, Riker simplifies the goal of political man to one that involves achievement of a specifiable outcome—winning—where all power accrues to the victors.[7] I shall later describe situations in American politics to which Riker's model has been applied, but first consider what situations reflect a winner-loser mentality.

The word "mentality" underscores the fact that any statement made about a postulated goal is necessarily based on the *perceptions* of actors. Ordinarily, this causes no problem in political situations like elections, where the method of counting votes and the decision rule for selecting a winner are known and accepted by the contestants—at least in situations where information is assumed to be complete. But it should be noted that although elections usually distinguish unambiguously the winner from the losers, the winner may not be perceived as the true victor.

The Democratic presidential primary in New Hampshire in 1968 is a case in point. The incumbent president, Lyndon Johnson, captured 50 percent of the vote to Eugene McCar-

6. William H. Riker, *The Theory of Political Coalitions* (New Haven, Conn.: Yale University Press, 1962), p. 22.

7. Much of the material that follows in this and the next two sections is a somewhat simplified and condensed discussion of the analysis, and examples from American electoral politics, in Steven J. Brams, *Game Theory and Politics* (New York: Free Press, 1975), pp. 215–40.

thy's 42 percent, with the remaining 8 percent split among minor candidates. Despite the fact that Johnson's candidacy was unannounced (his name did not even appear on the ballot), and he never set foot in New Hampshire, a majority of voters took the trouble to write in his name. Nonetheless, McCarthy was hailed as the victor by political pundits and the press since he surpassed his "expected" vote.[8] In such situations, expectations become the benchmark against which reality is tested.

Besides positing the goal of winning, Riker makes several assumptions in his game-theoretic model (the mathematical details of which will be ignored here):

1. *Rationality.* Players are rational, which means that they will choose the alternative that leads to their most-preferred outcome—namely, winning.[9] Riker does not argue, however, that all political actors are rational with respect to this goal but rather that the winner-loser mentality pervades, and conditions the behavior of, participants in such situations as elections.

2. *Zero-sum.* Decisions have a winner-take-all character—what one coalition wins the other coalition(s) loses—so the sum of payoffs to all players is zero. In other words, the model embraces only situations of pure and unrelieved conflict where all value accrues to the winner; cooperation among participants that redounds to the mutual benefit of all is excluded.

3. *Complete and perfect information.* Players are fully informed about the state of affairs at the beginning of the game and the moves of all other players at all times.

4. *Allowance for side payments.* Players can communicate

8. Richard M. Scammon and Ben J. Wattenberg, *The Real Majority: An Extraordinary Examination of the American Electorate* (New York: Coward, McCann and Geoghegan, 1970), pp. 27, 85–93.

9. Strictly speaking, it is not necessary to postulate winning as the most-preferred outcome. Rather, "rationality" may be defined in terms of the choice of the *most valued* outcome, where the value associated with winning coalitions and the payoffs to their members are stipulated by assumptions 5 and 6 in the text.

with each other and bargain about the distribution of payoffs in a winning coalition, whose value is divided among its members. ("Side payments" simply refer to individual payments players transfer to each other in dividing up the value.)

5. *Positive value.* Only winning coalitions have positive value. (However, the grand coalition, consisting of all players, has zero value, since there are no losers from whom to extract value, and so do blocking coalitions, since the complement of a blocking coalition is a blocking coalition.)

6. *Positive payoffs.* All members in a winning coalition receive positive payoffs. This assumption, of course, provides an incentive for players to join a winning coalition.

7. *Control over membership.* Members of a winning coalition have the ability to admit or eject members from it.

The last three assumptions (5, 6, and 7)—besides the assumption that the goal of players is to form winning coalitions—are what Riker calls "sociological assumptions," as distinguished from the four previously postulated "mathematical assumptions" (1, 2, 3, and 4) standard in n-person game theory. The sociological assumptions specify more precisely the goal of winning and thereby enable Riker to derive the size of winning coalitions that is optimal and therefore likely to form.[10]

10. William H. Riker and Peter C. Ordeshook, *An Introduction to Positive Political Theory* (Englewood Cliffs, N.J.: Prentice-Hall, 1973), pp. 179–80. For further details, see Riker, *Theory of Political Coalitions*, pp. 40–46, 247–78; and William H. Riker, "A New Proof of the Size Principle," in *Mathematical Applications in Political Science, II*, ed. Joseph L. Bernd (Dallas: Southern Methodist University Press, 1967), pp. 167–74. It should be noted that several theoretical challenges have been mounted against the size principle. See Robert Lyle Butterworth, "A Research Note on the Size of Winning Coalitions"; William H. Riker, "Comment on Butterworth, 'A Research Note on the Size of Winning Coalitions' "; and Butterworth, "Rejoinder to Riker's 'Comment,' " all in *American Political Science Review* 65, no. 3 (September 1971): 741–48. In Kenneth A. Shepsle, "On the Size of Winning Coalitions," *American Political Science Review* 68, no. 2 (June 1974): 509–18, issues posed in the exchange between Riker and Butterworth are analyzed; although Shepsle finds support

Given these assumptions, Riker shows that there are no circumstances wherein an incentive exists for coalitions of greater than minimal winning size to form. On the other hand, the fact there is a positive value associated with winning coalitions (assumption 5), each of whose members receive positive payoffs from winning (assumption 6), is a sufficient incentive for such coalitions to form. The incentive for winning coalitions to form, but not to be of greater than minimal winning size, means that the realization of the goal of winning takes form in the creation of only minimal winning coalitions, which Riker calls the *size principle*.

More specifically, his reasoning is as follows. Given that only winning coalitions have positive value (assumption 5), the zero-sum assumption (assumption 2) implies that losing coalitions must have complementary negative value. Since such a coalition has no things of value to distribute among its members, it would form only as a pretender to eventual winning status. Indeed, the possibility that a losing coalition could eventually become winning provides a strong incentive for a winning coalition to pare off superfluous members (permitted by assumption 7), who would be vulnerable to

---

for the size principle in different solutions concepts of n-person game theory, he also shows that minimal winning coalitions are characterized by an instability somewhat akin to that of the 3/2's rule discussed in section 3.8. For further debate on this and related points, see Butterworth, "Comment on Shepsle's 'On the Size of Winning Coalitions,' " and Shepsle, "Minimum Winning Coalitions Reconsidered: A Rejoinder to Butterworth's 'Comment,' " *American Political Science Review* 68, no. 2 (June 1974): 519–24. Most recently, the generality of the size principle has been questioned in Russell Hardin, "Hollow Victory: The Minimum Winning Coalition," *American Political Science Review* 70, no. 4 (December 1976): 1202–14; for a rebuttal from Riker and a rejoinder from Hardin see "Communications," *American Political Science Review* 71, no. 3 (September 1977): 1056–61. Although the scope of this book does not permit a thorough airing of the technical issues in this debate, they certainly are relevant to model-building efforts. Since my focus here is on the empirical validity of the size principle in presidential politics, however, most of my criticism later is directed not at the mathematical class of games to which the size principle applies—the major concern of Riker's critics—but rather to a broader question: is the goal of winning an appropriate one to assume of political actors?

offers from a losing coalition that could promise them greater rewards in a (prospective) minimal winning coalition.

Alternatively, members of a minimal winning coalition may wish to acquire additional members if they are not certain their coalition is sufficiently large to be winning. But they have complete and perfect information (by assumption 3), so this cannot be the case.

Several things should be noted about Riker's derivation of the size principle. First, the goal of winning is implicit in the assumptions of the model, particularly the assumption of rationality (assumption 1) that motivates players to obtain the benefits of being in a winning coalition, as stipulated in assumptions 5 and 6. Second, the size principle is a statement about an outcome—the size of winning coalitions—and not about the process of coalition formation, which I shall say more about later in this chapter. And finally, since winning by whatever amount is the sole determinant of value (assumption 5), the ejection of superfluous members means that the same total amount can be divided among fewer members, to the advantage of at least one of these (remaining) members.[11]

One might argue that the formalism of a mathematical model is not required to grasp the idea that the smaller the size of a winning coalition, the more each of its members individually profits and would therefore be expected to work to reduce its size; hence, the expected result would be minimal winning coalitions. Yet this commonsensical "explanation" of the size principle suffers from a difficulty endemic to all proverbial wisdom: it does not offer limiting conditions on the veracity of the size principle that a mechanism suggested by the assumptions of a model does.

I have already reviewed how the assumptions of Riker's

11. But when the spoils dispensed are some collective good, which is not perfectly divisible (implicit in assumption 4), but instead is equally available to all members, there will be no incentive for a coalition to eject members since the payoff to each member will by definition remain the same whatever the size of the winning coalition. See Thomas S. McCaleb, "The Size Principle and Collective Consumption Payoffs to Political Coalitions," *Public Choice* 17 (Spring 1974): 107–09.

model lead to a situation in which the realization of the goal of winning takes form in the creation of only minimal winning coalitions. As an explanation of why the size principle should hold, however, this argument has logical force only. To connect Riker's model with reality, consider now how its assumptions can be interpreted as conditions that limit the operation of the size principle when its theoretical concepts are operationally defined and it is posited as an empirical law. In translating the size principle from a theoretical statement derived from the assumptions of a game-theoretic model into a descriptive statement about the real world that is capable of empirical confirmation or disconfirmation, Riker interprets it as follows:

> In social situations similar to n-person games with sidepayments, participants create coalitions just as large as they believe will ensure winning and no larger.[12]

The introduction of the beliefs or perceptions of individuals about a subjectively estimated minimum simply acknowledges the real-world fact that players do not have complete and perfect information about the environment in which they act and the actions of other players. Consequently, players are inclined to form coalitions that are larger than minimal winning size as a cushion against uncertainty, and oversized winning coalitions thus become a quite rational response in an uncertain world.

In this manner, complete and perfect information serves as a limiting condition on the truth of the size principle: in its absence, coalitions will *not* tend toward minimal winning size.[13] The other assumptions of the model also restrict the

12. Riker, *Theory of Political Coalitions*, p. 47.
13. Another related reason why they may not form is that when there is incomplete or imperfect information, maximizing the probability of minimum winning coalitions may not be consistent with maximizing the probability of winning, especially in small groups. See Richard G. Niemi and Herbert F. Weisberg, "The Effects of Group Size on Collective Decision Making," in *Probability Models of Collective Decision Making*, ed. Richard G. Niemi and Herbert F. Weisberg (Columbus, Ohio: Charles E. Merrill, 1972), pp. 140–43.

applicability of the size principle in the real world, but Riker
singles out the effect of information on the operation of the
size principle for special attention probably because it is the
concept most easily interpreted, if not operationalized, of
those embodied in the assumptions of his model.

The enlargement of coalitions above minimal winning size
due to the effects of incomplete or imperfect information is
what Riker calls the *information effect*. Since this effect is endemic in an uncertain world, there naturally exist many
examples of nonminimal winning coalitions. For Riker these
examples represent situations in which coalition leaders mis-
calculated the capabilities, or misread the intentions, of
opponents—given that the other assumptions of his model
were reasonably well met—not because they were irrational
but rather because they lacked accurate and reliable information on which to act.

4.7. *Applications of the Size Principle to American Politics*

However oversized coalitions come into existence, the prediction of the size principle is that they will be relatively
short-lived. In seeking out evidence that supports the principle, Riker examined all instances of "overwhelming majorities" in American politics in which one party effectively de-
molished another party in a presidential election—and the
losing party virtually disappeared from the national scene.

The period of one-party dominance following such elections, Riker found, is soon undercut by party leaders who
force out certain elements in policy and personality disputes.
This leads to the dominant party's shrinkage and eventual
displacement by another party. Since victory in elections is
indivisible, elections, Riker argues, can properly be modeled
as zero-sum games, where the players are individuals and
groups that unite behind the banners of political parties.

The three instances of overwhelming majorities in American politics analyzed in *The Theory of Political Coalitions* are the
Republican party after the 1816 election that destroyed the
Federalist party, the Democratic party after the 1852 election
that destroyed the Whig party, and the Republican party after

the 1868 election that signaled the temporary demise of the Democratic party, at least outside the South. Because Riker's book was published in 1962, there is of course no mention of the 1964 election, in which Lyndon Johnson wiped out Barry Goldwater with a 16-million-vote popular majority, but Riker and Ordeshook have since analyzed the aftermath of this election in terms of the size principle. Arguing that Johnson dissipated his overwhelming majority by progressively alienating (1) many Southerners with his strong pro–civil rights stance, and then (2) liberals with his escalation of the Vietnam war, Riker and Ordeshook contend that by 1968 Johnson probably did not have the support of even a minimal majority of the electorate and hence chose not to run for a second term.[14]

A similar fate befell Richard Nixon after his landslide victory in 1972. Unable to extricate himself from the albatross of Watergate—not to mention the energy crisis and a faltering economy—he was forced to resign eighteen months into his

14. Riker and Ordeshook, *Introduction to Positive Political Theory*, pp. 194–96. Whether or not Johnson was conscious beforehand of the effects his actions would have is irrelevant to the test of the size principle, which asserts that he could not have prevented the breakup of his grand coalition no matter how hard he tried. That is, the game-theoretic logic of the model says that some of his "excess" supporters would invariably have been disaffected and attracted to the opposition coalition, whomever he tried to please with his policies. That Johnson was aware of the dilemma he faced is suggested by the following remarks he made to Doris Kearns:

> "I knew from the start," Johnson told me in 1970, describing the early weeks of 1965, "that I was bound to be crucified either way I moved. If I left the woman I really loved—the Great Society—in order to get involved with that bitch of a war on the other side of the world, then I would lose everything at home. All my programs. All my hopes to feed the hungry and shelter the homeless. All my dreams to provide education and medical care to the browns and the blacks and the lame and the poor. But if I left that war and let the Communists take over South Vietnam, then I would be seen as a coward and my nation would be seen as an appeaser and we would both find it impossible to accomplish anything for anybody anywhere on the entire globe."

Doris Kearns, *Lyndon Johnson and the American Dream* (New York: New American Library, 1977), p. 263.

second term (see chapter 5). It seems no accident that whatever the time and circumstance, every United States president or political party that has emerged with an overwhelming majority has always faced a mounting tide of opposition to which the president or political party has succumbed in the end. In zero-sum politics, it seems, an instability occasioned by the miscalculations of leaders is unavoidable in a world enshrouded by uncertainty.

This evidence is historical in nature and not particularly susceptible to quantification and rigorous empirical testing. Nonetheless, it has the virtue of being systematic: Riker did not ransack American history for isolated examples that support the size principle but rather considered all instances of relevant cases within the spatially and temporally defined limits he set. To the extent that these cases—and the class of events they are drawn from—are representative of zero-sum situations generally, they allow him to draw more general conclusions than could be adduced from anecdotal evidence alone. Yet, one is still perhaps left with a sense of uneasiness about what exactly is being tested if none of the key concepts has been operationally defined.

The appeal of the size principle may be better appreciated from a quantitative example that Riker offers, which also illustrates the "dynamics" of coalition-formation processes.[15] I enclose the word "dynamics" in quotation marks, however, because—for reasons discussed later in this chapter—the goal of winning does not seem to provide an adequate foundation on which to build a dynamic theory of coalition-formation processes. Nevertheless, it is instructive to consider a coalition situation unfolding over time wherein the participants acted as if they repeatedly invoked the size principle, even if repeated application of the size principle does not constitute a dynamic theory.

Following the demise and eventual disappearance of the Federalist party, James Monroe was reelected president almost unanimously in 1820—only one vote was cast against

15. Riker, *Theory of Political Coalitions*, pp. 149–58.

him in the Electoral College. But the grand coalition of Republicans that he headed soon fell into disarray, consistent with the size principle, and as the presidential election of 1824 approached, factions formed around five candidates, whom Riker and Ordeshook characterized as follows:

> John Quincy Adams, of Massachusetts, Secretary of State, favorite of the former Federalists, although, as a moderate, he had been driven out of the Federalist Party in 1808.
>
> William Crawford, of Georgia, Secretary of the Treasury, was the candidate of that alliance of Jeffersonians which had produced a series of presidents from Virginia and vice-presidents from New York.
>
> John C. Calhoun, of South Carolina, Secretary of War, was the candidate of South Carolina and himself.
>
> Andrew Jackson of Tennessee, the hero of New Orleans, governor of the Florida territory, and later senator from Tennessee, turned out to be the most popular candidate.
>
> Henry Clay, of Kentucky, representative and leader of the opposition in the House, ultimately became the founder of the Whig Party.[16]

Calhoun settled for the vice presidency, narrowing the list to four candidates, none of whom won a majority of electoral votes in the Electoral College:

Jackson:	Carried 11 states with 99 electoral votes;
Adams:	Carried 7 states with 84 electoral votes;
Crawford:	Carried 3 states with 41 electoral votes;
Clay:	Carried 3 states with 37 electoral votes.

Consequently, the election was thrown into the House of Representatives, where each state had a single vote that went to the candidate favored by a plurality of its representatives. Following considerable bargaining in the House, Adams replaced Jackson as the leader in the standings:

16. Riker and Ordeshook, *Introduction to Positive Political Theory*, p. 199.

Adams:	10 votes (states);
Jackson:	7 votes (states);
Crawford:	4 votes (states);
Clay:	3 votes (states).

Riker suggests that the desertion of representatives from states that Jackson carried was not surprising because the coalition of Adams, Crawford, and Clay initially constituted (see the first distribution) a unique minimal winning coalition with thirteen votes (there were twenty-four states), making Jackson "strategically weak."

Because the Twelfth Amendment limits the number of candidates in the House to the three with the highest electoral-vote totals, Clay was eliminated. To whom would his three votes go? If Clay threw his support to Jackson, he would create a deadlock between Adams and Jackson, with Crawford then controlling the critical votes. By supporting Adams instead, he could himself be critical and elect Adams president with a minimal winning coalition.

This is exactly what he did in exchange for Adams's promise to appoint him secretary of state, at that time traditionally a stepping-stone to the presidency. Thus was struck the so-called corrupt bargain of 1825, which also happens to be the outcome predicted by the size principle. In sum, both the desertions from Jackson and the Adams-Clay alliance, each of which involved the selection of coalition partners according to the size principle, triumphed over considerations of friendship, personal loyalty, and ideology (which are detailed in Riker's more extended historical treatment).

One puzzling question is why, given the size principle, overwhelming majorities occur in the first place. In section 4.4 I suggested one reason based on the maximization of EU: a candidate will adopt an extremist position if his activist support quickly dries up as he moves toward the median position. An opponent with more moderate activist support could then adopt a position near the median which would assure him of a lopsided victory (see section 4.5).

A second reason for overwhelming majorities is due to the information effect described in section 4.6. Besides miscalculations induced by uncertainty, however, overwhelming majorities may also occur when a player holds out to potential coalition members the promise of large side payments. Should he renege on such a promise once he has won (e.g., as did Lyndon Johnson on the military policy he said he would pursue in Southeast Asia, creating the much-ballyhooed "credibility gap"), it may lose him later support but not take away his initial victory.

If side payments cannot be extravagantly promised, but must instead be delivered before the outcome is decided—or irrevocably committed, which amounts to the same thing (e.g., Adams's commitment of the secretary of state post to Clay for his votes)—then coalition leaders must be selective in their commitments from the start and overwhelming victories are much harder to bring off. If they form on the basis of extravagant promises, however, the size principle says that they will not last: there always exist forces that move coalitions toward minimal winning (equilibrium) size, whether from "above" or "below." Thus, the size principle is really a statement about an equilibrium, which may or may not be immediately realized.

Since the publication of *The Theory of Political Coalitions*, the size principle has stimulated many efforts aimed at testing its truth in a variety of empirical settings.[17] It has also been the target of much criticism, with one of the most frequently voiced complaints being its lack of specificity in describing how long an oversized coalition may be expected to persist. To respond that this will depend on how incomplete or imperfect information is is not helpful when no time-dependent functional relationship between this variable and the size principle is specified. Will the excess majority of an oversized coalition be dissipated in weeks, years, or decades?

Riker himself admitted that the model is "quite vague" on this point and that specifying a pattern in the growth of coalitions "may be regarded as the main task of a dynamic theory of coalitions."[18] To probe more deeply into the

17. This literature is critically reviewed in Brams, *Game Theory and Politics*, pp. 226–32.
18. Riker, *Theory of Political Coalitions*, pp. 107–08.

dynamic nature of transitions from stage to stage, goals different from "winning" to which rational actors might aspire must be postulated and their implications developed. I shall consider an alternative goal in section 4.8—which was previously defined in section 2.5 for national party conventions—and sketch what implications its satisfaction has on time-dependent, sequential aspects of coalition-formation processes.

4.8. An Alternative Goal: Maximizing One's Share of Spoils

Although the study of coalition behavior has been vigorously pursued in recent years, little attention has been devoted to the construction of theoretical models of coalition-formation processes that occur over time. Rather, studies of coalition behavior have focused more on *static outcomes* than on the *dynamic processes* that produced them *prior* to the point at which one coalition has gone on to win. Even in the relatively well-structured context of voting bodies, to which the subsequent analysis will be confined, the development of dynamic models has only recently been initiated.

This gap in the literature is due in considerable part to the failure of theorists to postulate goals for rational actors that raise questions about the *timing* of their actions—and therefore about political processes that occur over time. Before I reintroduce such a goal in this section, I shall first outline a verbal model of coalition-formation processes in voting bodies.

The analysis will be restricted to the study of coalition-formation processes involving as active opponents only two *protocoalitions*—coalitions not of sufficient size to win—that vie for the support of uncommitted members in a voting body so that they can become winning coalitions (which are decisive, given some decision rule). As previously, it is useful to distinguish all winning coalitions from the subset of winning coalitions that are minimal winning—coalitions in which the subtraction of a single member reduces them to (nonwinning) protocoalitions.

My main interest is in studying the formation of winning

coalitions including one or the other of the two protocoalitions, but not both. I assume that the two protocoalitions are totally at odds with each other and seek victory only through securing the commitment of uncommitted members, not through switching members' commitments from one protocoalition to the other. I thus preclude members of the two protocoalitions from combining to form a winning coalition, as the joining together of the two leading candidates in national party conventions was precluded in chapter 2.

To illustrate this model, consider the final stage of the coalition-formation process in the U.S. House of Representatives prior to the election of John Quincy Adams as president in 1825 (see section 4.7). Recall that the standing of the four candidates before voting began was

Adams:	10 votes (states),
Jackson:	7 votes (states),
Crawford:	4 votes (states),
Clay:	3 votes (states),

which would have forced the elimination of Clay under the Twelfth Amendment, which allows only three runoff candidates.

Realizing that the votes Clay controlled were open for bidding, Crawford's managers, it seems fair to suppose, might also have considered selling their votes since their candidate ranked well below the two front-runners.[19] If we assume that the two leading candidates, Adams and Jackson, represent the two protocoalitions in the model I have described, and the "uncommitted" votes are the blocs controlled by Clay and Crawford, it is simple to determine how each of the two leading candidates could have won (the decision rule is thirteen out of twenty-four states):

Adams, with the support of (1) Clay, (2) Crawford, or (3) both Clay and Crawford;

Jackson, with the support of (4) both Clay and Crawford.

19. If a deadlock had developed, this appears indeed to have been their intention. See John Spencer Bassett, *The Life of Andrew Jackson*, 2d ed. (New York: Macmillan, 1925), p. 368.

Without any additional information about coalitions that might form in this situation, it is reasonable to assume that each of these four outcomes is equally likely (I shall modify this assumption later in light of the size principle). Hence, the complementary probabilities (Ps) that each of the two leading candidates (i.e., protocoalitions) would become winning can be calculated:[20]

$$P(\text{Adams}) = \frac{3}{4} = 0.75; \; P(\text{Jackson}) = \frac{1}{4} = 0.25.$$

In fact, of course, Clay threw his support to Adams as a result of the "corrupt bargain," making Adams the winner (with probability equal, in effect, to 1.00). If Clay had instead supported Jackson, then Jackson and Adams would have tied with ten votes each. If, at this hypothetical juncture, Crawford had been equally likely to have given his support to either leading candidate, then each would have had a probability equal to 0.50 of going on to win.

The two choices open to Clay—support Adams or support Jackson—are pictured in figure 4.3, with the probabilities that each of the main contenders, Adams and Jackson, would win before and after Clay's commitment to one of them.[21] Along each branch in figure 4.3 are shown the *probabilistic contributions* that Clay's support makes to raising the probability of winning of Adams (from 0.75 to 1.00, or an increment of 0.25) and of Jackson (from 0.25 to 0.50, or an increment of 0.25). The fact that these probabilistic contributions are both

20. Probabilities like these based on equiprobability assumptions are common in the natural sciences. For their use in the Maxwell-Boltzman and Bose-Einstein statistics in physics, and analogous applications in political science, see William Feller, *An Introduction to Probability Theory and Its Applications*, 2d ed. (New York: Wiley, 1957), pp. 20–21, 38–40; and Steven J. Brams, "The Search for Structural Order in the International System: Some Models and Preliminary Results," *International Studies Quarterly* 13, no. 3 (September 1969): 254–80.

21. I have assumed that Clay made the first commitment not only because as low man he was eliminated from the contest in the House but also because Crawford's supporters felt bound to vote for their candidate on the first ballot. Bassett, *Life of Andrew Jackson*, p. 363.

Figure 4.3
Probabilities of Becoming Winning, and Probabilistic
Contributions, in 1824–25 Presidential Election
Uncommitted: Clay, Crawford
(Adams, Jackson)
0.75, 0.25

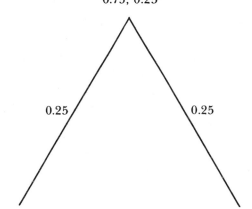

0.25   0.25

Uncommitted: Crawford   Uncommitted: Crawford
(Adams and Clay, Jackson)   (Adams, Jackson and Clay)
1.00, 0   0.50, 0.50

equal to 0.25 means that no advantage would accrue to Clay
from supporting one candidate over the other if his goal were
to maximize his probabilistic contribution to a contender.[22]

The goal I postulate, however, is that uncommitted actors
seek to maximize their *share of spoils* (*SS*), which is defined as
the probabilistic contribution (*PC*) an uncommitted actor
makes to a protocoalition times the probability (*P*) that, with
this contribution, the protocoalition will go on to win. Thus

$$SS(\text{Clay} \rightarrow \text{Adams}) = PC(\text{Clay} \rightarrow \text{Adams})P(\text{Clay} \rightarrow \text{Adams})$$
$$= (0.25)(1.00) = 0.25,$$
$$SS(\text{Clay} \rightarrow \text{Jackson}) = PC(\text{Clay} \rightarrow \text{Jackson})P(\text{Clay} \rightarrow \text{Jackson})$$
$$= (0.25)(0.50) = 0.125,$$

22. If an uncommitted actor's probabilistic contribution can be taken as a
measure of the resources he brings to a protocoalition, then Gamson predicts
that payoffs after winning will be distributed according to these contribu-

where the actor before the arrow indicates the uncommitted "giver" and the actor after the arrow the protocoalition "receiver." Assuming Clay's goal was to maximize his share of spoils, then it was rational by this calculation for him to support Adams rather than Jackson (as he in fact did), since the former action would yield twice as much in "spoils" as the latter.

I computed above the probabilities that the two leading candidates would become *any winning* coalitions—that is, coalitions with *at least* a simple majority of members—before and after the commitment of Clay. If we restrict coalitions to those which are *minimal winning* with *exactly* a simple majority of members, then consonant with the size principle there is only one way that Adams can win with exactly thirteen of the twenty-four votes (i.e., by gaining the support of Clay), but no way Jackson can win with this bare majority. Since the Adams-Clay alliance is the only possible minimal winning coalition, it will become minimal winning with probability equal to 1.00 *before* Clay's commitment, given that only minimal winning coalitions form. *After* Clay's commitment, the coalition will be winning (with probability equal, in effect, to 1.00), so Clay's probabilistic contribution, and share of spoils that he can expect to receive from Adams, is zero.

This may seem a rather artificial result, especially in light of the fact that Clay became secretary of state under Adams and was importuned by all parties for support before the House vote.[23] Apparently, not everybody was aware of the size principle, for if they had been all except Adams's supporters should have given up hope!

Despite its artificialty, however, this result points up one nonobvious fact about coalition formation: to the extent that an uncommitted actor is constrained in the range of choices open to him, his influence will be diminished. Indeed, in the extreme case where he is a captive of one protocoalition, his probabilistic contribution and share of spoils are effectively

tions. See William A. Gamson, "A Theory of Coalition Formation," *American Sociological Review* 26, no. 3 (June 1961): 372–82.

23. Bassett, *Life of Andrew Jackson*, pp. 350–51.

zero since he is not truly uncommitted. This was the case in the 1824–25 presidential election, for if Clay adhered to the size principle, he could support only Adams.

In other words, the size principle, like friendship, ideology, and other constraints on free association, may cut down an actor's range of choices and force his hand before all alternatives but one are foreclosed to him. In fact, one month before the actual balloting in the House, Clay confided to intimates that he would support Adams,[24] which became public knowledge two weeks before the election.[25] But there was still great uncertainty about what the outcome would be because the New York delegation (counted earlier in Adams's total) was deadlocked up to the day of voting. The election eventually turned on the vote of one of the thirty-four representatives from New York, who on the day of voting broke the deadlock and gave New York to Adams.[26]

How do these historical details bear on models of coalition formation? First, I have shown that an alternative goal— maximization of share of spoils based on the any winning model—also retrodicts that Clay would support Adams over Jackson. In the example I have been considering, this goal is perhaps more realistic than the goal of winning because it directly incorporates the notion of private and divisible benefits that uncommitted actors may realize in addition to the public and indivisible benefits of winning that all members of the winning coalition share. Second, I have shown some curious implications of the share-of-spoils calculation when the size principle is invoked. If all but minimal winning coalitions are disallowed, the share-of-spoils calculation suggests that Clay's votes were not essential to Adams, for the size principle precludes their going to anybody else. Manifestly, the situation was not viewed this way by the participants, although

24. Bassett, *Life of Andrew Jackson*, p. 352.

25. Marquis James, *Andrew Jackson: Portrait of a President* (New York: Gosset and Dunlap, 1937), p. 120.

26. Riker views skeptically an interesting (and possibly apocryphal) story about the intense pressure exerted on this representative and how he made his decision. Riker, *Theory of Political Coalitions*, pp. 155–57.

Clay's votes were committed before the day of the election and it fell to somebody else to make the critical choice on that day. This leads me to ask: what makes a player's choices critical?

Choices of players are *critical*, it seems, if (and only if) they are preceded by prior choices of other players that make them decisive in the determination of outcomes. For this reason, it is useful to view coalition-formation processes as *sequences of moves* on the part of players. In most real coalition-building situations, however, it is no easy task to abstract any set of general contingencies.[27] Even in a particular situation, the possible alignments, and the ways in which they can form, are manifold. What can be offered, however, is a prescription of how protocoalitions should grow *at all stages* in the coalition-formation process to maximize their attractiveness to uncommitted actors.

Intuitively, it seems clear that uncommitted actors who wish to maximize their share of spoils in the previously described model would be interested in joining the protocoalition with the greater probability of winning. Otherwise, their probabilistic contributions would be cut by more than half in the share-of-spoils calculation. On the other hand, if the probability that one of the two protocoalitions would become winning were overwhelming (i.e., close to 1.00), the probabilistic contribution that an uncommitted actor would make by joining it would be necessarily small, even though the contribution itself would not be heavily discounted in the share-of-spoils calculation.

27. Although the calculations are rather complicated, some attempt at generalization has been made through the utilization of lattice structures for arraying the step-by-step buildup of protocoalitions in ten-member voting bodies and computer-simulation techniques for larger bodies. See Steven J. Brams and William H. Riker, "Models of Coalition Formation in Voting Bodies," in *Mathematical Applications in Political Science, VI*, ed. James F. Herndon and Joseph L. Bernd (Charlottesville: University Press of Virginia, 1972), pp. 79–124; Steven J. Brams, "A Cost/Benefit Analysis of Coalition Formation in Voting Bodies," in *Probability Models of Collective Decision Making*, pp. 101–24; and Steven J. Brams and John G. Heilman, "When to Join a Coalition, and with How Many Others, Depends on What You Expect the Outcome to Be," *Public Choice* 17 (Spring 1974): 11–25.

It turns out that if there are two protocoalitions, one of which grows faster than the other, an uncommitted actor should join the one he thinks is growing faster—as measured by its larger size at any stage—when its probability of becoming *minimal winning* is 2/3.[28] That is, he should wait until the probability that one protocoalition becomes minimal winning is exactly twice that of the other before committing himself to what he perceives to be the faster-growing protocoalition. This advice is applicable whether this point (or points) is reached early or late in the coalition-formation process.

From the viewpoint of the coalition leaders, an awareness of this strategy provides no guarantee of victory. For example, a protocoalition may simply not have the resources to pull ahead of another protocoalition so that it is perceived as the two-to-one favorite. Given that it is able to accomplish this feat, however, the "2/3's rule" prescribes that it should not attempt to increase these odds in its favor still further, for then it will become less attractive to uncommitted actors who desire to maximize their share of spoils. One would expect, therefore, that a protocoalition will maximize the commitments it receives from uncommitted actors when it enjoys a two-to-one probabilistic advantage over the other protocoalition.

Of course, an opposition protocoalition would be attempting to achieve the same kind of effect, which means that neither protocoalition has a surefire winning strategy unless additional assumptions are made about the total resources possessed by each side, the manner in which they are allocated, their effects, and so on. By the same token, uncommitted actors cannot anticipate if and when optimal commitment times will occur in the absence of additional assumptions. The 2/3's rule as such says only that there exist optimal commitment times, but it says nothing about instrumental strategies for realizing them.

28. Steven J. Brams and José E. Garriga-Picó, "Bandwagons in Coalition Formation: The 2/3's Rule," *American Behavioral Scientist* 18, no. 4 (March/April 1975): 472–96. This article is reprinted in *Coalitions and Time: Cross-Disciplinary Studies*, ed. Barbara Hinckley (Beverly Hills, Calif.: Sage Publications, 1976), pp. 34–58.

Still, this rule offers a precise quantitative statement of when bandwagons would be expected to develop and provides, in addition, a rationale for their existence based on the assumptions of the model from which it is derived (which I shall not try to develop rigorously here). As Philip D. Straffin Jr., has argued, however, the assumptions underlying the 2/3's rule are quite restrictive, and he has proposed an alternative model to analyze coalition formation in large voting bodies.[29]

4.9.   The Bandwagon Curve

Straffin's model is based on the application of a modified Shapley-Shubik power index to "oceanic games," in which there are two—or possibly more—"large players" (major candidates), who control the committed voters, and an "ocean" of uncommitted voters in an infinite-size voting body.[30] To illustrate the meaning of these curves in the finite case, consider a voter in a five-member voting body in which two members are already committed to candidate X and one member to candidate Y. If a majority of three votes is needed to win, is it in the interest of one of the two uncommitted members to join X, Y, or stay uncommitted?

Consider all possible orders of X (two committed members), Y (one committed member), and the two uncommitted members (each designated by "1"):

*X (Y) 1 1	*Y 1 (X) 1	1 1 (X) Y
X (1) Y 1	Y 1 (1) X	1 Y (1) X
X (1) 1 Y	1 (X) 1 Y	*1 Y (X) 1
*Y (X) 1 1	1 (X) Y 1	1 1 (Y) X

29. Philip D. Straffin Jr., "The Bandwagon Curve," *American Journal of Political Science* 21, no. 4 (November 1977): 695–709.

30. See L. S. Shapley and Martin Shubik, "A Method of Evaluating the Distribution of Power in a Committee System," *American Political Science Review*, 48, no. 3 (September 1954): 787–92, for a description of the Shapley-Shubik index; and Lloyd Shapley and John Milnor, "Values of Large Games II: Oceanic Games," Research Memorandum RM-2649 (Santa Monica, Calif.: RAND Corporation, 1961), for the application of this index to oceanic games.

In each ordering, the actor [commited or uncommitted member(s)] who casts the third or *pivotal vote* is shown in parentheses. Following Brams and Riker,[31] Straffin excludes as illegal the four orderings (marked by an asterisk) in which *both* X and Y are members of the winning coalition—by being pivotal or to the left of the pivot—under the assumption that uncommitted members will form a winning coalition only with either X or Y but not both. Of the eight remaining orderings, X is pivotal in three, Y in one, and the two uncommitted members in four, or two each.

Define the *pivotal power* of a member to be the fraction of (legal) orderings in which he is pivotal. Thus, the pivotal power of the uncommitted members is $2/8 = 1/4 = 0.250$, and the pivotal power of X is $3/8 = 0.375$. On the other hand, the pivotal power of Y is $1/8 = 0.125$.

If an uncommitted member joins X, he makes X winning with three members, giving X (now with three members) pivotal power of 1.000. This makes the uncommitted member's *incremental contribution* to X

$$1.000 - 0.375 = 0.625.$$

(If the uncommitted member joined Y instead, his incremental contribution would be

$$0.250 - 0.125 = 0.125,$$

since after he joins Y, X and Y each have two members and pivotal power of 0.250.) This means that an uncommitted member does best by joining X, giving him an incremental contribution of 0.625, which is more than he contributes by joining Y (0.125) and more power than he has by remaining uncommitted (0.250).

Applying this reasoning in the infinite case, Straffin is able to construct "bandwagon curves" for the major candidates, X and Y, from his model (see figure 4.4). These curves divide the region in figure 4.4 into subregions in which uncommitted voters should commit to X, commit to Y, or stay uncom-

31. Brams and Riker, "Models of Coalition Formation in Voting Bodies."

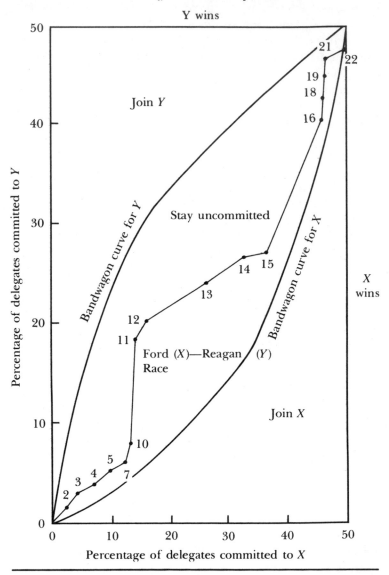

Figure 4.4
Bandwagon Curves, with Week-by-Week Delegate Commitments to Ford and Reagan in 1976 Republican Race

Y wins

Join Y

Stay uncommitted

Bandwagon curve for Y

Bandwagon curve for X

X wins

Ford (X)—Reagan (Y) Race

Join X

Percentage of delegates committed to Y

Percentage of delegates committed to X

Source: Philip D. Straffin Jr., "The Bandwagon Curve," *American Journal of Political Science* 21, no. 4 (November 1977): 701, figure 3; reprinted with permission.

mitted. Thus, an uncommitted voter should stay uncommitted—not join X or Y—if the percentage of voters committed to X and Y is a point that falls in the subregion between the bandwagon curves of X and Y in figure 4.4. Otherwise, he should join X or Y, respectively, depending on whether (1) X is the larger protocoalition—has more committed voters—and the situation is defined by a point in the subregion below the bandwagon curve for X, or (2) Y is the larger protocoalition and the situation is defined by a point in the subregion above the bandwagon curve for Y.

Thus, unlike the model to analyze commitments in national party conventions discussed in chapter 2, an uncommitted voter should *always* join the larger protocoalition if its lead is "sufficiently great."[32] *How great* is given precisely by the curves, but for rough guidance Straffin provides the following rules of thumb: the advantage that the larger protocoalition needs to start a bandwagon in its favor is

4:1 if 10 percent of the members are committed;
3:1 if 20 percent of the members are committed;
2:1 if 40 percent of the members are committed;
3:2 if 60 percent of the members are committed.[33]

The acid test of a model, of course, is how well it works, and Straffin's model worked remarkably well in predicting the outcome of the race for the Republican presidential nomination between Gerald Ford and Ronald Reagan in 1976. As shown in figure 4.4, Straffin plotted the delegate totals of candidates Ford (X) and Reagan (Y) on a week-to-week basis, as reported in *Congressional Quarterly Weekly Reports* and *The New York Times* between February and July 1976.

Beginning with the New Hampshire primary in week 1 and continuing for the next ten weeks, Ford was ahead but still within his bandwagon curve. Then, after the Texas and In-

32. In the chapter 2 model, however, the calculations were for *blocs* of *all* uncommitted delegates in a national party convention, not for individual uncommitted actors, which Straffin uses as the basis of calculation in his model.

33. Straffin, "Bandwagon Curve," p. 700.

diana primaries in weeks 11 and 12, Reagan was ahead—but by not nearly enough to shoot past his bandwagon curve—and his momentum petered out. Slowly, once again, Ford began to gain strength, and in week 22—specifically, on July 17 when the Connecticut delegation gave Ford thirty-five votes—Ford moved past his bandwagon curve into the bandwagon region (see figure 4.4). Common perceptions soon matched the mathematics of the bandwagon curve:

> On July 19, the *Washington Post* headlined "Privately, Some Aides See Reagan at End of Trail," and the story was picked up across the country. On the same day the *Los Angeles Times* reported a change in tactics by the Ford delegate hunters: "The message Ford people are now sending to uncommitted delegates is simple and direct: you had better get aboard—the train is about to leave without you."[34]

Despite Reagan's best efforts first to dispute the figures and then to muddy the waters with his surprise announcement of Richard Schweiker, a liberal Republican senator from Pennsylvania, as his choice for running mate, Ford went on to win the nomination on the first ballot of the Republican convention on August 18. Straffin makes the following trenchant observations about the effects of the Schweiker announcement:

> The bandwagon curve analysis suggests that the Schweiker announcement was valuable not as pressure on Gerald Ford to make a similar announcement, or as a bridge to liberal Republicans, or as an attempt to gain Pennsylvania delegates, but as a successful move to divert attention from bandwagon-starting delegate counts. It also helped make those counts seem less reliable by centering speculation on how the Schweiker announcement would alter delegate commitments. The bandwagon curve provides a framework in which to view the remarkable events of July and August 1976.[35]

34. Straffin, "Bandwagon Curve," p. 702.
35. Straffin, "Bandwagon Curve," p. 703.

To conclude this analysis, it seems fair to say that goals like winning, which apply to a coalition as a whole, tend to shut off inquiry into the dynamic analysis of what offers protocoalitions are likely to make, and uncommitted actors accept, at particular times in the formation and disintegration of winning coalitions. Simply to say that uncommitted actors seek to obtain the benefits of winning does not by itself entail the choice of a particular strategy on their part. By contrast, postulating the goal of not just obtaining the benefits of winning, but maximizing one's portion of these benefits[36]—as measured by the share of spoils or pivotal power—directs one's attention to the optimal timing of strategic choices (e.g., when to join a protocoalition), and hence the unfolding of events (e.g., bandwagons) over time.

4.10. Conclusions

In this chapter I have developed a variety of coalition models and applied them to the study of presidential politics. In the case of each model, an attempt was made to determine the optimal strategies that players would follow to maximize some postulated goal and compare these with the actual behavior of parties and candidates in presidential elections.

The historical evidence considered in this chapter strongly suggests that coalitions in American politics are none too permanent and may be indeed quite fragile. The models indicate several reasons why this is the case, including

(1) the influence exerted by activists who favor extremist candidates, which has led in the recent past to stunning victories and defeats for both political parties;

(2) incomplete and imperfect information about what strategies will produce minimal winning coalitions,

36. This idea is incorporated in Adrian and Press's reformulation of the size principle. See Charles H. Adrian and Charles Press, "Decision Costs in Coalition Formation," *American Political Science Review* 62, no. 2 (June 1968): 557. More recently, "satisfaction" has been distinguished from "power" in dynamic coalition models, which also incorporate assumptions about ideological structure. See Philip D. Straffin Jr., Morton D. Davis, and Steven J. Brams, "Power and Satisfaction in an Ideologically Divided Voting Body" (mimeographed, Beloit College, 1978).

which has encouraged miscalculations resulting in oversized coalitions that eventually succumbed to the size principle;

(3) the unattractiveness to uncommitted actors of proto-coalitions with overwhelming odds in their favor (based on the share-of-spoils calculation that says a two-to-one probabilistic advantage is optimal), which may on occasion help the underdog (as was shown in chapter 2).

To be sure, the pivotal-power calculation *always* favors the front-runner over the second-leading candidate, but not necessarily over staying uncommitted if his (the front-runner's) lead is not too large. Thus, even this model says that there is a basic fragility about a leader's position, which small shifts may suddenly upset.

For these and probably other reasons, there seems little danger that winners will become permanently institution-alized in American politics—given, of course, that the basic rules of the game allowing for the formation and disin-tegration of coalitions do not change. Hence, despite the occasional humiliation of a Goldwater or a McGovern at the polls, the competitive two-party system does not seem about to disappear in presidential politics.

5   The Unmaking of a President: How an Election Mandate Was Upset

5.1.   Introduction

The assessment I offered at the end of chapter 4 of the resilience of the two-party system to the ups and downs of each party is perhaps most seriously challenged in recent times by the events of Watergate. All the presidential abuses of power evoked by the name "Watergate" certainly cast doubt on the ability of the election process to displace an incumbent president determined to hold onto power.

Incumbent Richard Nixon did in fact swamp George McGovern in the 1972 election with almost no campaigning; McGovern won only one state, Massachusetts, and the District of Columbia. Yet, while the "dirty tricks" of some Nixon campaigners probably contributed to his victory, it is almost impossible to conceive of Richard Nixon's losing on the issues—among them, Vietnam, law and order, and busing—in 1972. All the polls at the time showed him to be the most popular choice by a wide margin.

In section 4.7, I suggested how the size principle inevitably exacts its toll on American presidents who run up huge electoral victories. But more than the operation of the size principle was at work in Richard Nixon's case after the 1972 election. A confluence of more proximate causes connected with Watergate brought about his ultimate humiliation, in the end forcing him to be the first president ever to resign from office.

The outcome of one game played out in the final stages of Watergate—Nixon's confrontation with the Supreme Court—was probably the most immediate cause of Nixon's resignation. Although nothing quite like this game will probably ever be repeated, it does provide both general insights into the workings of the American constitutional system and more specific insights into how a presidential mandate can be upset after an election.

Whereas the resignation of a prime minister in parliamentary systems of government almost always leads to new elections, the resignation of a president in the United States leads to the elevation of the vice president to the highest office in the land. In a sense, this may be thought of as a kind of surrogate election—with the alternatives the incumbent president and the vice president—though neither the people nor the Congress (by impeachment and conviction) make a direct choice in the case of a presidential resignation. This is not to say that the political pressure they exert is inconsequential; quite the contrary, it seems to have been decisive in President Nixon's decision to resign—as he put it, "I no longer have a strong enough political base [to complete the term of office]."[1]

When Nixon resigned and Gerald Ford took over, there was a feeling that a new chapter had been opened. Indeed, the new president sought to wipe the old slate clean by proclaiming in his inaugural statement that "our long national nightmare is over."[2] How this nightmare was ended is the subject of this chapter.

5.2. *Game Theory and the White House Tapes Case*

A decision is formally rendered by a simple majority of the nine justices on the Supreme Court.[3] On some occasions, however, it appears that members of the Court act *as if* a unanimous decision were required.

A case in point is *Brown* v. *Board of Education,* the 1954 school desegregation decision in which the Court split six to three in its preruling deliberations only to present a unani-

1. Staff of The New York Times, *The End of a Presidency* (New York: Bantam Books, 1974), p. vii.

2. Staff of The New York Times, *End of a Presidency*, p. 75.

3. Material in the remainder of this chapter is based largely on Steven J. Brams and Douglas Muzzio, "Game Theory and the White House Tapes Case," *Trial* 13, no. 5 (May 1977): 48–53; and Brams and Muzzio, "Unanimity in the Supreme Court: A Game-Theoretic Explanation of the Decision in the White House Tapes Case," *Public Choice* 32 (Winter 1977): 67–83; the permission of *Trial* and *Public Choice* to adapt material from these articles is gratefully acknowledged.

mous ruling to the nation.[4] Anticipating strong opposition to the decision, Chief Justice Earl Warren redrafted his opinion several times before it gained the approval of all the justices.[5]

Yet there have been recent major constitutional cases in which the Court has split. For example, in *Baker* v. *Carr* (1962), the first of the reapportionment cases, the Court split six to two, though strong opposition to this decision could be anticipated. Nonetheless, the Court did not act to undercut this opposition by presenting a united front.

When will members of the Court be willing to submerge individual differences and speak with a single voice? As the *Brown* and *Baker* decisions show, this question is not satisfactorily answered by saying in major constitutional cases in which the Court is likely to be opposed or threatened.[6] Because this response does not answer the question of *who* is opposed or threatened on these cases—or, more important, *why*—it does not provide an explanation for the Court's behavior.

Using the tools of game theory, I shall try to explain the Court's decision, and Richard Nixon's response to its decision, in the landmark case of *United States* v. *Nixon*. In this case, the Supreme Court unanimously ruled on July 24, 1974, to end President Nixon's efforts to withhold evidence from Special

4. Rowland Evans and Robert Novak, "A Unanimous Court against Mr. Nixon?" *Washington Post*, July 23, 1974, p. C7. For further details, see Richard Kluger, *Simple Justice: The History of Brown vs. Board of Education and Black America's Struggle for Equality* (New York: Knopf, 1976), chaps. 25–26. It is interesting that the day following the unanimous decision in *United States* v. *Nixon*—the case analyzed here—the Court reverted to a more characteristic five-to-four conservative-liberal split in striking down a metropolitan-area school integration plan for Detroit.

5. David W. Rohde and Harold J. Spaeth, *Supreme Court Decision Making* (San Francisco: W. H. Freeman, 1976), p. 201.

6. The best analysis of the proposition that threats induce unanimous or lopsided Court majorities is Rohde and Spaeth, *Supreme Court Decision Making*, pp. 195–203. The authors admit, however, that "it does not seem possible, short of interviewing the justices, to derive an objective indicator of threat situations" (p. 195). For this reason, it seems useful not to try to define "threats" as such but instead show how the norm of unanimity can be derived as a consequence of rational choices in a particular situation.

Prosecutor Leon Jaworski in the so-called Watergate cover-up case. That same day the president, through his attorney, James St. Clair, announced his compliance with the ruling— he would release the White House tapes the special prosecutor sought. Fifteen days later the Nixon presidency ended in ruins, a direct result of the Court's action.

In my reconstruction of the White House tapes case, I shall provide only the historical details that seem necessary to justify the later game-theoretic analysis. After setting the stage for the game played, I shall identify the players and their strategies. The possible outcomes of the game, and the preference rankings of the players for these outcomes, will then be described. Finally, the optimal strategies of the players will be analyzed, and a paradoxical consequence of their "rationality" will be discussed.

5.3. The Players and Their Preferences

The immediate history of the White House tapes decision began on March 1, 1974, when the Watergate grand jury indicted seven former White House and campaign aides for attempting to cover up the Watergate scandal (*United States* v. *Mitchell et al.*). On April 16, the special prosecutor petitioned Judge John Sirica to subpoena tapes and documents of sixty-four presidential conversations with Dean, Haldeman, Ehrlichman, and Colson; the subpoena was issued on April 18.

On May 1, St. Clair announced that his client, the president, would refuse to submit the subpoenaed materials, and St. Clair sought an order quashing the subpoena. After hearing arguments, Judge Sirica confirmed the subpoena order on May 20. On May 24, St. Clair filed an appeal in the Court of Appeals, which, it seemed, would probably result in the postponement of the cover-up trial.[7]

---

7. For reasons, see Frank Mankiewicz, *U.S.* v. *Richard M. Nixon: The Final Crisis* (New York: Random House, 1975), pp. 87–88; for an explanation of the president's strategy, see George V. Higgins, *The Friends of Richard Nixon* (Boston: Little, Brown, 1975), pp. 166–67, and Clark Mollenhoff, *Game Plan for Disaster* (New York: W. W. Norton, 1976), p. 376.

The prosecutors moved quickly to prevent delay. On the same day that the appeal by St. Clair was filed in the Court of Appeals, Leon Jaworski, using a seldom-invoked procedure, went to the Supreme Court and sought a writ of *certiorari before judgment* that would leapfrog the appeals process. Citing the imminent cover-up trial date, Jaworski also noted the necessity to settle expeditiously an issue that was paralyzing the government. He requested the Court not only to issue the writ but also, because of the "imperative public importance" of the case, to stay in session into the summer.[8] This way the case could be decided in sufficient time that the tapes could be used as evidence at the trial—should Judge Sirica's ruling be upheld.[9] The Supreme Court agreed on May 31 and heard oral arguments on July 8.

When the justices went into conference on July 9, each of the eight who were to consider the case had basically two choices—decide for or decide against the president. (Associate Justice William Rehnquist withdrew from the case evidently because of his previous service at the Justice Department under John Mitchell, though he never publicly stated a reason for disqualifying himself.) It appears from the available record that six of the justices reached an early consensus against the president on all three of the major issues:[10]

8. J. Anthony Lukas, *Nightmare: The Underside of the Nixon Years* (New York: Viking Press, 1976), p. 495.

9. For a detailed discussion of the elements that went into the special prosecutor's decision to seek the writ, see Bob Woodward and Carl Bernstein, *The Final Days* (New York: Simon and Schuster, 1976), pp. 182–83.

10. The Supreme Court is the most secretive of all American institutions; it is virtually unheard of for a justice to reveal anything specific about the Court's case work. [The only such breach of secrecy on record occurred in 1857 when the thrust of the *Dred Scott* v. *Sanford* decision was leaked in advance by Justice Catron to President Buchanan. See Henry Abraham, *The Judicial Process*, 3d ed. (New York: Oxford University Press, 1975), p. 345.] Law clerks, too, are sworn to secrecy. To say anything authoritative about the workings of the Court in any specific case is therefore fraught with difficulties. Reports on the tapes case are contradictory concerning Burger's (and Blackmun's) role. See, for example, *Newsweek*, August 5, 1974, pp. 23–26; *Time*, August 5, 1974, pp. 20, 25; *The New York Times*, August 5, 1974, p. 18; *National Review*, August 16, 1974, p. 906; Nina Totenberg, "Behind the

(1) whether the Court had jurisdiction in the case—standing to sue—since Jaworski was an employee of the executive branch; (2) whether executive privilege was absolute; and (3) whether Jaworski had demonstrated a sufficient need for the subpoenaed materials.[11]

Justices Burger and Blackmun, while concurring with the majority on limiting executive privilege, believed that the special prosecutor lacked legal standing to sue the president.[12] For this reason, it appears, they voted originally against granting the case *certiorari*.[13]

Justices Burger and Blackmun are conceived of as one player. This is so because it is almost axiomatic that Blackmun votes with Burger: in the first five terms (1970–74) that Burger and Blackmun served together on the Court, they agreed on 602 of the 721 cases they both heard (83.5 percent), which is the highest agreement level of any pair of justices who served over these five terms.[14] They are referred to as the "Minnesota Twins" by the Supreme Court staff.

Burger and Blackmun had a choice of two strategies:

1. To decide against the president, joining the other six justices to create a unanimous decision.

Marble, Beneath the Robes," *New York Times Magazine*, March 16, 1975, pp. 15 ff; and Woodward and Bernstein, *The Final Days*, p. 262.

11. *Time*, July 22, 1974, pp. 10–17.

12. *Newsweek*, August 5, 1974, p. 24.

13. Although votes for *certiorari* are secret, and the reasons for a decision on *certiorari* are "seldom, if ever, disclosed" (Abraham, *Judicial Process*, p. 179), it is reported by Totenberg, "Behind the Marble, Beneath the Robes," p. 58, that Justices Burger, Blackmun, and White all voted against granting the writ. I do not include White with Burger and Blackmun as a player in the subsequent analysis because he is not a Nixon appointee and there is no evidence from reports of the predecision deliberations that he ever considered supporting the president. Instead, it seems reasonable to infer that he preferred that the case proceed through the usual judicial process (i.e., go next to the Court of Appeals).

14. Data on case agreement can be found in the November issues of *Harvard Law Review* (1971–75). On the concurrence of Burger and Blackmun, see *The New York Times*, July 1, 1974, p. 10; and Totenberg, "Behind the Marble, Beneath the Robes."

2. To decide for the president, forming a minority to create a six-to-two "weak" decision.

President Nixon's possible response to an adverse Supreme Court ruling was long a matter of doubt—and one which, it will be argued here, Burger and Blackmun could not afford to ignore. On July 26, 1973, deputy White House press secretary Gerald Warren stated that President Nixon would abide by a "definitive decision of the highest court." Nixon, at a news conference on August 22, 1973, endorsed the Warren formulation but neither he nor White House spokesmen would expand on the original statement.[15] These statements were made in reference to the president's refusal to obey a subpoena from the first special prosecutor, Archibald Cox, for nine White House tapes.

That case never reached the Supreme Court. The Court of Appeals ruled against the president, who, after a delay of eleven days, agreed to submit the tapes—but not before he had dismissed Cox. The question of what "definitive" meant then became moot.

The issue arose again on May 24, 1974, when Jaworski filed his appeal with the Supreme Court. On July 9, St. Clair made it clear that the president was keeping open the "option" of defying the Court. The question of compliance, he stated, "has not yet been decided."[16] Since the expectation at the time was that the Court would rule against the president,[17] President Nixon had two strategies:

1. Comply with an adverse Court ruling.
2. Defy an adverse Court ruling.

Several factors help to explain President Nixon's refusal to make a definite commitment concerning his response to a Court decision. If he stated that he would not comply, his statement might be used as a ground for impeachment. If he stated that he would comply, then the House Judiciary Com-

15. *The New York Times*, July 25, 1974, p. 22.
16. *The New York Times*, July 10, 1974, p. 1.
17. *Newsweek*, July 22, 1974, p. 18; *Time*, July 22, 1974, pp. 15–17.

mittee might argue that the president would either have to comply with its subpoenas, too, or be impeached.[18]

More important, though, the president's refusal to assure his compliance with an adverse decision was designed to threaten the Court and lead the justices to render either a favorable decision or, at worst, a closely divided adverse split decision which he could claim was insufficiently "definitive" for a matter of this magnitude. Rowland Evans and Robert Novak reported at the time: "The refusal of St. Clair to say Nixon would obey an adverse decision has disturbed the judicial branch from the high court on down."[19]

If the president's intent were to threaten the Court, the threat backfired. But why? To explain why Justices Burger and Blackmun departed from their apparent personal preferences and eventually sided with the Court majority, I shall next describe the game they and President Nixon played.

5.4. The Outcomes and Their Preference Rankings by the Players

The probable outcomes of the four possible strategy choices of the two players are presented in tabular, or matrix, form in figure 5.1. To justify these outcomes, first consider the consequences associated with Nixon's defiance of an adverse Supreme Court ruling.

Unquestionably, if the president defied the Court, his defiance would represent a direct assault on the Supreme Court's constitutional place as the "principal source and final authority of constitutional interpretation" and thereby threaten the very structure of the American political system.[20] Indeed, it seems highly probable that Nixon would have plunged the country into its deepest constitutional crisis since the Civil War. No previous president had ever explicitly defied an order of the Supreme Court, though such action had apparently been contemplated.[21]

18. *The New York Times*, July 10, 1974, p. 1.

19. Rowland Evans and Robert Novak, "Mr. Nixon's Supreme Court Strategy," *Washington Post*, June 12, 1974, p. A29.

20. D. Grier Stephenson, Jr., " 'The Mild Magistracy of the Law': U.S. v. Richard Nixon," *Intellect* 103, no. 2363 (February 1975): 292.

21. Robert Scigliano, *The Supreme Court and the Presidency* (New York: Free Press, 1971), chap. 2.

Figure 5.1
Outcome Matrix of White House Tapes Game

		Nixon	
		Comply with Court	Defy Court
Burger and Blackmun	Decide for president; create a "weak" 6–2 decision	A. Constitutional crisis averted; Nixon not impeached for noncompliance; majority-rule principle preserved	B. Constitutional crisis; Nixon impeached but conviction uncertain
	Decide against president; create a unanimous 8–0 decision	D. Constitutional crisis averted; Nixon not impeached for noncompliance; majority-rule principle possibly weakened	C. Constitutional crisis; Nixon impeached and conviction certain

Source: Steven J. Brams and Douglas Muzzio, "Game Theory and the White House Tapes Case," *Trial* 13, no. 5 (May 1977): 50, figure 1; reprinted with permission.

Note: The only impeachment charge being considered here is non-compliance with the Supreme Court decision on the tapes, not any of the other charges voted by the House Judiciary Committee in July 1974.

At the time of the decision in *United States* v. *Nixon,* it appeared that the result of presidential defiance would be impeachment by the House of Representatives. While the outcome in the Senate was less certain than in the House, a unanimous adverse decision by the Court that included three conservative Nixon appointees (Burger, Blackmun, and Powell; I do not include Powell in the present analysis for reasons discussed later) would preempt charges that the president was the victim of what presidential counselor Dean Burch called a "partisan lynch mob."[22] Indeed, St. Clair warned the president on the day of the decision that he would be surely impeached and swiftly convicted if he were to defy the unanimous ruling of the Court.[23]

On the other hand, Jaworski believed that "if the vote against him [the president] was close he would go on television and tell the people that the presidency should not be impaired by a divided Court."[24] A "weak" decision from which at least some of the more conservative Nixon appointees dissented would also allow the president to continue his "one-third plus one" strategy in the Senate to avoid conviction and removal from office.

Consider now the consequences associated with Nixon's compliance with an adverse Supreme Court decision. Clearly, compliance would avert a constitutional crisis, and President Nixon would avoid immediate impeachment in the House on the ground of withholding evidence from the special prosecutor and/or violation of the separation-of-powers principle. However, compliance posed problems for the president; he had reason to believe that the subpoenaed materials, if released, would prove damaging to his impeachment defense in Congress. Indeed, upon learning of the Court's decision, Nixon, who was at San Clemente, telephoned White House special counsel Fred Buzhardt in Washington. "There may be some problems with the June 23 tape," Nixon said.[25]

Although the revelation of this tape ultimately forced his resignation, President Nixon apparently did not fully realize at the time the incriminating nature of the recorded conversations. In *The Final Days,* Woodward and Bernstein report that Buzhardt felt that the tape was "devastating"; Nixon, on the other hand, felt that Buzhardt was "overreacting," that it was "not that bad."[26] Even as late as August 5, in his statement

22. Lukas, *Nightmare*, p. 510.
23. Lukas, *Nightmare*, p. 519.
24. Leon Jaworski, *The Right and the Power: The Prosecution of Watergate* (New York: Reader's Digest Press, 1976), p. 164.
25. *Washington Post*, September 9, 1974, p. A1.
26. Woodward and Bernstein, *The Final Days*, p. 276.

accompanying the public release of the tape transcripts, Nixon reflected his mixed evaluation of the tape's impact: "I recognize that this additional material I am now furnishing may further damage my case. . . . I am firmly convinced that the record, in its entirety, does not justify the extreme step of impeachment and removal from office."[27]

Compliance or, more accurately, the announcement of compliance would allow the president to fall back on his long-used strategy of delay, though it would not necessarily remove the threat of impeachment and ultimate conviction, especially if the Court were unanimous in its judgment. For Justices Burger and Blackmun, who had voted originally against granting the case review, supporting the majority (possibly against their convictions) to counter a presumed threat might possibly weaken the majority-rule principle that *any* majority is sufficient for a ("definitive") decision.[28] But voting their convictions would be hazardous should the president use a divided decision as a pretext to defy the Court.

I shall now attempt to combine these conflicting considerations into a ranking of the four outcomes by the two players. It should be stressed that I attempt only a ranking, not an assessment of *how much* each player preferred one outcome over another.

Clearly, President Nixon preferred the *risk* of conviction and removal to its virtual certainty. Thus, the president would prefer to defy a weak decision (outcome B in figure 5.1) than to defy a unanimous decision (C), which I indicate by the (partial) preference scale (B, C). For the same reason, he would prefer to comply with any adverse decision (A or D) than to defy a unanimous decision (C)—his worst outcome—

---

27. Staff of The New York Times, *End of a Presidency*, p. 324.

28. For a discussion of the importance of the majority-rule principle in the Court, see Thomas J. Norton, "The Supreme Court's Five to Four Decisions," *American Bar Association Journal* 9 (July 1923): 417–20; John H. Clarke, "Judicial Power to Declare Legislation Unconstitutional," *American Bar Association Journal 9* (November 1923): 689–92; Herbert Pillen, *Majority Rule in the Supreme Court* (Washington, D.C.: Georgetown University, 1924); and Charles Warren, *The Supreme Court in United States History*, vol. 1 (Boston: Little, Brown, 1924), pp. 664–70.

so $(A\text{-}D, C)$, where the hyphen indicates indifference (for now).

Defying a weak decision (B) is considered preferable to complying with any adverse decision $(A$ or $D)$, for such defiance would preclude the release of potentially devastating evidence and at the same time present Nixon with the possibility of avoiding conviction and removal for noncompliance; hence $(B, A\text{-}D)$. Between the two compliance outcomes $(A$ and $D)$, I assume that the president "preferred" to comply with a weak decision (A) than with a unanimous decision (D), so (A, D). A weak decision with some justices dissenting would leave the issue confused and subject to interpretation; a weak decision would leave room to maneuver for partial compliance.[29]

Putting the partial preference scales together, the president's presumed ranking of the four outcomes is: B preferable to A preferable to D preferable to C, or (B, A, D, C). Given these rankings by the president, what are the corresponding rankings of Justices Burger and Blackmun?

Although it was previously suggested that Burger and Blackmun would have preferred to decide for the president on at least one of the strictly legal questions (standing to sue by the special prosecutor), there is no doubt that the justices believed that compliance by the president with any adverse Court ruling $(A$ or $D)$ would be preferable to defiance $(B$ or $C)$; hence, their (partial) preference scale is $(A\text{-}D, B\text{-}C)$. Indeed, in the Court's opinion, which Burger drafted, the chief justice quoted Chief Justice John Marshall in *Marbury* v. *Madison* (1803): "It is emphatically the province and duty of the Judicial department to say what the law is."

It also seems reasonable to assume that if the president complies, the justices would prefer to decide for him (A) rather than against him (D); hence, (A, D). After all, the notion that the Court must be unanimous or close to it to

29. It can reasonably be argued that the president preferred to comply with a unanimous decision (D) than an "indefinitive" ruling that he had been threatening to ignore (A), so (D, A). This reversal of the ranking of the two compliance outcomes leads to essentially the same results that I shall subsequently describe, except that the equilibrium outcome becomes $(3, 3)$ rather than $(3, 2)$, and the paradox of rational choice discussed later disappears.

make a decision credible, and thereby induce compliance, is an undesirable restriction on the Court's authority and might establish an unhealthy precedent. Finally, I assume that the justices "preferred" the president to defy a unanimous decision (C) than to defy a weak decision (B)—on which his chances of success would be higher—so (C, B).

Putting the partial preference scales together, the justices' presumed ranking of the four outcomes is: A preferable to D preferable to C preferable to B, or (A, D, C, B). If we represent the best outcome for each player by 4, the next-best outcome by 3, the next-worst outcome by 2, and the worst outcome by 1, the rankings of the four outcomes in the figure 5.1 outcome matrix will be as shown in the figure 5.2 matrix. (Thus, the higher the number, the higher the ranking of the outcome by a player.) I shall refer to this matrix as the *payoff matrix*—though the "payoffs" are only ranks and do not say how much more one outcome is valued over another—where the first

Figure 5.2
Payoff Matrix of White House Tapes Game

Nixon

		Comply with Court	Defy Court
Burger and Blackmun	Decide for president	A. (4,3)	B. (1,4)
	Decide against president	D. (3,2)	C. (2,1)

Source: Steven J. Brams and Douglas Muzzio, "Game Theory and the White House Tapes Case," *Trial* 13, no. 5 (May 1977): 52, figure 2; reprinted with permission.

Note: The first entry of each ordered pair is the ranking by the row player (Burger and Blackmun), the second entry the ranking by the column player (Nixon).

entry of the ordered pair associated with each outcome gives the payoff to the row player (Burger and Blackmun), the second entry the payoff to the column player (Nixon).

5.5. The Game Tree and Revised Payoff Matrix

Because the players in the White House tapes game did not make simultaneous choices in ignorance of each other, the payoff matrix in figure 5.2 does not provide an accurate representation of this game. Justices Burger and Blackmun—and the Court—acted first, and only then did President Nixon have to make a strategy choice, as depicted in the *game tree* in figure 5.3 (read from top to bottom).

The game tree depicts the step-by-step sequence of moves. It clearly shows that Burger and Blackmun had two choices open to them, and—depending on how the Court ruled—

Figure 5.3
Game Tree of White House Tapes Game

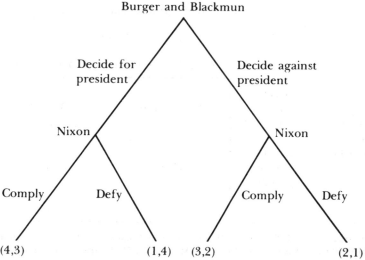

Source: Steven J. Brams and Douglas Muzzio, "Game Theory and the White House Tapes Case," *Trial* 13, no. 5 (May 1977): 52, figure 3; reprinted with permission.

there were four possible choices open to Nixon. That is, before the Court rendered its verdict, any of the four outcomes could occur.

The payoffs associated with these outcomes are shown as the endpoints of the four lower branches of the game tree in figure 5.3. In figure 5.4, the *revised* payoff matrix of this game is given, wherein Burger and Blackmun have two strategies but Nixon now has four strategies. This is so because each of Nixon's two original strategies, "Comply" and "Defy," are contingent on what Burger and Blackmun decide ("Decide for President," "Decide against President"), which yields 2 · 2 = 4 strategies for the president.

The payoffs in figure 5.4 can be easily derived from the payoffs given in either figure 5.2 or figure 5.3. For example, assume Burger and Blackmun choose strategy A (decide

Figure 5.4

Revised Payoff Matrix of White House Tapes Game

Nixon

		Comply (C) regardless	Defy (D) regardless	C if F, D if A	D if F, C if A
	Decide for president (F)	(4,3)	(1,4)	(4,3)	(1,4)
Burger and Blackmun	Decide against president (A)	(3,2)	(2,1)	(2,1)	(3,2)
					Dominant

Source: Steven J. Brams and Douglas Muzzio, "Game Theory and the White House Tapes Case," *Trial* 13, no. 5 (May 1977): 53, figure 4; reprinted with permission.

Note: The circled outcome (3,2) is in equilibrium; Nixon's D if F, C if A strategy is dominant.

against president), and Nixon chooses C if A, D if F (comply if Burger and Blackmun decide against, defy if Burger and Blackmun decide for). Since Burger and Blackmun choose A, this choice implies that Nixon's choice will be C, which yields the payoff (3,2) associated with the "Decide against President"/"Comply" outcome in both the payoff matrix of figure 5.2 and the game tree of figure 5.3.

Now consider the White House tapes game shown in figure 5.4. It is easy to see that D if F, C if A is a *dominant strategy* for Nixon: it yields payoffs as good as, and in at least one case better than, the payoffs yielded by any of his other three strategies, whatever the strategy choice of Burger and Blackmun (F or A).

Given this unconditionally best strategy choice on the part of Nixon, it is reasonable to assume that Burger and Blackmun will anticipate its choice, assuming they (as well as Nixon) have complete information about the figure 5.4 revised payoff matrix. To maximize *their* payoff, Burger and Blackmun will choose the strategy which yields for them the highest payoff in that column associated with Nixon's dominant strategy (the fourth column in figure 5.4). Since 3 is better than 1 for Burger and Blackmun in this column, we would therefore expect that they would choose their strategy A.

As we already know, the Supreme Court did decide unanimously against President Nixon. Nixon was reportedly shocked by the Court's ruling, feeling himself "sold out" by his three appointees, Chief Justice Burger and Associate Justices Blackmun and Powell. (I did not include Powell along with Burger and Blackmun as the Court player since he originally favored granting *certiorari*; also, Powell "demonstrated the highest level of independence within the Nixon Bloc"[30] and has been described as "one of the least predictable of the eight and most flexible of the Nixon appointees."[31]) Charles Colson claims that the president counted on all three

30. *The New York Times*, July 1, 1974, p. 10.
31. *Time*, July 22, 1974, p. 16.

justices. Others say he was certain of Burger and Blackmun. When he learned of the decision, Nixon used expletive-deleted language to describe Burger. The president could not believe that the Court's ruling had been unanimous. "Significantly, the President's greatest fury seems to have been directed not at the decision itself but at the three Justices who 'deserted' him."[32]

In any event, the decision was unanimous with no dissenting or concurring opinions. "It was the Court's seamless unity which made defiance so difficult."[33] Eight hours after the decision was handed down, the president, through St. Clair, announced his compliance with the decision "in all respects."

In summary, the game-theoretic analysis seems to explain well, in terms of the foregoing reconstruction of the players' strategies and preferences for outcomes, why the players acted as they did. Yet not only is the outcome that occurred not the most desirable from the viewpoint of either player, but both players might have done better had the president been a little more reassuring.

5.6. A Paradox of Rational Choice

It is worth noting that the payoff $(3, 2)$ associated with the strategies A, and D if F, C if A, is not only the outcome one would expect on the basis of the reasoning presented earlier, but it is also the only outcome in figure 5.4 that is *in equilibrium*: once chosen by both players, neither player has an

32. This account is drawn from Lukas, *Nightmare*, p. 519. One of the more intriguing allegations concerning Burger's role in the case is provided by Charles Colson, who quotes President Nixon as stating, "I think we'll really win in the Supreme Court. Burger thinks this whole thing is a disgrace." Colson does not claim to know whether Nixon had spoken directly with Burger or whether the president had drawn a conclusion based on second-hand information (*Washington Post*, January 18, 1975, p. A4). According to a report in *The New York Times* (January 15, 1975, p. 16), "The Supreme Court information officer, Barrett McGurn, denied that the chief justice had discussed the pending case with Mr. Nixon. . . . According to the NBC broadcast, 'a source close to Richard Nixon' also denied that any conversation between Mr. Nixon and Mr. Burger had occurred."

33. Lukas, *Nightmare*, p. 519.

incentive to depart unilaterally from it because he will do no better, and perhaps worse, if he does. Yet, paradoxically, *both* players could have done better if they had chosen strategies associated with either of the two (4, 3) payoffs in the figure 5.4 matrix. The outcomes that yield these payoffs both involve the choice by Burger and Blackmun of deciding for the president, and the choice by Nixon of compliance. The president can "arrive at" this choice either by selecting Comply (C) regardless or C if F, D if A in the figure 5.4 matrix.

Unfortunately for the players, however, neither of the outcomes that yield (4, 3) as a payoff is in equilibrium: Nixon in each case has an incentive to depart unilaterally from the strategies associated with (4, 3) to try to bring about his best outcome, (1, 4).[34] Not only are the (4, 3) outcomes not in equilibrium, but Nixon's two strategies associated with these outcomes are dominated by his (dominant) strategy, D if F, C if A.

For these reasons, therefore, it is hard to see how both players could have done better, even though the opportunity existed. Only if Burger and Blackmun had believed that their dissent would not trigger presidential defiance could they have voted their (presumed) convictions with greater equanimity.[35]

The public record shows that Burger and Blackmun never received any assurance that the president would comply if the Court split. Quite the contrary: Nixon and his spokesmen, as I indicated earlier, continually held out the possibility of defying a Supreme Court decision that was not "definitive." Thus, Burger and Blackmun had no choice—despite their disagreement with some arguments of the special prosecutor—but to decide against the president. Thereby the Supreme

34. Interestingly, *no* outcomes in the figure 5.2 matrix representation— neither those which yield payoffs (4, 3) nor (3, 2)—are in equilibrium, but this fact is not relevant to the present analysis because I have already established that this representation does not depict the game that was played.

35. For a more detailed development of this logic and other game-theoretic arguments in this chapter, see Brams and Muzzio, "Unanimity in the Supreme Court."

Court decision was rendered unanimous and both players in the White House tapes game lost out, in a sense, on greater payoffs that—at least in principle—were attainable.

The public probably gained from this "noncooperative" solution, however. If we identify the public with the special prosecutor in the White House tapes case, it seems likely that the special prosecutor, who set up the game that I have described though he was not himself a player, would rank the outcome that actually occurred as the best of the four possible outcomes. This is certainly a reasonable inference from Jaworski's remarks immediately after the Court decision: "I feel right good over what happened. We can move ahead now. . . . I'm especially pleased it was a unanimous decision. It doesn't leave any doubt in anyone's mind."[36]

5.7. Conclusions

In this chapter I have shown how a president was forced from office by the unanimous adverse decision of the Supreme Court. The game-theoretic analysis indicated not only why the players in the White House tapes game acted as they did but also why they were unable to do better, despite the existence of a mutually "cooperative" solution. Of course, it is too early after the event to be absolutely confident about the reconstruction of outcomes, or the players' preferences for these outcomes, but for the purposes of this analysis the record seems reasonably complete.[37]

By way of conclusion, it seems worth pointing out that a variety of bizarre motives ("need to fail," "death wish") and personality traits ("self-destructive") have been attributed to Richard Nixon. The analysis in this chapter, however, suggests that his rhetoric in the White House tapes case that

36. *The New York Times*, July 25, 1974, p. 22.

37. Since this analysis was written, H. R. Haldeman has corroborated Jaworski's view (see section 5.5) about the consequences of a nonunanimous Court decision: "If the Supreme Court had handed down a [nonunanimous] majority decision, Nixon would have defied the Court and refused its order to turn over the tapes." H. R. Haldeman with Joseph DiMona, *The Ends of Power* (New York: Times Books, 1978), p. 310.

pushed his confrontation with the special prosecutor and then the Supreme Court beyond the point of no return was not at all strange. Rather, Nixon was simply caught up in an intractable game that, with perhaps greater prescience, he could have avoided.

That he did not possess such prescience seems quite understandable. Political leaders of all different stripes have similar failings. The consequences of these failings, I believe, can be well understood within the rationalistic framework that has been used to analyze other aspects of the presidential election game.

6 Approval Voting:
A New Election Reform

6.1. Introduction

It is traditional to conclude a book on presidential elections with calls for reform. I shall not depart from this tradition, but neither shall I rehearse the usual complaints about the hurdles to voter registration that still exist in many states, the inordinately large number of state primaries, lax controls at the ballot box in certain jurisdictions that encourage election fraud, the faithless elector in the Electoral College who does not vote for the winning candidate in his state, and so on. These are legitimate complaints that can be made about our present system of electing a president, but they are not its central problems.

There are two central problems. The first is the Electoral College, whose effects I have already discussed in detail in chapter 3. Because it seriously violates the one-man, one-vote principle— both in theory and in practice—I recommended in section 3.13 that it be replaced by the popular-vote election of a president.

The second problem occurs in multicandidate races and is not peculiar to presidential elections. In a race with three or more candidates, a candidate not favored by a majority may be elected. In fact, as a real-life example discussed in section 6.8 will show, it is possible that a candidate who wins in a three-way plurality contest would lose in two-way contests to each of the other candidates and hence be the least popular candidate in the race.

This problem with multicandidate elections has long been recognized, but it admits of no solution short of running several two-way elections to find the most popular candidate in pairwise contests (if one exists). This, of course, is not a practicable solution, so the problem is to design a system that minimizes the likelihood that a nonmajority candidate will be elected and that is relatively easy to implement.

There are other criteria which a good voting system should satisfy that will be discussed presently. I shall advocate adoption of a system, called "approval voting," that seems better to satisfy these criteria than any other practicable and easy-to-understand system.

Since approval voting is not yet well known, I shall devote considerable space to analyzing its properties. Many examples will be given throughout this chapter to illustrate the analysis, which builds up gradually to include general results called theorems. In most but not all cases, once a theorem is stated, a proof is offered to establish its validity.

Although this style of analysis is still uncommon in political science, it is being more and more used in rigorous scientific treatments of a variety of subjects. Its main advantage is that it allows one to make statements that are valid, or logically true—that is, that can be derived step by step from a set of assumptions and are always true if the conditions of the theorem are met. To the extent that these statements describe a real-life situation or class of events, they offer generalizations—not just specific illustrations—of what will follow under the given conditions.

These generalizations are particularly important when we compare voting systems and try to establish which are superior according to specified criteria. When we look at an actual election, on the other hand, our interest is not in general results but in specific changes that might have occurred had a different voting system been used. This is precisely the question asked in section 6.9, where I report on an attempt made to reconstruct from survey data what the outcome would have been in the 1968 presidential election had approval voting been used.[1]

1. Much of the material in the remainder of the chapter is based on Steven J. Brams, *One Man, n Votes*, Module in Applied Mathematics, Mathematical Association of America (Ithaca, N.Y.: Cornell University, 1976); Brams, "When Is It Advantageous to Cast a Negative Vote?" *Lecture Notes in Economics and Mathematical Systems (Mathematical Economics and Game Theory: Essays in*

6.2.   Preview of the Analysis

It has been proposed by George A. W. Boehm that voters in an election be allowed either to cast a vote for or a vote against one candidate, but not both.[2] A candidate's "negative" votes would be subtracted from his "positive" votes to determine his *net vote,* and the candidate with the highest net vote would win.

Boehm argues that the introduction of negative votes in United States presidential elections would force the candidates to appeal to the voters with positive programs, not just try to be the least unpopular candidate in the race. To prevent a candidate from winning who had little popular appeal, but who otherwise might be preferred because he attracted few negative votes, Boehm suggests that a threshold (say, at least 10 percent of the total votes cast) be set that a winning candidate's net vote would have to exceed for him to be elected.

In this chapter, I shall show that there is never any incentive for a voter to cast a negative vote in a two-candidate race, except to register his dissatisfaction with one of the candidates or possibly prevent the leading candidate from obtaining the number of net votes required to be elected (if there is a minimum threshold that must be met). Because a voter can always bring about the same outcome with a positive vote as with a negative vote in a two-candidate race without a minimum threshold, negative votes are superfluous in such a contest.

To be sure, the psychological impact of negative votes may be considerable, especially in the case where the net vote of

---

Honor of Oskar Morgenstern, ed. R. Henn and O. Moeschlin), vol. 141 (Berlin: Springer-Verlag, 1977), pp. 564–72; Brams, *Comparison of Voting Systems,* Instructional Module (Washington, D.C.: American Political Science Association, 1978), which also includes exercises and their solutions; and Brams and Peter C. Fishburn, "Approval Voting," *American Political Science Review* 72, no. 3 (September, 1978). Permission to adapt material from these articles is gratefully acknowledged.

2. George A. W. Boehm, "One Fervent Vote against Wintergreen" (mimeographed, 1976).

the "winner" is negative. However, if one's reason for casting negative votes is to ensure or prevent the election of a candidate, then a negative vote against a candidate always has the same effect on the outcome as a positive vote for the other candidate if there is no minimum threshold.

In three-candidate races, by contrast, negative votes may be uniquely advantageous: a voter can definitely do better, in some circumstances, by casting a negative vote against a candidate rather than a positive vote for either of the other two candidates. This fact will be demonstrated both in the case in which the candidate with a plurality wins and the case in which there is a runoff election between the top two vote-getters in the plurality contest if no candidate wins a majority of votes.

In races with more than three candidates, some of the advantages of negative voting break down, and it is useful to ask whether the *idea* of negative voting can be incorporated in a voting scheme that allows for the fuller expression of voter preferences. Indeed, a simple generalization of the idea of negative voting that allows a voter to cast "approval" votes for one *or more* candidates is equivalent to a negative voting strategy in specific cases.

More generally, however, approval voting opens up possible voting strategies for a voter that a single positive or a single negative vote does not permit. Not only may it lead to more desirable strategy choices for individual voters but it may also produce more desirable outcomes for a plurality or majority of voters than could be achieved by restricting voters to a single positive or single negative vote. According to criteria that I shall set forth later, several general results for approval voting will be established that allow comparisons with other systems that permit voters to vote for no more than one, no more than two, . . . , candidates, without ranking them according to their preferences.

The possible effects of poll announcements on the voting behavior of individuals, and on election outcomes, will then be discussed and illustrated for an actual election. Finally, an application of the theoretical analysis to voting in the 1968 multicandidate presidential election in the United States will be presented.

6.3. Negative Voting in Two-Candidate Contests

To fix ideas, first consider the effect of negative voting in a two-candidate contest. Assume that X and Y are two candidates running for office, and every voter has a preference scale defined over these candidates. He may prefer X to Y, which I indicate by the scale (X, Y), Y to X, which I indicate by the scale (Y, X), or be indifferent between the two candidates, which I indicate by the scale $(X\text{-}Y)$.

Given negative voting, every voter has four *strategies*: (1) vote for X (X); (2) vote against X ($\bar{X}$); (3) vote for Y (Y); (4) vote against Y ($\bar{Y}$). (I ignore the strategy of abstaining, because it cannot change the outcome of voting by all other voters, which is the focus of the subsequent analysis.) A voter is *rational* if he chooses a strategy that is *undominated*: there is no other strategy that is as good in all contingencies and better in at least one contingency.

"Contingencies" are the *states of nature* that can arise from the voting of all the *other* voters. If there are n voters, there are 4^{n-1} states of nature since the $n - 1$ other voters can each choose one of their four possible strategies.

However, many of these states of nature lead to the same *result*, which I define to be the ordered pair (x, y), where x is the net vote cast for X and y is the net vote cast for Y by the $n - 1$ other voters. In fact, to determine the undominated strategies of a voter, only a relatively few results—those in which the vote of a single voter can make a difference in the outcome—must be examined.

A voter's vote can make a difference if and only if it makes or breaks a tie. In a two-candidate race, a voter can break a tie (of the $n - 1$ other voters) if the result is $x = y$, he can make a tie if $x = y - 1$ or $y = x - 1$. For all other results (i.e., where $|x - y| > 1$), a voter's vote would not change the *outcome*, which I define to be the candidate—or candidates, in the case of a tie—who receives the larger net vote and is thereby elected.

If there is a tie, presumably one candidate will eventually be selected, perhaps by some random device. In evaluating this outcome, I assume that a voter allows for the possibility that either candidate will eventually be selected. Thus, if his preference scale is (X, Y), it follows that he will rank the tied outcome X/Y "in the middle"—$(X, X/Y, Y)$; if his preference scale is $(X\text{-}Y)$, then $(X\text{-}X/Y\text{-}Y)$ since indifference between X and Y implies indifference among X, X/Y, and Y.

I have already indicated that in two-candidate contests there are only three results of voting by the $n - 1$ other voters in which a voter's vote is decisive: $x = y$; $x = y - 1$; $y = x - 1$. Since the strategy a voter chooses cannot change the outcome associated with any other result, these are the only results relevant to the determination of undominated strategies. The outcomes generated by a voter's four strategies for these results in a two-candidate contest are shown in table 6.1.

Notice that the outcomes associated with strategy $\bar{X}$ are exactly the same as those associated with strategy Y, and the outcomes associated with strategy $\bar{Y}$ are exactly the same as those associated with strategy X, for all relevant results. Since a voter who casts a negative vote against one candidate can always do as well by casting a positive vote for the other candidate, both these strategies are undominated and a negative vote is not uniquely advantageous in a two-candidate contest.

Table 6.1
Outcomes in Two-Candidate Contest
with Negative Voting

Strategies of voter	Relevant results for $n - 1$ other voters		
	$n - 1$ even	$n - 1$ odd	
	$x = y$	$x = y - 1$	$y = x - 1$
X	X	X/Y	X
$\bar{X}$	Y	Y	X/Y
Y	Y	Y	X/Y
$\bar{Y}$	X	X/Y	X

In section 6.4 I shall show that in a three-candidate contest among X, Y, and Z, there is one situation in a plurality election in which casting a negative vote is definitely preferable to casting a positive vote. Even when the plurality election is followed by a runoff election between the top two vote-getters, negative voting may still be advantageous. But first I analyze the case without a runoff.

6.4. Negative Voting in Three-Candidate Contests without a Runoff

Consider three-candidate contests in which the candidate with the most votes wins (plurality elections). If there is no single plurality winner, a voter evaluates tied outcomes in the manner described earlier.

In table 6.2 outcomes associated with the sixteen relevant results and six strategies of each voter are shown for a plurality election. Numerical examples are also given in table 6.2 for the subsets of relevant results that are the same except for the order in which x, y, and z are listed in the triple (x, y, z).

Thus, for example, there are three relevant results in which two candidates are tied with the same number of votes and the third candidate has one more vote than the other two. These results are indicated in the first three columns of table 6.2: Z has the extra vote in column 1, Y in column 2, and X in column 3. The numerical example given above these three columns in table 6.2, $(x, y, z) = (0, 0, 1)$, illustrates the case in which Z has the extra vote.

In table 6.3 the undominated strategies of a voter are given for four different preference scales. The four preference scales given in table 6.3 include all preference scales indistinguishable except for order. Thus, while the three outcomes X, Y, and Z can be permuted in six different ways $(3! = 3 \cdot 2 \cdot 1 = 6)$, the five permutations different from (X, Y, Z) are indistinguishable except for order. Similarly, there are two preference scales indistinguishable from $(X, Y\text{-}Z)$ except for order (either Y or Z is ranked first), and two indistinguishable from $(X\text{-}Y, Z)$ except for order (either X or Y is ranked last). If the order in which indifference is indicated is irrelevant, indif-

Table 6.2
Outcomes in Three-Candidate Contest with Negative Voting

Relevant results (and examples) for $n-1$ other voters

Strategies of voter	$(x, y, z) = (0, 0, 1)$			$(x, y, z) = (1, 1, 0)$			$(x, y, z) = (0, 0, -2)$			$(x, y, z) = (2, 1, 0)$						$(x, y, z) = (0, 0, 0)$
	1	2	3	4	5	6	7	8	9	10	11	12	13	14	15	16
	x $=y$ $=z-1$	x $=z$ $=y-1$	y $=z$ $=x-1$	$x-1$ $=y-1$ $=z$	$x-1$ $=z-1$ $=y$	$y-1$ $=z-1$ $=x$	$x-1$ $=y-1$ $>z$	$x-1$ $=z-1$ $>y$	$y-1$ $=z-1$ $>x$	$x-1$ $=y$ $>z$	$x-1$ $=z$ $>y$	$y-1$ $=x$ $>z$	$y-1$ $=z$ $>x$	$z-1$ $=x$ $>y$	$z-1$ $=y$ $>x$	x $=y$ $=z$
X	X/Z	X/Y	X	X	X	X/Y/Z	X	X	X	X	X	X/Y	Y	X/Z	Z	X
$\overline{X}$	Z	Y	X/Y/Z	X	Z	Y/Z	Y	Z	Y/Z	X/Y	X/Z	Y	Y	Z	Z	Y/Z
Y	Y/Z	Y	X/Y	Y	X/Y/Z	Y	Y	X/Z	Y	X/Y	X	Y	Y	Z	Y/Z	Y
$\overline{Y}$	Z	X/Y/Z	X	X/Y/Z	X/Z	Z	X	X/Z	Z	X	X	X/Y	Y/Z	Z	Z	X/Z
Z	Z	Y/Z	X/Z	X/Y	Z	Z	X/Y	Z	Z	X	X/Z	Y	Y/Z	Z	Z	Z
$\overline{Z}$	X/Y/Z	Y	X	X/Y	X	Y	X/Y	Z	Y	X	X	Y	Y	X/Z	Y/Z	X/Y

Table 6.3
Undominated (Dominant) Strategies for Four Preference
Scales with Negative Voting

Preference scales	Undominated (dominant) strategies
(X, Y, Z)	$X, \bar{Z}$
$(X, Y\text{-}Z)$	(X)
$(X\text{-}Y, Z)$	$(\bar{Z})$
$(X\text{-}Y\text{-}Z)$	$X, \bar{X}, Y, \bar{Y}, Z, \bar{Z}$

ference among the three outcomes is obviously given by one scale: $(X\text{-}Y\text{-}Z)$.

In the subsequent analysis, I assume that the preference relation (P) and indifference relation (I) that underlie the scales of individual voters are *transitive*: if A, B, and C are any three candidates, $A \underline{P} B$ and $B \underline{P} C$ implies $A \underline{P} C$; and $A \underline{I} B$ and $B \underline{I} C$ implies $A \underline{I} C$. This assumption ensures that for a voter with preference scale (X, Y, Z) or $(X\text{-}Y\text{-}Z)$, for example, it is always true that (X, Z) in the case of the former, $(X\text{-}Z)$ in the case of the latter.

For two of the four preference scales in table 6.3, $(X, Y\text{-}Z)$ and $(X\text{-}Y, Z)$, there is only one undominated strategy of a voter. A unique undominated strategy of a voter is necessarily *dominant*—as good as, and in at least one contingency better than, any other strategy—which means it is an unequivocally best choice, whatever result shown in table 6.2 occurs.

This can be verified for a voter with preference scale $(X, Y\text{-}Z)$. To do so, the outcomes associated with his dominant strategy X must be compared with the outcomes associated with his five other strategies for the sixteen relevant results. To begin with, note that the outcomes associated with strategy X are at least as good as the outcomes associated with his five other strategies. Thus, for example, if strategy X does not yield his first choice, X, as an outcome, neither do his other strategies.

Is strategy X better than every other strategy in at least one contingency? For result 5, it yields X, which is a better outcome for our voter than strategies $\bar{X}$, Y, $\bar{Y}$, and Z—which all can lead to nonpreferred outcomes Y or Z—offer. But strategy X is also better than strategy $\bar{Z}$, because even though it leads to the same outcome as X for relevant result 5, X leads to a better outcome than $\bar{Z}$ for relevant result 6 ($X/Y/Z$ versus Y). In this contingency, strategy X allows for the possibility that outcome X will be chosen, but strategy $\bar{Z}$ always ensures that nonpreferred outcome Y will be chosen. Thus, I have shown that X is a dominant strategy for a voter with preference scale $(X, Y\text{-}Z)$: it leads to outcomes at least as good as, and sometimes better than, any other strategy.

The fact that $\bar{Z}$ is dominant when the preference scale of a voter is $(X\text{-}Y, Z)$ demonstrates that a negative vote is uniquely advantageous in this situation. While it leads to no better an outcome than strategy X or strategy Y for thirteen of the sixteen relevant results, it leads to a definitely superior outcome for three results (better than X for results 6, 9, and 15; better than Y for results 5, 8, and 14). We say that $\bar{Z}$ dominates X and Y (as well as all other strategies) for a voter with preference scale $(X\text{-}Y, Z)$.

In words, the preference scale $(X\text{-}Y, Z)$ of a voter says that he is indifferent between two candidates (X and Y) but definitely prefers them to the third candidate (Z). In such a situation, it is always rational for a voter to cast a negative vote against Z rather than a positive vote for either of the two candidates, X and Y, that he prefers.

6.5. *Negative Voting in Three-Candidate Contests with a Runoff*

What if the election is not decided in the three-candidate plurality contest but in a runoff between the top two vote-getters? To compare negative voting in a single plurality contest with voting in a plurality contest followed by a runoff, assume for now that—consistent with most present-day procedures—a voter cannot cast a negative vote in the plurality contest. Then the undominated (dominant) strategies for the four preference scales, given earlier in table 6.3, are shown in table 6.4. Comparing undominated and dominant strategies in the two tables, it is clear that when a voter's strategy of voting against his last choice ($\bar{Z}$) is unavailable, it

Table 6.4
Undominated (Dominant) Strategies for Four Preference
Scales without Negative Voting

Preference scales	Undominated (dominant) strategies
(X, Y, Z)	X, Y
$(X, Y\text{-}Z)$	(X)
$(X\text{-}Y, Z)$	X, Y
$(X\text{-}Y\text{-}Z)$	X, Y, Z

may be advantageous for him to vote for his second choice [Y if his preference scale is (X, Y, Z)], or either one of his first choices [X or Y if his preference scale is $(X\text{-}Y, Z)$].

Can a voter's choice of these apparently inferior strategies, when he is restricted to casting only a positive vote, be rectified in a runoff? When the runoff occurs if and only if no candidate in the plurality election receives a majority of votes—as is common in many jurisdictions—the answer is not necessarily. In other words, the restriction of voters to a single positive vote may again force them to choose inferior strategies—compared with strategies available under negative voting—even when a runoff is permitted.

An example will help to clarify this point. Assume there are five voters, whose preference scales are as follows: (1) $(X, Y\text{-}Z)$; (2) $(X, Y\text{-}Z)$; (3) $(Y, X\text{-}Z)$; (4) $(Y, X\text{-}Z)$; (5) (X, Y, Z). From table 6.4 we know that voters 1 and 2 and voters 3 and 4 have dominant strategies: vote for X and vote for Y, respectively. Now, if voters are restricted to a single positive vote in the plurality election, voter 5 has two undominated strategies (given that he has no information about the preference scales of the other voters and therefore cannot predict how they will vote): vote for X or vote for Y (see table 6.4). Clearly, strategy X would be preferable if X and Y were tied and Z were out of the running; on the other hand, strategy Y would be preferable if Y and Z were tied and X were out of the running.

Regardless of which undominated strategy voter 5 chooses, either X or Y will receive a majority of votes and there will be no runoff. If voter 5 chooses strategy Y, however, and Y

thereby obtains a majority of votes, three of the five voters (1, 2, and 5) will be dissatisfied. For X is the so-called *Condorcet winner*—the candidate preferred by a majority of voters in pairwise contests between each of the other candidates, Y and Z (see section 1.8 for an example in which there is no alternative that is a Condorcet winner). In a pairwise contest between X and Y, X would be preferred by voters 1, 2, and 5; similarly, these voters would also prefer X to Z in a pairwise contest between those two candidates. Yet, if all voters but voter 5 choose their dominant strategies, and voter 5 chooses his undominated strategy Y, Y will defeat the Condorcet winner X.

Would negative voting have prevented the choice of Y in a plurality election with a runoff if there were no majority winner (of net votes)? The answer is yes, because, whichever of his undominated strategies voter 5 chose in the plurality election—X or $\bar{Z}$ (see table 6.3)—he would have prevented the election of Y. If he had voted for X, X would have defeated Y by three votes to two, and there would have been no runoff. If he had voted against Z, the plurality contest would then have resulted in a two-to-two tie between X and Y (with Z's net vote being -1), and X would have won in the runoff since voter 5 prefers him to Y.

Clearly, allowing for a runoff in a plurality contest restricted to positive voting does not necessarily recapture the advantages of negative voting—specifically in this example, lead to the election of the Condorcet winner. Permitting negative voting, on the other hand, does lead to the election of the Condorcet winner, at least in this example, if there is a runoff between the top two vote-getters when neither finalist receives a majority of votes. In addition, the example suggests that if there is a Condorcet winner, negative voting is better able to find him, though I postpone a further discussion of this question until a generalization of negative voting is offered in section 6.6.

In summary, although negative voting offers no unique advantage to a voter in two-candidate contests, negative votes in a plurality contest among three candidates—with or without a runoff between the top two—may be uniquely advantageous for a voter, depending on his preference scale. In addition, negative voting can ensure the selection of a Condorcet winner when a runoff does not.

As I shall show in section 6.6, however, the apparent advantages of negative voting do not carry through to plurality contests with more than three candidates. Yet, a simple generalization of negative voting in more populous contests can prevent the most undesirable outcomes from occurring, given voters can make a dichotomous division of the candidates. In particular, if all voters can divide the candidates into two categories—"acceptable" and "unacceptable"—the candidate who is acceptable to the most voters will be elected when the voters choose their dominant strategies. Such strategies, it will be proved in section 6.6, always exist.

6.6. Advantages of Approval Voting

Consider a four-candidate contest among the set of candidates $\{W, X, Y, Z\}$. If a voter has preference scale $(W\text{-}X, Y\text{-}Z)$, and he can cast either one positive or one negative vote, whom should he vote for or vote against?

It is not necessary to construct a table of relevant results for four-candidate plurality contests to show that this voter has four undominated strategies: cast a positive vote for W or X (strategies W and X) or cast a negative vote against Y or Z (strategies $\bar{Y}$ and $\bar{Z}$). Clearly, if the result of voting by the $n - 1$ other voters is $(0, 0, 0, 0)$, casting a positive vote for either W or for X are the only strategies that ensure the election of a preferred candidate (W or X). If the results are either $(1, 0, 1, 0)$ or $(0, 1, 1, 0)$, casting a negative vote against Y is the only strategy that ensures the election of a preferred candidate in both contingencies; similarly, if the results are $(1, 0, 0, 1)$ or $(0, 1, 0, 1)$, casting a negative vote against Z is the only strategy that ensures the election of a preferred candidate in both contingencies. In both the latter cases, negative votes eliminate a nonpreferred candidate and thereby make a preferred candidate the winner.

But in these examples there is a strategy, if a voter can cast more than one positive vote, that is as good as, and for at least one relevant result better than, any of the four "best" (undominated) strategies described above. For a voter with preference scale $(W\text{-}X, Y\text{-}Z)$, this strategy is to cast two positive votes, one for W and one for X.

For the two results $(1, 0, 1, 1)$ and $(0, 1, 1, 1)$, this strategy ensures the election of one of one's more-preferred candidates, whereas none of the four undominated strategies under negative voting can offer this assurance for both results. In the case of all other results—including those described previously for which the four undominated negative voting strategies are best—casting two positive votes for W and X is a strategy that cannot be improved upon.

Thus, the strategy of casting two positive or "approval" votes for W and X is as good as, and in at least one contingency better than, any of the four undominated strategies described earlier of casting a single positive or a single negative vote. Hence, it dominates these four strategies. If there are m candidates, voting that allows a voter to cast m or fewer positive or approval votes—but no more than one vote for each candidate—is called *approval voting*.

Negative voting does not yield as good a set of outcomes for all relevant results as approval voting in this example because it restricts a voter to only one positive or one negative vote. If there are m candidates, this means that a voter can cast a positive vote in m ways, and a negative vote in m ways, giving him a total of $2m$ strategies. (If the abstention strategy of casting no positive votes for all candidates, or the equivalent strategy of casting no negative votes for all candidates, is also included, a voter has $2m + 1$ strategies.)

By contrast, under approval voting, a voter can cast either an approval vote or no vote for each of the m candidates, giving him 2^m voting strategies. (Since, however, the abstention strategy of casting no approval votes is equivalent to the strategy of casting m approval votes for all the candidates, a voter has $2^m - 1$ nonequivalent strategies.) Because $2^m - 1 > 2m + 1$ if $m > 3$, approval voting in general allows a voter more voting strategies in multicandidate races.

When $m = 3$, $2^m - 1 = 2m + 1 = 7$, and negative voting yields the same outcomes as approval voting. The reason is that, eliminating the abstention strategy, six strategies remain under both types of voting. Clearly, the three positive voting strategies in which one positive vote is cast for one of the three candidates are also approval strategies, and the three negative voting strategies in which one vote is cast against one of the three candidates are equivalent to approval strategies in which two positive votes are cast for the other two candidates. Thus, when there are three candidates, the strategies and outcomes under negative voting and approval voting are equivalent.

It might be noted that "disapproval" voting (negative voting for more than one candidate) is in general equivalent to approval voting, given that the candidate with the fewest negative votes wins. The reason is evident: a voter who casts positive votes under approval voting for one subset of candidates would cast negative votes for the complementary subset under disapproval voting. Since both forms of voting change the difference in the vote between the approved and disapproved candidates by one vote, they both yield the same outcomes.

It may be feared that since the number of approval voting strategies increases exponentially with the number of candidates, approval voting may well overwhelm voters with a wealth of options. For example, if there are as few as four candidates, there are $2^4 - 1 = 15$ approval voting strategies. However, if the salient consideration for a voter with a given preference scale is the number of these voting strategies that are undominated or dominant, then this number is not necessarily greater under approval voting than under the other forms of voting considered here.

To illustrate this fact, define a strategy for a voter with a given preference scale to be *admissible* if and only if it is either undominated or dominant. Then the number of admissible voting strategies for plurality voting (no runoff), negative voting, and approval voting among a set of four candidates $\{W, X, Y, Z\}$ are shown in table 6.5 for all distinct preference scales (except that indicating indifference among all candidates). Note that three scales are *dichotomous* (divide candi-

Table 6.5
Numbers of Admissible Voting Strategies for Three
Voting Systems with Four Candidates

		Number of admissible strategies		
		---	---	---
Preference scale		Approval voting	Negative voting	Plurality voting
Dichotomous:	$(W, X\text{-}Y\text{-}Z)$	1	1	1
	$(W\text{-}X\text{-}Y, Z)$	1	1	3
	$(W\text{-}X, Y\text{-}Z)$	1	4	2
Trichotomous:	$(W\text{-}X, Y, Z)$	2	4	3
	$(W, X, Y\text{-}Z)$	2	4	2
	$(W, X\text{-}Y, Z)$	4	2	3
Multichotomous:	(W, X, Y, Z)	4	4	3

dates into two subsets, among whose members a voter is indifferent), three are *trichotomous* (divide candidates into three subsets), and one is *multichotomous* (divide candidates into more than three subsets).

It is apparent from table 6.5 that approval voting generally offers fewer admissible strategies to a voter than the other voting systems when a voter's preference scale is dichotomous. When a voter's preference scale is trichotomous, approval voting offers more admissible strategies than the other two systems for one preference scale, $(W, X\text{-}Y, Z)$. In the case of the single multichotomous scale, approval voting and negative voting offer a voter the same number of admissible strategies. Thus, although approval voting may offer more admissible strategies than the other systems, as when a voter's preference scale is $(W, X\text{-}Y, Z)$, it may also offer fewer admissible strategies than the others, as when a voter's preference scale is dichotomous. Hence, it is not generally true that approval voting will overwhelm voters with a wealth of *viable* options.[3]

3. Brams and Fishburn, "Approval Voting"; for more details, see Peter C. Fishburn, "A Strategic Analysis of Nonranked Voting Systems," *SIAM Journal on Applied Mathematics* (forthcoming, 1978).

6.7. General Results for Approval Voting

The first general results I shall establish for approval voting relate to optimal strategies.

THEOREM 6.1. If a voter has dichotomous preferences, he has a dominant strategy under approval voting: vote for all members of his preferred subset. This strategy is called his *approval strategy*.

Proof. Consider a strategy (N) in which a voter does *not* vote for all members of his preferred subset. Then this strategy is dominated by a voter's approval strategy (A), because for at least one result of voting by the $n - 1$ other voters, A would give a preferred candidate who did not receive a vote under N more votes than any other candidate and hence make him the winner. For results in which A would not make this preferred candidate the winner, it would either create a tie between him and another winning candidate or have no effect on the outcome. Thus, a voter's approval strategy cannot prevent the choice of another candidate (if a tie is created or the outcome is unaffected), but it will ensure the choice of a preferred candidate for at least one result. Hence, this strategy dominates a strategy of not voting for all members of one's preferred subset.

Consider a strategy (M) in which a voter votes for all members of his preferred subset *plus* one or more candidates who are members of his nonpreferred subset. Then this strategy is dominated by his approval strategy, because for at least one result of voting by the $n - 1$ other voters, M would give a nonpreferred candidate more votes than any other candidate and hence make him the winner. For results in which M would not make this nonpreferred candidate the winner, it would either create a tie between him and another winning candidate or have no effect on the outcome. Thus, a voter's approval strategy cannot prevent the choice of another candidate (if a tie is created or the outcome is unaffected), but it will prevent the choice of a nonpreferred candidate for at least one result. Hence, this strategy dominates a strategy of voting for all members of one's preferred subset plus one or more candidates who are members of one's nonpreferred subset.

By a similar argument, one can show that a voter's approval strategy dominates his strategy of voting for some (but not all) members of his preferred subset and some (but not all) members of his nonpreferred subset. Since this strategy dominates all other voting strategies under approval voting, it is a dominant strategy.

Theorem 6.2 reverses the implication of Theorem 6.1.

THEOREM 6.2. If a voter has a dominant strategy under approval voting, his preferences are dichotomous.

Proof. The proof is by contradiction. Assume that a voter's preferences are *not* dichotomous. Then there are two possibilities:

1. He is indifferent among all the candidates, in which case he does not have a dominant strategy since all his strategies are undominated.
2. He can divide the set of candidates into more than two disjoint subsets—with at least one member— such that the following preference ordering holds: each member of a first subset, among whom the voter is indifferent, is preferred to each member of a second subset; each member of the second subset, among whom the voter is indifferent, is preferred to each member of a third subset; and so on.

In fact, for possibility 2, the division into subsets can be read off directly from a voter's preference scale. The first subset contains the candidate(s) that the voter most prefers but among whom he is indifferent; the second subset contains the candidate(s) the voter next most prefers but among whom he is indifferent; and so on.

By assumption, there are at least three nonempty disjoint subsets into which the candidates can be divided for possibility 2. Without loss of generality, assume that the voter's preferences are trichotomous, and let candidates X, Y, and Z be the only members of the first, second, and third subsets, respectively. For a voter with preference scale (X, Y, Z), consider the following results (x, y, z) of voting by the $n - 1$ other voters: (1) $(2, 2, 0)$; (2) $(0, 2, 2)$. For result 1, a voter has no better strategy than to vote for X, thereby making his most preferred candidate the winner; for result 2, a voter has no better strategy than to vote for Y, or for X and Y, thereby making his next most preferred candidate the winner. Now, for a strategy of a voter with preference scale (X, Y, Z) to be dominant, he *must* vote for Y in the case of result 2, but he *cannot* vote for Y in the case of result 1, so there is a contradiction.

Thus, no strategy exists that is best for a voter for all results of voting by the other voters. Hence, a voter does not have a dominant strategy if his preferences are not dichotomous. Consequently, only if a voter has dichotomous preferences will he have a dominant strategy under approval voting.

Taken together, Theorems 6.1 and 6.2 establish the logical equivalence between dichotomous preferences and the existence of a dominant strategy under approval voting. Theorem 6.1 also says what this strategy is for a voter with dichotomous preferences—vote for all members of his preferred subset.

To be sure, not all voters may have dichotomous preferences. Assume, however, instead of asking voters to rank candidates, they are asked simply to distinguish acceptable from unacceptable candidates—and not to discriminate among candidates within these two classes. If this division of candidates into two classes meets the conditions of Theorem 6.1—that is, if all voters are truly indifferent among members of each class, however they make the division—they will have dominant strategies under approval voting: their approval strategies of voting only for the candidates they deem acceptable.

I shall next characterize the nature of outcomes under approval voting, given that all voters can divide the set of candidates into acceptable and unacceptable classes, among whose members each voter is indifferent. (If all voters make only a two-way division, of course, they have dichotomous preferences.)

> THEOREM 6.3.   If all voters have dichotomous prefer-
> ences, and they choose their approval strategies, a candi-
> date wins under approval voting if and only if he is a
> Concorcet winner.
> *Proof.*   By definition, a winning candidate under ap-
> proval voting is judged acceptable by more voters than
> any other candidate. Given that voters who consider each
> candidate acceptable in a plurality election do not change
> their judgment in a pairwise contest, a winning candidate
> in the plurality election will remain a winner in each
> pairwise contest, and vice versa.

Thus, unlike many other voting procedures—under which a winning candidate may not be a Condorcet winner—approval voting always produces a Condorcet winner, given that voters only distinguish between acceptable and unacceptable candidates (i.e., they have dichotomous preferences). Of course, a winning candidate under approval voting—even when voters are able to divide the candidates into acceptable and unacceptable classes and choose their dominant strategies—may not be acceptable to a majority of voters. The most that can be said of the winning candidate in such a situation is that (1) he will be acceptable to more voters than any other candidate; and (2) in a pairwise contest with every other candidate, he will be acceptable to a majority of voters who consider either one or both candidates of the pair acceptable.

Approval voting has other desirable properties if all voters have dichotomous preferences. To describe these, first some definitions are necessary. A voting *strategy* is *sincere* if and only if, whenever it includes voting for some candidate, it also includes voting for all candidates preferred to him. A voting *system* is *sincere* for a set of voters if and only if no voter in the set has an admissible strategy that is insincere.

THEOREM 6.4. If all voters have *dichotomous* preferences, every system is sincere; if some voters have *trichotomous* preferences but none multichotomous preferences, approval voting is uniquely sincere; if some voters have *multichotomous* preferences, no voting system is sincere.

The proof of this theorem, which applies to all voting systems in which a voter cannot rank candidates but can only vote for one candidate, one or two candidates, . . . , m or fewer candidates, is beyond the scope of this book and is given elsewhere.[4] I can, however, illustrate it by referring to the results for the three nonranked voting systems given in table 6.5.

It can be verified by the reader that (1) for the three dichotomous preference scales given in table 6.5, admissible strategies under approval voting, negative voting, and single plurality are all sincere; (2) for the three trichotomous scales, only the admissible strategies under approval voting are all sincere. To illustrate the third part of Theorem 6.4, consider the four admissible approval voting strategies for the multichotomous scale: vote for (1) $\{W\}$; (2) $\{W, X\}$; (3) $\{W, Y\}$; (4) $\{W, X, Y\}$. Clearly, (3) is not sincere since it does not include voting for X, who is preferred to Y.

To show when it would be advantageous for a voter to choose his insincere admissible strategy, $\{W, Y\}$, assume that he thinks that the result of voting by the other voters might be either (1) (1, 1, 0, 0), or (2) (0, 0, 1, 1). Then his only admissible strategy that simultaneously ensures the election of W in the case of (1), and the election of Y (and the defeat of Z) in the case of (2), is $\{W, Y\}$.

The problem with such an insincere strategy is that if the result of voting by the other voters is, say, (0, 1, 1, 1), the

4. Brams and Fishburn, "Approval Voting."

voter's next worst choice, Y, is elected. On the other hand, if the voter had chosen his sincere admissible strategy $\{W, X, Y\}$, the voter's next best choice, X, would have been elected. Thus, the voter has reason to regret his insincerity.

This cannot happen, however, if the voting system is sincere and voters choose admissible strategies. Although a voter may not obtain his best choice under such a system, after the election he cannot regret having failed to vote for a candidate (X in the previous example) preferred to the lowest-ranked candidate he voted for (Y in the previous example).

There is still a stronger criterion than sincerity that may be used to characterize voting systems. A voting system is *strategyproof* for a set of voters if and only if every voter in the set has exactly one strategy that is admissible (in which case this strategy must be sincere).

THEOREM 6.5. If all voters have *dichotomous* preferences, approval voting is uniquely strategyproof; if some voters have *trichotomous* or *multichotomous* preferences, no voting system is strategyproof.

Like Theorem 6.4, the proof of Theorem 6.5 is beyond the scope of this book and is given elsewhere.[5] From table 6.5, however, it can readily be ascertained that for the four-candidate case and the three voting systems under consideration, (1) approval voting is the only system in which a voter has just one admissible strategy for all dichotomous preferences—namely, his approval strategy; (2) no system, including approval voting, limits a voter to just one admissible (sincere) strategy when preferences are trichotomous or multichotomous.

Like sincerity, strategyproofness seems a desirable property of a voting system. If a voter has only one admissible strategy,

5. Brams and Fishburn, "Approval Voting." Other sets of properties that approval voting uniquely satisfies are delineated in different axiomatizations of approval voting in Peter C. Fishburn, "Symmetric and Consistent Aggregation with Dichotomous Voting," in *Aggregation and Revelation of Preferences*, ed. J.-J. Laffont (Amsterdam: North-Holland, forthcoming, 1978); and Fishburn, "Axioms for Approval Voting" (mimeographed, Pennsylvania State University, 1977).

he will never have an incentive to deviate from it for strategic reasons even if he knows the result of voting by all the other voters.

Sincerity, on the other hand, does not imply such stability but rather says that whatever admissible strategy a voter chooses, he will vote for all candidates above the lowest-ranked candidate that his admissible strategy includes. Thus, if a candidate that a sincere voter votes for wins, the sincere voter can rest assured that he could not have brought about the election of a more preferred candidate by choosing a different admissible strategy.

A voting system that encourages sincere voting, it seems, would probably produce higher voter turnout. By allowing voters to tune their preferences more finely, and by forcing them to make insincere choices for strategic reasons less often, approval voting may well stimulate more voters to express themselves at the polls and enhance their attitudes toward the system.

Taken together, Theorems 6.4 and 6.5 establish that approval voting is the most sincere and strategyproof of all systems in which a voter can vote for, but not rank, candidates. Yet, the limitations of these and the previous results should not be forgotten; strategyproofness, as well as the existence of dominant strategies (Theorems 6.1 and 6.2)—which is closely related—depends entirely on the preferences of all voters being dichotomous. So does the assured selection of a Condorcet winner under approval voting (Theorem 6.3). Only the weaker criterion of sincerity extends to trichotomous preferences under approval voting; for multichotomous preferences, there seem to be no significant desiderata that distinguish approval voting strategies and outcomes from those that other nonranked voting systems offer the voter.

Despite the restriction of the foregoing positive results to dichotomous and trichotomous preferences, multicandidate races in which voters make only two- or three-way preference divisions of the candidates seem quite common. I shall say more about the relationship of these theoretical results to empirical data in section 6.9, but first some possible effects of poll announcements on voting strategies and outcomes will be assessed.

6.8.   *The Possible Confounding Effects of a Poll*

Theorem 6.3 demonstrates that if not all voters have dichotomous preferences, a candidate who is not the Condorcet winner (if one exists) may be elected under approval voting.[6] As an example, consider an election among a set of four candidates $\{W, X, Y, Z\}$, where the electorate consists of four voters whose preference scales are as follows: (1) (Y, W, X, Z); (2) (Y, W, X, Z); (3) (Y, X, W, Z); (4) (Z, X, W, Y). Assume that each voter judges the three candidates he ranks highest to be "acceptable," his last choice "unacceptable." Then, under approval voting, W and X will each receive 4 votes, Y 3 votes, and Z 1 vote. Yet, Y is the Condorcet winner if the complete preference scales of the voters are taken into account, though he loses to both W and X under approval voting.

Curiously, if a pollster announced these results before the election, and voters changed their votes to distinguish between the two likely winners, W and X, each voter would have an incentive to divide acceptable and unacceptable candidates as follows (indicated by a slash): (1) $(Y, W \ / X, Z)$; (2) $(Y, W \ / X, Z)$; (3) $(Y, X \ / W, Z)$; (4) $(Z, X \ / W, Y)$. By voting only for his favorite candidate of the two, either W or X, each voter would make his vote "count" for one of the likely winners (but not the other).

Now the results of the election would be that W and X would each receive 2 votes, Y 3 votes, and Z 1 vote, so Y, the Condorcet winner, would be elected. However, if the preferences of voters 3 and 4 were (Y, W, X, Z) and (Z, W, X, Y), respectively, W would defeat the Condorcet winner Y by 4 votes to 3 after the results of the poll were announced.

So far I have shown by examples that if the preferences of voters are not dichotomous, a Condorcet winner may not be

---

6. Much of the material in this section was suggested to me by Philip D. Straffin Jr.

elected under approval voting. Neither is a Condorcet winner guaranteed election by a poll that induces voters to adjust their voting strategies to distinguish between the top two candidates in the poll. However, one general result that relates Condorcet winners and polls can be proved.

THEOREM 6.6.   If one of the top two candidates indicated by a poll is a Condorcet winner, this candidate will always defeat the other top candidate if voters adjust their voting strategies after the poll.

Proof.   By assumption, voters adjust their strategies to distinguish between the top two candidates. But this is the same distinction they would make in a pairwise contest between these two candidates, so the Condorcet winner (who by definition defeats every other candidate in a pairwise contest) will defeat the other top candidate after the poll announcement.

Note that the sufficient condition for this theorem—that the Condorcet winner be one of the top two candidates indicated by the poll—was not met by the earlier examples. That this condition is not necessary is shown by the previous example in which the Condorcet winner is elected after the poll announcement, though he is not one of the top two candidates in the poll.

The restriction of voters today to only one vote in plurality elections probably leads to the election of non-Condorcet winners more frequently than would approval voting. To see how approval voting might have counteracted this problem in a real-life case—though not a presidential election—consider the 1970 New York race for the United States Senate among James R. Buckley, Charles E. Goodell, and Richard L. Ottinger. Although the conservative candidate, Buckley, won this election, probably a majority of voters would have preferred either of the more liberal candidates—Goodell or Ottinger—who collectively got 61 percent of the vote to Buckley's 39 percent.[7]

7. For reasons why voters support third-party candidates under plurality

Suppose one-half of the 24 percent who supported Goodell and the 37 percent who supported Ottinger had felt truly indifferent between these two candidates. Had they been able to cast approval votes for both Goodell and Ottinger (their dominant strategy under approval voting), then Goodell would have received about 42 percent of the vote, Ottinger 49 percent, and Buckley would have finished last. Likewise, a runoff election between Buckley and the leading liberal candidate, Ottinger, probably also would have resulted in the defeat of Buckley. Therefore, in a real-life instance either approval voting or a runoff election would probably have prevented the will of the majority from being thwarted. (As I showed in section 6.5, however, negative [and approval] voting may not produce the same outcome as a runoff election.)

In the 1970 Senate race in New York, it seems plausible to assume that the preference scales of supporters of Buckley (B), Goodell (G), and Ottinger (O) were (B, G, O), (G, O, B), and (O, G, B), respectively. Also, if Buckley supporters considered only B acceptable, but Goodell and Ottinger supporters considered both G and O acceptable, then G and O would have tied with the most votes, and Buckley again would have finished last under approval voting.

If, however, in addition to the mutual support that Goodell and Ottinger supporters confer on each other, Buckley supporters considered Goodell acceptable, then Goodell would have emerged as the clear-cut winner. In fact, William C. Stratmann estimates that under approval voting, Goodell would have won with about 59 percent of the vote to about 55 percent each for Buckley and Ottinger: whereas Buckley and Ottinger would have received significant support from Goodell voters, Goodell would have benefited from the support of *both* Buckley and Ottinger voters.[8]

---

voting, see William H. Riker, "The Number of Political Parties: A Reexamination of Duverger's Law," *Comparative Politics* 9, no. 1: 93–106; also, Steven J. Brams, "The Entry Problem in a Political Race" (mimeographed, New York University, 1978).

8. Personal communication, William C. Stratmann, September 21, 1977, based on work reported in Stratmann, "The Calculus of Rational Choice," *Public Choice* 18 (Summer 1974): 93–105, esp. 98–99.

Now if there were a poll that indicated Goodell and Ottinger to be the top two candidates, supporters of each of the three candidates would be motivated to make the following divisions between acceptable and unacceptable candidates in their preference scales: B—$(B, G / O)$; G—$(G / O, B)$; O—$(O / G, B)$. Paradoxically, Goodell, the candidate with the fewest supporters, would get the most votes—from both his and Buckley's supporters.

This result is not as paradoxical as it first seems when one realizes that Goodell is the Condorcet winner: he would defeat both Buckley and Ottinger in pairwise contests by getting the votes of the third candidate. In fact, as the Condorcet winner, and one of the top two candidates in the poll, Goodell *must* defeat the other top candidate in the poll (Ottinger), after the poll announcement, according to Theorem 6.6.

Surprisingly, it is possible for a candidate who is not one of the top two in the poll to defeat, after the poll announcement, one of the top two in the poll. Even if one of the top two is a Condorcet winner—who by Theorem 6.6 will always defeat the other top candidate—he may still lose after the poll to a third and lower-standing candidate. As an example of this bizarre circumstance, assume there are a set of three candidates, $\{X, Y, Z\}$, and six classes of voters with the following numbers of members and preference scales for the candidates:

1. 10: (X, Y, Z)
2. 10: (X, Z, Y)
3. 9: (Y, X, Z)
4. 10: (Y, Z, X)
5. 15: (Z, X, Y)
6. 11: (Z, Y, X)

If all voters consider the top two candidates acceptable under approval voting, the outcome is Z—46, X—44, and Y—40. (Note: Z also wins under plurality voting—all voters vote only for their top single candidate—getting 26 votes to X's 20 and Y's 19. Moreover, Z is the Condorcet winner, defeating both X and Y 36 to 29; Y again comes in last, losing to X in a pairwise contest 35 to 30.)

After the poll announcement identifying Z and X as the top two candidates, the six classes of voters will make the following divisions between acceptable and unacceptable candidates:

1. 10: $(X, Y / Z)$
2. 10: $(X / Z, Y)$
3. 9: $(Y, X / Z)$
4. 10: $(Y, Z / X)$
5. 15: $(Z / X, Y)$
6. 11: $(Z, Y / X)$

(Note that if the previous division of voting for the top two candidates already distinguished between Z and X, the voter makes no adjustment in his previous strategy.) Now Y, the former last-place candidate, wins with 40 votes, Z—the Condorcet winner—gets 36 votes, and X gets 29 votes!

Clearly, poll announcements that voters react to in the manner I have postulated may drastically alter election outcomes. As in the previous example, they may elevate last-place candidates to first place, and, in the process, may even topple Condorcet winners (Z in the example). Indeed, in the 1970 New York race for Senate, there is good reason to believe that Goodell was the Condorcet winner (as I suggested earlier), but in the election he came in a poor third. At least in part his poor showing seems attributable to some of his supporters who—viewing the real contest in the end to be one between Buckley and Ottinger (as the polls indicated)—drifted toward one or the other of the two front-runners.

To recapitulate, I have shown in this section that four combinations of outcomes are possible—winning and losing, with or without a poll—under approval voting. In fact, all voting systems of the kind discussed are vulnerable to possible manipulation by the publication (or nonpublication) of poll results. Although it is hard to assess the degree to which poll announcements actually affect voting behavior, and even change election outcomes,[9] the foregoing model of poll ef-

9. For a review of empirical evidence, see Steven J. Brams, *Paradoxes in*

fects at least shows up some potential problems of polling in a democratic society.

6.9. Approval Voting and Presidential Elections

Several desirable properties of approval voting in multi-candidate elections have been described in previous sections. As a practicable reform, John Kellett and Kenneth Mott have made a strong case that approval voting be adopted in presidential primaries, which, at least in the early stages, often involve several candidates running for their party's nomination.[10] When Kellett and Mott asked a sample of 225 Pennsylvania voters to "vote for any candidates whose nomination you can support" in the 1976 presidential primary (eight Democratic candidates and eight Republican candidates were listed on two sample ballots), 72 percent of those voting chose to support two, three, or four candidates.

A case for approval voting in national party conventions can also be made. As in primaries, the main effect would probably be to give comparatively more support to moderates that most delegates find acceptable, comparatively less to extremists who are only acceptable to ideological factions in their party.

If there had been approval voting in the 1972 Democratic convention, it seems at least doubtful that George McGovern would have been his party's nominee. Not only did he not have strong support from his party rank and file,[11] but he also was accorded little chance of winning in the general election.

Although most general elections are, for all intents and purposes, two-candidate contests, since 1900 there have been several serious bids by third-party candidates in presidential elections.[12] The most notable challenges in the first quarter of

Politics: An Introduction to the Nonobvious in Political Science (New York: Free Press, 1976), pp. 67–70.

10. John Kellett and Kenneth Mott, "Presidential Primaries: Measuring Popular Choice," *Polity* 9, no. 4 (Summer 1977): 528–37.

11. William R. Keech and Donald R. Matthews, *The Party's Choice* (Washington, D.C.: Brookings Institution, 1976), p. 212.

12. See Daniel A. Mazmanian, *Third Parties in Presidential Elections* (Washington, D.C.: Brookings Institution, 1974).

the century were in 1912, when Theodore Roosevelt won 27.4 percent of the popular vote, and in 1924, when Robert La Follette won 16.6 percent of the popular vote.

More recently, Harry Truman faced defections from both wings of the Democratic party in 1948. The Progressive candidate, Henry Wallace, and the States' Rights candidate, Strom Thurmond, each captured 2.4 percent of the popular vote. Nevertheless, Truman was able to win 49.6 percent of the popular vote to Republican Thomas Dewey's 45.1 percent.

The most serious challenge by a minor-party candidate since World War II was that of George Wallace in the 1968 presidential election. I shall shortly analyze this election in some detail to try to assess the possible effects of approval voting in a presidential election.

Most recently, Eugene McCarthy ran as a third-party candidate in the 1976 presidential election. Playing the spoiler role, McCarthy sought to protest what he saw to be the outmoded procedures and policies of the Democratic party, for whose nomination he had run in 1968 and 1972. Although McCarthy garnered only 0.9 percent of the popular vote, his candidacy may have cost Jimmy Carter four states, which Gerald Ford won by less than what McCarthy polled. In the end, of course, Carter did not need the electoral votes of these states; however, if he lost in a few states that he won by slim margins, these McCarthy votes could have made the difference in the election outcome.

I turn now to an analysis of the third-party challenge by George Wallace's American Independence party in 1968. As with Strom Thurmond's support twenty years earlier, Wallace's support was concentrated in the South. Although Wallace had no reasonable chance of winning the presidency, it seemed at the time that he had a very good chance of preventing both Richard Nixon and Hubert Humphrey from winning a majority of electoral votes, thereby throwing the election into the House of Representatives. There Wallace could have bargained with these candidates for major policy concessions—in particular, weaker enforcement of civil rights statutes and a halt to busing.

Wallace captured 13.5 percent of the popular vote and was the victor in five states, winning 46 electoral votes. He came close to denying Nixon, who got 43.4 percent of the popular vote to Humphrey's 42.7 percent, an electoral-vote majority.

Would this outcome have been different, or would its magnitude have significantly changed, if there had been approval voting in 1968? Presumably, all voters who voted for one of the three candidates would not have changed their votes. But how many would have cast second approval votes, and for whom would they have voted?

The best information available to answer this question was collected in the University of Michigan Survey Research Center's 1968 National Election Study. Data derived from a "feeling thermometer" assessment of candidates—whereby respondents are asked to indicate warm or cold feelings toward the candidates on a 100-degree scale—may be used to define an "acceptability" scale for candidates, from which plausible approval voting strategies of voters can be surmised.

Taking account of both the reported votes of the respondents (the survey was taken just after the election) and their feeling-thermometer assessments of the candidates, D. R. Kiewiet developed a set of ten rules for assigning approval votes to respondents.[13] After adjusting reported voting by the sample to reflect the actual voting results, he estimated that Nixon would have increased his vote total to 69.8 percent (a 58 percent increase over the 44.1 percent in the survey who reported voting for Nixon), Humphrey would have increased his vote total to 60.8 percent (a 44 percent increase over the 42.3 percent in the survey who reported voting for Humphrey), and Wallace would have increased his vote total to 21.3 percent (a 58 percent increase over the 13.5 percent in the survey who reported voting for Wallace).

Kiewiet draws several conclusions from his analysis. First,

13. D. R. Kiewiet, "Approval Voting: The Case of the 1968 Presidential Election" (mimeographed, Yale University, 1977). For a related effort, applied to primaries, to translate 1972 feeling-thermometer data into electoral outcomes under a variety of decision rules, see Richard A. Joslyn, "The Impact of Decision Rules in Multi-Candidate Campaigns: The Case of the 1972 Democratic Nomination," *Public Choice* 25 (Spring 1976): 1–17.

plurality voting nearly deprived Nixon of his victory: although many voters were certainly not wildly enthusiastic about Nixon, more than a two-thirds majority probably considered him at least acceptable. Second, although most of the additional approval votes Nixon and Humphrey would have received would have come from each other's supporters, Wallace supporters—according to the rules used for assigning approval votes—would have cast more than twice as many approval votes for Nixon as for Humphrey.

It is this factor which largely explains Nixon's 9 percent approval-voting edge over Humphrey. Wallace also would have benefited from approval voting. In fact, his estimated 21 percent approval voting share exactly matches the percentage who reported they would vote for him two months before the election.[14] If there had been approval voting, Wallace almost surely would not have lost most of his original supporters, and probably would have picked up some support from the major-party voters as well, to capture approval votes from more than one-fifth of the electorate.

Perhaps the most interesting conclusion that can be derived from these estimates is that Nixon was undoubtedly the Condorcet winner. Kiewiet estimates that Nixon would have defeated Wallace in a pairwise contest 81.5 percent to 18.5 percent and would have defeated Humphrey 53.4 percent to 46.6 percent, given the propensity of Wallace voters to favor Nixon.

Several objections can be raised against Kiewiet's estimates and indeed against virtually any estimates based on assumptions about how the attitudes or "feelings" of voters would translate into voting behavior. Rather than dwelling on these, however, consider a rather different set of estimates made by Kiewiet based on more "strategic" assumptions.

These assumptions reflect the view of most voters in 1968 that only Humphrey and Nixon stood a serious chance of winning the election. After all, even at his high point in the

14. Richard M. Scammon and Ben J. Wattenberg, *The Real Majority: An Extraordinary Examination of the American Electorate* (New York: Coward, McCann and Geoghegan, 1970), pp. 171–72.

polls, Wallace commanded the support of barely more than one-fifth of the electorate. Consistent with the poll model in section 6.8, then, it is plausible to assume that voters would cast approval votes to distinguish between Humphrey and Nixon.

More specifically, Kiewiet assumed that (1) Humphrey and Nixon supporters would vote for Wallace, if they also approved of him, but would not vote for the other major-party candidate; (2) all Wallace voters would vote for either Humphrey or Nixon, but not both, in addition to Wallace. As he put it,

> In effect, a poll indicating Wallace had no chance of winning would, under approval voting, turn the election into two elections: the first, a pairwise contest between Nixon and Humphrey, wherein all voters would choose one or the other; the second, a sort of referendum for Wallace, who would receive approval votes from voters who wished to support him even if he could not win the election.[15]

In operational terms, Kiewiet postulated that Humphrey and Nixon supporters would vote for their first choice and, in addition, for Wallace if the latter's thermometer rating exceeded 50. Wallace supporters, on the other hand, were assumed always to cast a second approval vote for the major-party candidate they gave the highest thermometer rating to, no matter what this rating was. Thereby Wallace voters were "forced" to be rational in accordance with the assumptions of the poll model.

What estimates does this set of assumptions yield? Nixon would have received 53.4 percent of the popular vote and Humphrey 46.6 percent—the same percentages given earlier had they been in a pairwise contest—and Wallace 21.3 percent. Thus, the approval voting percentages of Humphrey and Nixon would have been substantially reduced over those estimated earlier (69.8 and 60.8 percent, respectively), but

15. Kiewiet, "Approval Voting: The Case of the 1968 Election."

Wallace would have come out exactly the same (21.3 percent estimated earlier) since the "strategic" assumptions do not alter the voting behavior of Wallace supporters for Wallace.

The two sets of estimates for Humphrey and Nixon probably bracket the percentages the candidates would actually have received had there been approval voting in 1968. Whichever set gives the better estimates, Nixon in either case would have been the clear-cut winner in the popular-vote contest because of the much broader support he, rather than Humphrey, would have received from Wallace supporters.

The Electoral College also magnified Nixon's narrow popular-vote victory because he won by slim margins in several large states. However, speaking normatively, I believe this fact should have no bearing on the outcome. Much more significant is the fact that Nixon was the first or second choice of most voters and hence more acceptable than any other candidate. This, I believe, is the proper criterion for the selection of a president—and other democratically elected officials as well.

It is also interesting to note that approval voting would probably obviate the need for a runoff election in most multi-candidate presidential elections if the Electoral College were abolished. No winning candidate in a presidential election has ever received less than 40 percent of the popular vote, with the exception of Abraham Lincoln in 1860, who got 39.8 percent. It seems highly unlikely that a candidate who is the first choice of 40 percent of the electorate would not be approved of by as many as one-sixth of the remaining voters and thereby receive at least 50 percent support from the electorate.

The legitimacy of election outcomes in the eyes of voters would certainly be enhanced if the winning candidate received the support of a majority of the electorate. This would be true even if he was the first choice of fewer voters than some other candidate, because this fact would not show up in the approval-voting returns.

By comparison, the proposed popular-vote amendment to

abolish the Electoral College provides for a runoff between the top two vote-getters if neither receives at least 40 percent of the vote (see section 3.3). This seems an unnecessary provision if more than 50 percent approve of the winning candidate. Of course, if no candidate wins even a majority of approval votes, then a runoff can still be conducted to ensure a majority winner.

But this would probably not be necessary in most presidential elections unless approval voting itself produces major changes in candidate strategies and election outcomes. Beyond these changes, however, approval voting could affect a fundamental alteration in the two-party system itself by encouraging additional parties or candidates to enter the fray. Fringe candidates, it seems, would probably drain little support from centrist candidates because, for strategic reasons, fringe candidate supporters would probably also tend to vote for a centrist. Additional centrist candidates, on the other hand, might draw support away from major party candidates if they (the new centrists) were perceived as serious contenders.

The question that is hard to answer, in the absence of experience, is whether such contenders could position themselves in such a way as to displace the major-party candidates. If so, presumably they would be motivated to run, giving voters more viable alternatives from which to choose and, in the process, weakening the two-party system. Their election, however, would probably not produce drastic changes in public policy since they would not be viable if they were unacceptable to numerous middle-of-the-road voters.

Barring unforeseen changes, it seems likely that at the same time approval voting would give some additional support to strong minority candidates like George Wallace, it would also help centrist candidates—including perhaps nominees of new parties—both in winning their party's nomination in the primaries and conventions and prevailing against more extreme candidates in the general election. Coupled with the greater opportunity it affords voters to express their preferences, and the greater likelihood it provides the winning candidate of obtaining majority support, approval voting would seem to be an overlooked reform that now deserves to be taken seriously.

6.10. Conclusions

Approval voting offers important advantages in multican-didate presidential elections—both at the nomination stage in primaries and party conventions and at the general-election stage. Among other things, it would probably (1) increase voter turnout, (2) increase the likelihood of a majority winner in plurality contests and thereby reinforce the legitimacy of election outcomes, and (3) help centrist candidates without, at the same time, denying voters the opportunity to express their support for more extremist candidates.

Approval voting might encourage additional candidates to run, however, and thereby weaken the two-party system. While it would probably make more centrist candidates via-ble, it seems unlikely that it would produce drastic policy shifts.

Evidence for the centrist bias of approval voting was pro-vided by two sets of estimates made of the likely outcome in the 1968 three-candidate presidential election had there been approval voting. Both sets of estimates indicated that Nixon would have won decisively, though Wallace would have made a much stronger showing than he did.

In a way, approval voting is a compromise between plural-ity voting and more complicated schemes like the Borda count which require voters to rank candidates.[16] In my opin-ion, the latter schemes are both too complicated and unneces-sary in elections in which there is only a single winner. (Elec-

16. For a very different theoretical argument in support of approval voting, as well as some empirical observations on its practicability, see Robert James Weber, "Comparison of Voting Systems" (mimeographed, University of Connecticut, 1977); and Robert James Weber, "Multiply-Weighed Voting Systems" (mimeographed, University of Connecticut, 1977); see also Samuel Merrill, III, "Approval Voting: A 'Best Buy' Method for Multi-candidate Elections?" *Mathematics Magazine* (forthcoming, 1978).

tions in which there are multiple winners, such as to a committee or council, would also seem well suited for approval voting, but that is a subject for another work.) On the other hand, approval voting is not only quite easy to understand—even if some of its theoretical implications are not so obvious—but it also seems an eminently practicable scheme that could readily be implemented on existing voting machines.[17]

17. Several new theoretical results have recently been proved for approval voting, including the following: (1) among all nonranked voting systems, approval voting is the only system that guarantees the existence of sincere admissible strategies that elect a Condorcet winner (if one exists); (2) allowing for a runoff election between the top two candidates under plurality voting also ensures the existence of admissible strategies that elect a Condorcet winner, but they are not necessarily sincere; (3) if plurality voting (with or without a runoff) leads to the election of a Condorcet winner whatever admissible strategies voters choose, so does approval voting, but the reverse is not true: there are situations in which approval voting guarantees the election of a Condorcet winner but plurality voting (with or without a runoff) does not. The last statement says, in effect, that approval voting does a better job of *ensuring* the election of a Condorcet winner than its main competitors, plurality voting with and without a runoff; I consider this result on a par with the sincerity and strategyproofness results in that it establishes the "dominance" of approval voting—but in this case with respect to the Condorcet criterion. Steven J. Brams and Peter C. Fishburn, "Runoff Elections" (mimeographed, New York University, 1978).

Index